# GUARDIANS
# OF THE
# GREAT
# COMMISSION

# GUARDIANS OF THE GREAT COMMISSION

## THE STORY OF WOMEN IN MODERN MISSIONS

RUTH A. TUCKER

Academie Books Grand Rapids, Michigan
Zondervan Publishing House

Front cover: The Heavenly Mission. From Daniel C. Eddy, *Daughters of the Cross; or, Woman's Mission* (Boston: Dayton and Wentworth, 1855).

Guardians of the Great Commission
Copyright © 1988 by the Zondervan Corporation
Grand Rapids, Michigan

ACADEMIE BOOKS is an imprint of Zondervan Publishing House,
1415 Lake Drive, S.E., Grand Rapids, Michigan 49506

**Library of Congress Cataloging in Publication Data**

Tucker, Ruth, 1945–
    Guardians of the Great Commission : the story of women in modern missions / Ruth A. Tucker.
        p.    cm.
        Bibliography : p.
        Includes index.
        ISBN 0-310-41471-7
        1. Women missionaries.        I. Title.
BV2610.T8 1988
266'.0088042—dc 19

88-16800
CIP

*Printed in the United States of America*

88  89  90  91  92  93 / DH / 10  9  8  7  6  5  4  3  2  1

For
Arti Dixon
who
has sacrificially served
as a Guardian of the Great Commission
but who
like the nameless and forgotten missionary heroines
of generations past
would consider herself utterly unworthy of recognition

# CONTENTS

## PART III. MINISTRY CHALLENGES

# INTRODUCTION

"I longed to be a martyr, to be one of that 'noble army' . . . I longed to do something. I had a strong desire to be a missionary, to give myself up to some holy work, and I had a firm belief that such a calling would be mine." These were the words of Ann Martin Hinderer, who from her youth felt compelled to heed the command of the Great Commission, no matter what the risk. Her longing "to be a martyr" reflected the reality of missionary life in Africa. The fact that most missionaries died within a few short years after their arrival could not have escaped her. Yet it was with anticipation that she married German-born David Hinderer in 1852 and joined him in his work with the Church Missionary Society in West Africa.[1]

As a childless woman, Ann maintained a full schedule of mission activities, and like all nineteenth-century Africa missionaries suffered countless bouts of fever. Yet, she continued to speak forth as a guardian of the Great Commission:

> When I see what is the need, I feel that if I had twenty lives I would gladly give them to be the means of a little good to these poor but affectionate and well-meaning people who, though black enough their skins may be, have never-dying souls, which need to be led to the Saviour, to be washed clean in the blood of the Lamb.[2]

The role of women in the modern missionary movement has been phenomenal. No other public ministry in the church has so captured the interest and commitment of women in the past two hundred years. There are a number of reasons for this, but two particularly stand out: opportunities for women were and are restricted in the institutionalized church at home, and mission leaders, because of their compulsion to reach a lost world for Christ, have been less restrictive than church leaders in this respect.

These two factors are related. The male-dominated institutionalized church has deeply entrenched concepts of power, authority, and office—and women have not fit into the scheme. The overriding motivation of the modern missionary movement, on the other hand, has been world evangelism, and in that framework women became a very necessary component—indeed, the most noted evangelical missionary statesmen of the past century and more have strongly advocated active female involvement in the cause.

From the very beginning of the modern missionary movement,

women played an active role—either in home-front support efforts or by working alongside their husbands in overseas ministries. As the nineteenth century progressed, their involvement deepened, in part because of the perception, widely held in society at large, that women were the guardians of religion. They were expected to keep the home fires of faith burning, and in doing so they instilled a missionary impulse in their children and became the guardians of the Great Commission. By the early decades of the twentieth century, women outnumbered men on the mission field by a ratio of more than two to one, and the women's missionary movement itself had become the largest women's movement in the country—larger than the Women's Christian Temperance Movement—with more than three million dues-paying members in America alone.[3]

Despite their active involvement in missions, however, women have been largely forgotten by the missions historians. In her research on women in missions Patricia Hill found this to be true: "As so frequently happens in the writing of history, the women have simply disappeared." Women often played crucial roles in pioneering new regions or in developing new programs, but they were granted little credit either at the time or by posterity. Women were involved in missions in large numbers, but it is important to point out that the numbers do not necessarily reflect their actual contribution to the cause. The married women who constituted more than thirty percent of the missionary force were often consumed with domestic duties and had less time than men for outreach ministries. Likewise, women rarely had leadership roles and, as is true in any field of history, the leaders are the ones who draw the attention of researchers.

But the accomplishments of married women in ministry should not be overlooked or minimized. Despite their heavy domestic responsibilities they made significant contributions to the missionary enterprise. This is acknowledged by Helen Barrett Montgomery in her classic, *Western Women in Eastern Lands*:

> In the history of the United States there are hundreds of pages devoted to the Pilgrim Fathers to one devoted to the Pilgrim Mothers. You might almost think there were no women, to read the ordinary school history. So also in missionary history, there is a tendency to pass over lightly the contribution of missionary wives and mothers. Yet their contributions are many and varied.[4]

Montgomery's claim is supported by another writer—a man—who had known well the value of women to foreign missions: "American historians usually write with a male bias and ignore the role of women in our culture, but no one can ignore the role of the missionaries' wives and daughters without distorting the history of the missionary movement.[5]

# PART I

# MINISTRY PROBLEMS

Most problems women faced in overseas evangelism were problems they had in common with men, but in many instances the problems were of greater severity among women, and some problems were almost exclusively confined to the "weaker sex." As the "head of the home," husbands generally had a greater voice in determining the parameters of the couple's missionary involvement. In some cases, the wives would have much preferred to remain in the homeland but agreed to go abroad in order to keep the family together and to properly submit to their husbands. But such sacrifice did not transpire without an array of related problems, as is clearly seen in the lives of such women as Dorothy Carey and Mary Livingstone.

Women, likewise, more than men, suffered from disease and premature death. Childbearing was risky business in malaria-infested regions during the nineteenth century, and many young mothers, such as Ann Judson, died in their twenties and thirties. Others, like Elizabeth Freeman, were unable to escape persecution and political turmoil. The heaviest price these women had to pay, however, was in losing their little ones. As mothers they anguished over this sacrifice that at times seemed too heavy to bear.

Their single sisters missed all the joys and agonies of giving birth, but they too faced unique problems that escaped the male missionaries. Although they had far greater opportunities for ministry in mission work overseas than was afforded them in the church at home, they nevertheless faced sex discrimination, as is seen in the ministry of Lottie Moon. They were not alone in this. Married women also faced similar opposition, as the life of Carie Sydenstricker illustrates, but because of the restraints of marriage, their voices were seldom heard.

Loneliness was also a problem that was deeply felt by women. Single women longed for marriage, and sometimes related jealousies brought on dissension between them that only aggravated their loneliness, as was true in the case of Emily Blatchley and Jennie Faulding, who both loved the same man. For Narcissa Whitman, loneliness was aggravated because her husband could not live in harmony with the husband of her one female companion. The dissension that wreaked havoc in Martha Crawford's life was in her own marriage.

But there were other factors besides dissension that created loneliness and unhappiness for women missionaries. Married women, like their single sisters, often struggled with loneliness and home-sickness—probably far more than their husbands did. This was true of Helen Holcomb, who had willingly accompanied her husband to India. Yet she suffered the pangs of homesickness while he busied himself in ministry. Although she herself had an effective ministry with the women of India, she missed the companionship that she had enjoyed with women back home. Soon after she returned from furlough in 1882 she wrote:

> We are in our old home here. . . . Yet I have felt more lonely than ever before in India. So much was done during our visit to make our brief sojourn a delight, such loving welcomes from old friends were given us, such precious new friends were raised up for us, and so dear to us was the constant familiar intercourse with Christian hearts, that I feel the contrast keenly between life in this heathen land and life in a land radiant with the light of the gospel.[1]

*Chapter 1*

# Reluctant Missionaries: Serving Without a Commitment or Call

The "missionary call" has been the stuff of modern missions. There is little agreement on precisely what it is, but without it overseas missions could never have taken hold. It was the impetus and provided the staying power when rational thought and logical decision-making mocked the utter foolishness of the undertaking. It was God's voice, and though no one else—not even a wife—may have heard it, it was real. It had to be heeded. There was no alternative— except saying "no" to the One who had suffered and died on the cross and shed His blood for the salvation of all mankind.

It was this call that compelled the great pioneers like William Carey and David Livingstone to ignore the discouraging voices at home and to brave the deadly elements abroad in their life-long commitment to missions. It was this call that was heard over the pitiful cry of wives and children, who were constrained to follow a call they had never heard themselves. For them, it was an oner-

ous call that brought only misery and affliction, and some, such as Dorothy Carey, gave way under the strain. Others, like Mary Livingstone, managed to survive the hardships, but not without severe emotional stress and family discontinuity.

Some women initially opposed the idea of going abroad, but then reluctantly agreed to go, acquiescing in their husbands' call. In some instances their ministry proved to be a great asset to the work, as was true of Giertrud Rask (who never took her husband's name), the wife of Hans Egede, a Norwegian pastor who left his homeland in 1718 to serve as a missionary in Greenland. Giertrud's initial opposition to her husband's rash decision was natural. She was not a young woman—especially considering eighteenth-century life spans. Hans was thirty-two at the time of their departure, and she was thirteen years his senior. She had four children, the youngest barely a year old. When Hans first disclosed his plans, "his own and his wife's friends wrote to express their severest reprobation. . . . His mother-in-law further inflamed the feeling against him, and even his wife began to hint that she repented having attached herself to a man who by such plans was going to ruin himself and those belonging to him."[1]

Hans did not ignore his wife's feelings as some men had. He was convinced of his calling, but he wanted his wife to concur in his decision. He did all he could "to make his wife see the will of God . . . and to regard it as their bounden duty to show a more resolute self-denial by leaving their home and going forth to preach the Gospel among the heathens," and then "they both laid the matter before God in prayer." The result was "the bending of her will, so that she confidently promised to follow him wherever he went." It was Hans, however, who had misgivings about the decision he had made, and shortly before they were to set sail, "he was assailed by doubts as to whether he really had been justified in jeopardizing his and his family's welfare." It was at that moment that the strength of Giertrud rallied his spirits: "My dear wife gave a proof of her great faith and constancy by representing to me that it was too late to repent of what had been done. I cannot say how much she encouraged me by speaking in this way and by the fact that she, a frail woman, showed greater faith and manliness than I."[2]

During the many years of their ministry in Greenland, Giertrud was by his side helping in the ministry. In 1733, during a smallpox epidemic, she opened her home to the sick and nursed them in her own bedroom. It was a gesture of kindness that deeply impressed the Greenlanders, who had heretofore been reluctant to listen to the doctrinaire teaching of the uninvited Scandinavian Lutheran preacher. But it was a heavy price to pay. "Not only I," wrote Hans, "but also my beloved wife after that time suffered greatly in strength and health, nay, from that day she was never well, until God in his mercy called her to him." Her "superhuman efforts . . . had undermined her constitution." And yet she would continue performing acts of kindness until she died two years later. The Moravian missionaries, who did not get along well with her husband, had "nothing but praise for her motherly care of them. . . . She always sent refreshments to the Brethren when she herself had anything, so that they frequently felt misgivings at receiving the benefits which she so abundantly conferred on them."[3]

Giertrud Rask, wife of Hans Egede, missionary to Greenland.

That wives reluctantly served as missionaries without a sense of call did not mean that they could not be effective partners in the work. For some, such as Giertrud Rask and Edith Buxton, the author of *Reluctant Missionary*, overseas ministry was a heavy sacrifice that called forth inner strength that could only be found in a deep faith in God. These women persevered and prospered in their ministries. Others, like Dorothy Carey, were crushed beneath the weight of the affliction.

### Dorothy Carey

Dorothy Carey ("Dolly" as she was known by family and friends) has not fared well at the hands of historians and her husband's biographers. She was a common, ordinary woman of her day. She grew up in a deeply devoted Puritan family and became acquainted with William during his apprenticeship with her brother-in-law. She was several years older than William and in her mid-twenties when they were married in 1781. Undoubtedly she had already been relegated to a state of spinsterhood by many in that era who assumed that any respectable woman would have been married at a much earlier age.

There may have been reasons for her delay in marrying. She was illiterate, not even able to sign her name in the parish marriage register. Although higher education was not readily available to women during this period, basic literacy was common. Susanna Wesley, who was reared in a Puritan family more than two generations earlier, was not only literate but wrote books and volumes of correspondence, as did other women of that era. Why did William

marry her, considering the gap in their intellectual interests? Perhaps he felt an obligation to his master. Perhaps it was true love—although, according to a recent biographer, "there is no evidence as to whether the marriage was a love-match."[4]

The question might also be asked, Why did Dorothy marry William? He had very little to offer her, and married life proved to be very difficult. William was a poor journeyman shoemaker, and less than a year after they married he took on the additional task of preaching regularly at a tiny Baptist church, too poor to pay him "enough to pay for the clothes he wore out in their service." When his mother visited them at the death of their baby daughter, she was shocked to discover their abject poverty. Sometime later, when his master died, William not only inherited the debts of the business, but also the obligation to support his master's widow and her four children.[5]

Yet, in spite of her difficult circumstances, Dorothy apparently accepted her husband's commitment to ministry. Although his preaching among the Baptists consumed his time and brought little or no financial remuneration, she supported this role and with her three young boys submitted herself to baptism by immersion shortly after he was ordained. Carey's ordination led to a commitment to full-time pastoral ministry, though the salaries of both churches which he served had to be supplemented by outside employment. Little is known about Dorothy's role as a pastor's wife, except that once again she would endure the sorrow of seeing a baby daughter slip away from her. It was a hard life for her "with her young husband so completely absorbed in his preaching and studying—interests which it would be difficult for an unlettered girl to share. She must have felt at times very much alone."[6]

Despite Dorothy's busy home life of caring for little ones and trying to provide a healthful diet and environment on her husband's meager income, she took time out to overcome her illiteracy. She not only learned to sign her name, but some years later she was able to correspond with her husband. She no doubt regretted that she had grown up in a community that had no school and that she was so far behind her husband in scholarly pursuits, so she determined on her own to enlarge her world.[7]

Carey's avid interest in foreign missions began while he was serving as a pastor. He was one of several missionary-minded Baptist pastors who founded the Baptist Missionary Society in 1792. Dorothy was aware of his activities, but she was as shocked as his family and parishioners when he announced that he had offered himself as a missionary to India. She had three young children to care for and was pregnant with a fourth. Leaving her home and family and everything she had known since childhood to live for the rest of her life in an inhospitable climate and an unfriendly environment was unthinkable to her. Even the most ardent female missionary enthusiasts would have struggled with a sacrifice like that, and there is no evidence that Dorothy was enthusiastic about missions at all. It was an era when most Christians had little concern for the unconverted beyond their borders.

Not surprisingly, she adamantly refused to go.[8]

Dorothy was, in the words of S. Pearce Carey, a "home-bird." She lived the first twenty-nine years of her life in a small community and "was home-clinging to a degree. Her people, as the registers prove, had for a century at least kept close to one another, sharing all their sunshines and griefs within the bounds of the village." Is it surprising that the thought of going to India was so abhorrent to her? "The seas were infested with pirates. . . . Then how should she dwell at nearly forty amongst a folk of foreign speech, when only since her marriage had she learned to write her own?" And, in addition to those factors, she was within a month of childbirth.[9]

Carey was determined to go, even if it meant going without her. Amazingly, Dorothy acquiesced in her husband's decision to abandon her while she was late in pregnancy, and she went beyond that to make a deep sacrifice for his wellbeing: "During those last days," according to S. Pearce Carey, "Dorothy Carey could not bear to have her husband go utterly alone, so promised him Felix for solace; eight years old, bright and gifted; sure token also of her own eventual following."[10]

Carey would have gone all the way to India had not John Thomas, his partner, been stopped by creditors and forced to return home until his financial affairs were in order. The delay gave Dorothy time to have her baby, and it also gave Carey and others time to put added pressure on her to go. John Thomas warned her that if she did not go "she would repent it as long as she lived" because the family would be "dispersed and divided for ever." Finally she relented—provided that her younger sister, Kitty, accompany her to help with domestic responsibilities.[11]

The voyage to India was a very difficult one, and circumstances were little better after they arrived in India—at least for the Careys. As a medical doctor, John Thomas lived with his wife in relative luxury in Calcutta, while the Careys were forced to live in the interior in dire circumstances. Thomas, who was responsible for financial matters, "Had pitiably miscalculated . . . expenses," and at times the Careys faced such destitution that they were "unable to afford even bread." Sickness plagued the family from the beginning, and William wrote home that Dorothy and Kitty were "continually exclaiming against" him. In 1794, the year after they arrived, little five-year-old Peter died, and from then on Dorothy was never the same. "Her brain became the haunted chamber of morbid fancies and tormenting fears. She grew the opposite of all she naturally was." She was later described as being "wholly deranged."[12]

In 1907, after thirteen years of misery, Dorothy died. It was no doubt a relief to her husband. One of his co-workers had written that Carey worked on his translations in the mission house "while an insane wife, frequently wrought up to a state of most distressing excitement, was in the next room." The children were cared for by Hannah Marshman, the wife of one of Carey's co-workers, who kindly stepped in when she was needed.[13]

William Carey, in recognition of his powerful influence on missions, has been given the title "Father of Modern Missions." If modern missions ever had a mother, it certainly was not Dorothy. And yet, Dorothy, too, merits recognition. While other women willingly died for the cause, she suffered years of mental torture for a cause to which she was not committed. She was deprived of the simple joys of home and family and was later remembered only for her "reproachful tongue" and her "insanity." She deserved more.

## Mary Livingstone

If Dorothy Carey has not fared well at the hands of missions historians, neither has Mary Livingstone, the wife of the nineteenth century's most acclaimed missionary-explorer, David Livingstone. Yet Mary's situation was entirely different from Dorothy's. Mary never opposed missionary work *per se*. She had grown up on the mission field as the daughter of the great missionary pioneers at Kuruman, Robert and Mary Moffat, and it seemed only natural to her that she would carry on the family tradition.

Mary was single and twenty-three years of age when David Livingstone came into her life. He had come to Africa at the urging of her father, and he quickly carved out his own independent ministry. He was a loner who did not get along well with other missionaries, but he was nevertheless lonely for companionship—especially during a period of convalescence after an attack by a lion. That prompted him to "pay his addresses" to Mary, and during that visit he "screwed up . . . courage to put the question beneath one of the fruit trees." He described her as a "sturdy" and "matter-of-fact lady," and that is just what he was looking for in a wife.[14]

The husband Mary was probably looking for was a man like her father, who had been an effective evangelist and church planter in Africa as well as a dedicated husband and father of ten children. But David Livingstone was not that sort of man. He "could never by any stretch of the imagination be regarded as a warm man," writes Geoffrey Moorhouse. That lack of warmth was evident by the way he announced his planned marriage to his superiors at the London Missionary Society: "Various considerations connected with this new sphere of labour, having led me to the conclusion that it was my duty to enter into the marriage relation, I have made the necessary arrangements for union with Mary, the eldest daughter of Mr. Moffat."[15]

Livingstone was a travel enthusiast who relished exploration—who described the arduous travel in the uncharted interior of Africa as a "prolonged system of picnicking." Settling down on a mission station was not for him, though he attempted to combine mission—station work with exploration during the first several years of their married life. It was a very trying time, however, for Mary. On one occasion, when Livingstone was away on an extended exploratory trip, he wrote: "Mary feels her situation among the ruins a little dreary and no wonder, for she writes me that the lions are resuming possession and walk around our house at night."[16]

Sometimes Mary accompanied her husband on exploratory trips, but that only made her situation worse—especially when she had little children to care for and was pregnant besides. To her mother she wrote, "I must again wend my weary way to the far Interior, perhaps to be confined in the field." She was "confined in the field," along the Zouga River.[17] Livingstone briefly mentioned the event in his diary, but allotted much more space to his exciting discovery of crocodile eggs on that same day. He lamented his wife's frequent pregnancies, comparing her fertility to the output of the "great Irish manufactory."[18]

Not only was Mary Livingstone distressed by her husband's unwillingness to settle down, but so was her mother. In a letter scolding her son-in-law for his perilous wanderings with his family, she wrote, "O Livingstone what do you mean—was it not enough that you lost one lovely babe, and scarcely saved the others, while the mother came home threatened with Paralysis?"[19] Livingstone, for his part, sought to defend his actions: "It is a venture to take wife and children into a country where fever—African fever—prevails. But who that believes in Jesus would refuse to make a venture for such a Captain?"[20]

By 1852, after seven years of marriage, Livingstone was no longer able to defend the severe health risks to which his exploratory work exposed his family. Yet he chose not to settle down, but to send his family back to England and to continue his exploration alone. "Nothing but a strong conviction that the step will tend to the Glory of Christ," he wrote, "would make me orphanize my children." His exploration did have a powerful impact on missionary work in Africa, but he paid a heavy price for it—a price for which he himself showed remorse. To his wife he wrote:

My dearest Mary–How I miss you now, and the dear children. My heart yearns incessantly over you. How many thoughts of the past crowd into my mind. I feel as if I would treat you all more tenderly and lovingly than ever. . . . I never show my feelings; but I can say truly, my dearest, that I loved you when I married you, and the longer I lived with you, I loved you the better.[21]

In other correspondence to her, however, he evidenced very little remorse. One letter read: "My dearest Mary, I have very little to write about. Nothing but Africa news and these of no interest. I am thankful that you are where you are, and if you improve your opportunities you may have cause for gratitude throughout life." Then, with no apparent guilt for his own neglect of the children, he went on to say, "Hope you give much of your time to the children. You will be sorry for it if you don't."[22]

For Mary, it was a painful separation, and adjusting to life back in England was most difficult. She and the children had a miserable existence. They were "homeless and friendless" and "often living on the edge of poverty in cheap lodgings," and Mary was said to be drowning her sorrows in alcohol.[23]

Livingstone returned to England in 1856, and after three days with his family he began a widely acclaimed whirlwind tour, telling his fascinating stories of Africa. The following year he returned to Africa where he remained the rest of his life, except for one furlough. Mary sailed with him

but was unable to accompany him as she had planned, because once again she was pregnant and was too sick to travel. She spent some time with her parents, but after the birth of her sixth child she returned to Scotland to be with her other children. Alone again, she "suffered such spiritual darkness that she has been referred to as a 'dejected Christian.' "[24]

By 1862, Mary had recuperated enough to join her husband, but "it was not a happy reunion. That it took place at all was entirely at her insistence." She had never felt settled back in England. Her own parents were still living at their mission post at Kuruman, and her husband's family had not welcomed her in their circles. And Livingstone himself was not eager to have her join him. He had cynically sneered at Bishop Mackenzie's desire for female companionship. "He seems to lean on them," he wrote. "Most High Church people lean on wives or sisters. . . . I hope the Bishop will remain at his post; if he doesn't he is a muff to lean on a wife or a sister. I would as soon lean on a policeman."[25]

Despite his lack of enthusiasm, Mary was determined that this time she would stay with her husband, but the reunion was short lived. The fever-ridden Zambezi delta, combined with emotional stress, soon claimed her life. For all that she had suffered, it was a tragedy that her last three months were clouded with a personal moral scandal. Rumors had spread that she was involved in an extramarital affair with James Stewart, who had come to Africa with her to investigate possibilities for a new mission venture for the Free Church of Scotland. "From the moment the gossip got out along the Zambezi and inklings of it reached Livingstone's ear," writes Moorhouse, "Mary went into a decline from which she did not recover." Whether or not the rumors were true, her accuser, John Kirk, "may not be the ideal witness . . . for he clearly did not like Mary very much." She died at the age of forty-two and was survived by her parents, her children, and her husband. Following her death, Livingstone "attacked his explorations along the river with even greater frenzy."[26]

*Chapter 2*

# Ministries Cut Short: Disease, Persecution, and Premature Death

Disease, persecution, and death took an incredible toll on women missionaries of the nineteenth and early twentieth centuries. Women were more vulnerable to the physical hardships of the mission field than were their husbands—due largely to the complications of childbirth. One missionary to China buried seven wives before he ended his term of service there, and many are the missionaries who had at least three wives, among them Adoniram Judson and William Carey.

The deaths of these women was a harsh reality of missionary life that was sometimes romanticized to the point of making it appear to be a glorious way of dying. "When married women are mentioned in missionary reports, it is most often in connection with their cheerful and holy demise," writes Barbara Welter. "No matter how brief her labors, or how unrewarding her time in missionary life, the woman could be counted on to expire with the hope that her passing would not discour-age newcomers to the field, and with a heartfelt statement that she was glad that she had come ... even if only to die there."[1]

In eulogizing Mrs. Elizabeth Baker Dwight, who died of the plague while serving in the region of Constantinople, Phebe Hanaford wrote: "She was drooping and delicate, like a transplanted flower which pines for its own mountain home, and the fresh breezes and pure sunshine of its first blossoming. ... She was only twenty-nine years of age and had hardly become habituated to the missionary cross, when she was called to wear its crown." And of Sarah Lanman Smith she wrote: "She died Sept. 30, 1836, aged thirty-four, a little over three years from the time she left her own dear land. ... and in the burial-ground of the latter her precious dust reposes beneath a monument which does honor to America by showing the heroic and holy character of her missionary daughters."[2]

The fact is that these missionary women usually suffered immensely and often died a most ignoble death. But that was part of the price they willingly paid. Indeed, some of their critics suggested that they died too willingly. William Dean, who had himself buried two wives on the mission field, criticized Lucy Lord in his introduction to her *Memoirs* for admonishing missionary wives to expend "more time and strength for other and higher duties" than domestic concerns. He blamed the premature death of missionary women on their "attempting to do what they cannot perform," and in so doing "they sacrifice health and life in the vain endeavor, and what is more, neglect the duties of their sacred calling and domestic relations." These women would live longer, Dean was convinced, if they would recognize that "their principle and usually only duty is to render their home a heaven, and their husband happy by lightening his cares, training his children, soothing his sorrows, sympathizing in his stresses, and lending their counsel and support to his duties."[3]

It is doubtful whether large numbers of women succumbed to an early death because they were too involved in ministry. It was rather their frequent pregnancies and resulting childbirth—more closely related to domestic activities—that contributed most to their ill health and premature death. That wives died in great numbers is not surprising. What is amazing is the fruitful ministry many of them carried on despite hardships and short life spans.

Because women were in the forefront of the missionary advance, in many cases their persecution and premature death was a natural result of their occupation and had nothing to do with their sex. This was true in the opening of Africa. Referred to despairingly as "the white man's graveyard," it was a malaria-infested continent whose sting of death did not discriminate between the sexes and might equally have been termed "the white *woman's* graveyard." Sierra Leone received its first permanent missionaries in 1811—a group of three young men—and three years later a married couple, Mr. and Mrs. Davies, joined them. As the first white woman in that region of Africa, she served faithfully and "readily drew women around her and . . . soon had nearly 150 girls under her instruction." Ten months after their arrival, however, she died of fever.[4]

The following year, on the appeal of Mr. Davies, the Church Missionary Society sent another couple, Mr. and Mrs. Brown. "She died in July 1817, after spending but seven months in the field." The third woman to enter the field was widowed after two years of ministry and returned home to England. The deaths went on and on—male and female—and missionaries became "great" simply for being able to survive more than a term of ministry.[5]

China was another field where women died in large numbers alongside their male counterparts. The Boxer Rebellion of 1900 claimed the lives of nearly two hundred missionaries. During that uprising and in the years that preceded it the antiforeign fury raged against women with the same intensity that it raged against men, and sometimes with even greater intensity. "No sadder catastrophe is known in the history of

English missions," wrote Augustus Buckland in reference to the massacre at Ku-Cheng on August 1, 1895. It claimed the lives of a man and eight women—eight missionaries and a female nurse. Two of them were sisters from Australia, who had "lived in hope that their [widowed] mother might speedily join them in the field." The grim details of their death was reported in a *Times* telegram from Shanghai:

Mr. and Mrs. Stewart, Miss N. Saunders, and Miss Lena Irish were burnt in the house. Miss Hessie Newcombe was speared and thrown down a precipice. Miss Marshall's throat was cut. Miss Gordon was speared in the head. Miss Topsy Sanders was speared in the brain. Miss Lena Stewart died from shock.[6]

What is perhaps most significant about the story of the "girl martyrs of Ku-Cheng" is that, despite the threats and persecution they had endured prior to their martyrdom, they stayed on and witnessed success in their work. Indeed, shortly before their deaths "twenty families had cast away their idols and asked for baptism."[7] This was true in the case of vast numbers of women who laid down their lives in missionary service.

There was another way in which a woman's ministry was terminated on the mission field, and that was by the death of her husband. A husband's death—particularly during the nineteenth century—generally meant that the wife was expected to return home. Some widows remained in the field, but often over the objection of mission board officials. Most of them returned home, and with good rea-

son. The emotional trauma of being widowed was magnified on the mission field, where the cause of the man's death and the isolated circumstances of the widow often added to her anguish.

This is pathetically illustrated in the life of Mary Williams, who was married to the great South Seas pioneer missionary John Williams. Soon after her arrival in the island world in 1817 she had become actively involved in the ministry, "holding daily religious classes for the women . . . as well as showing them how to make clothes." Though separated from her family in England by thousands of miles, she was relatively content—until her husband began planning long exploratory expeditions to islands where cannibalism was still rife. Her initial reaction was "I cannot consent to your going. You must not expect it of me." She finally relented, however, but pleaded with him not to go to the island of Erromanga, where "the people are the most wild and cruel that ever we have heard of."[8]

John left in November of 1839, "with these reiterated warnings of Mary's ringing in his ears." But he did not heed them. Four months later "she was awakened in the middle of the night to hear the news that her fears had many times anticipated:"

Your husband landed on the beach at Erromanga two weeks after he left you. At first the natives seemed friendly. But suddenly they attacked him from behind and he was clubbed and pierced with arrows as he tried to reach the boat. The captain of the *Camden* was unable to recover his body. You will realize what that means. . . . A cannibal feast? . . . Under the protection of the *Favorite's* guns we managed to land

and have brought the skull and other bones for burial here.[9]

The native Christians mourned with Mary at the loss of her husband, and they also mourned the loss of her, for they knew well that she could not remain with them alone with three small children to care for.

### Ann Hasseltine Judson

Ann Hasseltine Judson (1789–1826) was the wife of the renowned American missionary Adoniram Judson. Unlike many early missionary wives she served with distinction in her own right. She was converted in a New England revival in the early nineteenth century and had a strong desire to join the foreign missionary crusade that was just beginning on this side of the Atlantic. Though married to one of America's most renowned missionaries, she considered herself much more than simply a missionary wife. She was committed to foreign missions prior to her marriage and insisted that her going abroad in 1812 was not influenced by her love for a man—"an attachment to an earthly object," but rather was prompted by an "obligation to God . . . with a full conviction of its being a call."[10] Her marriage to Judson was in a sense God's confirmation of that call because her serving abroad obligated her to be married. Thirteen days after their marriage they set sail for India.

After she arrived in Burma she wrote of her desire to have a fruitful ministry:

> I desire to no higher enjoyment in this life, than to be instrumental of leading some poor, ignorant females to the knowledge of the Saviour. To have a female praying society, consisting of those who were once in heathen darkness, is what my heart earnestly pants after, and makes a constant subject of prayer. [I am] resolved to keep this in view as one principal object of my life.[11]

In Burma she quickly learned the language and began teaching native women and doing translation work. She took her ministry seriously, as an excerpt from a letter to a friend indicates: "My mornings are busily employed in giving directions to the servants–providing food for the family, etc. At ten my teacher comes, when, were you present, you might see me in an inner room, at one side of my study table, and my teacher at the other, reading Burman, writing, talking, etc." Though she had "many more interruptions than Mr. Judson" because she had "the entire management of the family," she nevertheless found herself to be ahead of him in some respects. "I have found by a year's experience, that it was the most direct way I could have taken to acquire the language; as I am frequently obliged to speak Burman all day. I can talk and understand others better than Mr. Judson, though he knows more about the nature and construction of the language."[12]

As she learned the language, Ann shared her faith with the Burmese she came in contact with. The most common response was that her religion was for foreigners and theirs was for Burmese. As she had anticipated, her ministry was directed mainly toward the women. After the Judsons became settled in their home in Rangoon, they arranged for the construction of a *zayat*, a shelter that offered neighbors an opportunity to stop and discuss the day's events or to listen to religious teachings—in this case Christian rather than Buddhist teaching. Speaking of the *zayat*, Ann wrote: "We have a place erected for public worship, where Mr. Judson and myself spend the day in conversing with all who call; he with the men, and I with the women."[13]

Her most important contribution to missions was her writing. She was the leading female missionary author of the early nineteenth century— indeed, she was the first woman missionary in modern times to attract a wide hearing on the subject of missionary life and the condition of the "heathen" overseas. Her letters and journal provided insight and inspiration to a generation of Americans whose knowledge of and commitment to overseas missions was very limited. She wrote gripping accounts of the problems of Burmese women and made a heartrending appeal for women's work. She told of the child marriages, female infanticide, and how women were kept under subjection by the "tyrannic rod" of their husbands. "The wife receives the appellation of *my servant*, or *my dog*, and is allowed to partake of what her lordly husband is pleased to give her at the *conclusion* of his repast."[14]

But worse than the ill-treatment they received was their "imbecility." They were "taught nothing" and spent their days in "listless idleness." The solution in Ann's mind was simple. Education would revolutionize their lives. Literacy would give them access to the Bible, and the Bible would free them from their chains of bondage:

> Shall we, my beloved friends, suffer minds like these to lie dormant, to wither in ignorance and delusion, to grope their way to external ruin, without an effort on our part, to raise, to refine, to elevate, and point to that Saviour who has died equally for them as for us? . . . Let us make a united effort . . . in attempting to meliorate the situation, to instruct to enlighten and save females in the Eastern world.[15]

Ann Hasseltine Judson, missionary to Burma and wife of Adoniram Judson.

Yet, important as her writing was, she did not delve into the crucial issues involving cross-cultural evangelism, nor did she seek to understand the Burmese worldview, as did some women missionaries of a later era. Speaking of women missionaries in India, Joan Brumberg writes, "With few exceptions, there was never any real analysis by evangelicals of the economic or social circumstances that contributed to the perpetuation of the practice of suttee. Rather the immolation of widowed women was cataloged as simply another highly dramatic example of 'Horrid Pagan Customs.' "[16]

Though she was considered a mere wife or "assistant" missionary, Ann had an independent ministry of her own, and in many ways her influence was as far-reaching as that of her famous husband. It was she who "first brought Thailand to the attention of Protestant missionaries." She initiated a ministry among the Thai prisoners of war in Rangoon— an unreached group that would have otherwise been utterly forgotten. She learned their difficult language and made translations of a catechism and the Gospel of Matthew, and she then made a plea for others to take the gospel to their homeland. "Two independently supported medical missionaries, Jacob Tomlin of England and Karl Augustus Guzlaff, a German, answered her call and arrived in Bangkok on August 23, 1828."[17]

Ann Judson's remarkable ministry in Burma was accomplished in spite of the many hardships that confronted virtually all married women missionaries in the nineteenth century. The disease-ridden climate and childbearing took their toll on her, and the pain of seeing baby Roger die and little Maria struggle for life was a heavy emotional burden. In addition, she had to contend with the family dislocation and physical privation caused by her husband's torturous internment in a filthy, vermin—infested Burmese prison house—an ordeal that drained her strength and made her more vulnerable to tropical fevers. In 1826, after only fourteen years of overseas service, she died, leaving behind a grief-stricken husband and little Maria, who hung on for only a few months before she died also.[18]

Was her life a tragic waste as some of her contemporaries suggested? Like other pioneer missionaries, she knew full well the risks to herself and her family. Yet she was convinced that she was precisely where God wanted her, and she served as a model for the countless missionary wives who would follow her. Though her life was filled with hardship and turmoil, she was fulfilled in her sense of calling, and that is what was paramount in her mind. She missed her family and "dear female friends" with whom she could "unite in social prayer," yet she could write, "I feel happy in thinking that I gave up this source of pleasure, as well as most others, for the sake of the poor heathen. Though I am unworthy of being allowed to do anything for Christ, I am happy that he has made it my duty to live among them, and labor for the promotion of the kingdom of heaven."[19]

Adoniram Judson married twice more and had many more children. Each subsequent birth brought risk to the mother's life in the inhospitable environment of Asia. Some people praised the courage and sacrifice involved, others deplored it. An editorial in the *Boston Evening Transcript* had only caustic remarks when Emily, Judson's third wife, was preparing to go abroad: "This is another case of *infatuation* which would almost seem to be for an untimely death. We really think there should be a law against the wholesale sacrifice of life which is continually chronicled amongst those who imagine they are 'called' to labor in unhealthy climes as the wives of missionaries."[20]

### Elizabeth Freeman

Elizabeth Freeman embarked on her missionary adventure to Northwest India in 1851, after a very short engagement and only five weeks of marriage to John Freeman, a twelve-year veteran missionary to India with the Presbyterian Board of Foreign Missions. Like so many other missionary women before her, John's first wife, Mary Ann, had died on the field, leaving two little children behind. Elizabeth quickly became involved in the mission work. She took language study on the sea voyage and began conducting women's and children's ministries after she arrived.[21]

She found it difficult to acclimate herself to the rigors of life in India, but she was convinced that her hardships were worth the cost. To her niece, who was yearning for missionary adventure, she wrote, "Let me tell you, my dear girl, unless you should come with your heart filled with love to God and these poor perishing heathens, you would be sadly disappointed." But she did not end her advice with that warning: "I hope you will be a missionary wherever your lot is cast, and as long as God spares your life; for it makes but little difference after all where we spend these few fleeting years, if they are only spent for the glory of God. Be assured there is nothing else worth living for!"[22]

That spirit of sacrifice would prove appropriate for the devastating turn of events that took place in 1858. The missionaries of the Futtehgurh Mission were aware of the impending danger. Word had reached them, as Elizabeth related, that "our companies of the ninth regiment of Allyghur had mutinied, murdered all the English, and left for Mynpoorie and Futtehgurh."

Elizabeth Freeman, missionary martyr to India.

The missionaries quickly realized they were stranded: "On Saturday," Elizabeth wrote, "we drove to the station, found all the ladies in tears, and their husbands pale and trembling. We all consulted together what was best to be done; but what could we do? Every place seemed as unsafe as this." The following Tuesday she wrote, "All safe this morning, though we spent a very anxious day yesterday; it was the last day of the great Mahammadan [sic] feast. They are always at that time in a very excited state; these are the most bitter opposers to the English rule and Christian religion, and would gladly exterminate both."[23]

A week later, on June 2, 1858, Elizabeth wrote that she had gone to bed the previous night with "a violent sick headache" after hearing that "two regiments from Lucknow had mutinied, and were on their way here." It was her last letter home, and her final words were poignant: "Can only say good-bye, pray for us, will write next mail if we live; if not you will hear from some other source. Your affectionate sister, E. Freeman." There would be another week of terror before the awful ordeal ended: "On the 13th of June, at seven o'clock in the morning, they were released, marched to the parade-ground, and ruthlessly shot. Their death was agonizing, but not long delayed. Thus died the Freemans, Campbells, Johnsons, McMillins, and dear little Fannie and Willie Campbell.'[24]

Elizabeth's death, like the deaths of so many other missionary wives, might have been considered a waste of precious humanity, and the editor of the *Boston Evening Transcript* could have used her death as one more reason why "there should be a law against the wholesale sacrifice of life." But for Elizabeth Freeman, her life was honorably spent because it was dedicated wholly to God.

## Chapter 3

# Paying the Highest Price:
# Losing Little Ones

The agonizing illnesses, torture, and death missionary women endured during the nineteenth century paled when compared to the anguish caused by the frequent deaths of their children. The lives of little ones were in constant jeopardy, and their mothers often suffered more than they while they witnessed their pain and death. This agony was graphically recounted by Bishop Samuel Gobat, who served with his wife Marie in the Middle East during the early decades of the nineteenth century. Due to the Bishop's ill health they were taking an overland journey for medical treatment—a harrowing journey that haunted them the rest of their lives:

One part of this journey in particular I can scarcely look back upon without shuddering and tears. We were still a long day's travel from the valley of the Nile, where water was to be found. Our strength was exhausted, and we were all more or less unwell. I begged that one of our Arabs would go and fetch water, but they all refused, though I offered to pay almost any amount; and so we were obliged to start early in the morning. Our child had grown worse in the night, and seemed to suffer great pain; her groans and cries pierced the heart of her mother, who was frequently obliged to take her in her arms and soothe her, though she herself was quite exhausted. . . .

A little before sunset we reached the longed-for well of pure water, where we . . . thought that the worst was over, but it was not so. The night was very cold, and our coverings very inadequate; moreover, the malady of our child reached the climax of its intensity. From the beginning of the night until daybreak she uttered piercing shrieks without respite. At daybreak the screams ceased and the child fell asleep; but consciousness had fled, only to return for one moment the next day, to revive in us a fading hope.

On arriving at Kena on the Nile, we hastened to engage a boat to take us to Cairo, where we hoped to find medical aid; but it was two days before the boat was ready. We then sailed day and night for eight days, during which time the sleeper was unconscious, sleeping most of the time until it pleased God to take her early on the eighth morning, three hours before reaching Old Cairo.[1]

The pain of helplessly watching a child die an agonizing death was only matched by the suffering caused by the death of a newborn baby—a scenario that was all too common for missionary mothers. Mary Williams, who would later lose her husband to the cannibals of the South Sea Islands, is an example. In 1831, she was pregnant again and "hoped, by a change of scene, that she might be 'spared the distress of consigning a seventh sweet babe to a premature grave.'" But, once again misfortune struck and "yet another still-born infant was 'planted' (in the language of five-year-old Sam) in the soil of yet another tropical island." The pain was nearly unbearable, but Mary had no choice but to pick up the pieces and go on with life.[2]

In reviewing missionary family life in the nineteenth century, it would be easy to conclude that separation, sickness, and death were the norm— that to serve abroad as a missionary meant to relinquish family stability. That was true of many of the well-known pioneer missionaries. William Carey, Adoniram Judson, David Livingstone, and Hudson Taylor are some notable examples. But there were other pioneer missionaries who had a much more balanced family life. Robert Moffat is a prime example. He and his wife Mary served for most of fifty years in Southern Africa. It was a very difficult life, and Mary barely survived some of her ten pregnancies, but despite the hardships, family life was maintained. The mission station at Kuruman was the only home the family ever knew, and it was described as an "oasis in the desert." Missionaries who visited spoke highly of the hospitality offered them:

> We stayed a short time at the station of that grand old patriarch of missionaries, Mr. Moffat, where we received all the kindly hospitality, attention and advice possible from him and Mrs. Moffat—verily the two best friends travelers ever came across. I shall never forget their affectionate courtesy, their beautifully ordered household, and their earnest desire to help us on in every way.[3]

There were times of separation in the Moffat household while Robert was away doing itinerant evangelistic work and when the children were at boarding school in Cape Town, but periodic trips to the coast helped maintain family closeness. As was so often true of missionary children, they were not alienated from missions because of the deprivations they endured. Indeed, all five of the Moffat children who survived to adulthood served in Africa as missionaries themselves, and they looked back with fondness to the family life they had known as children of pioneer missionaries. In many other instances, however, missionary children grew up hardly knowing the strangers who were their parents.

### Maria Taylor

Maria Taylor had no illusions about life on the mission field. She had been raised in China by missionary parents. She had seen death all

Maria Taylor, wife of J. Hudson Taylor, founder of the China Inland Mission.

around her and in her own family: her father died when she was a small child and her mother some years later. Following her mother's death, she returned home to England with her sister and brother, but for the two girls China had become home. They returned after they finished their schooling to work in a girls' school in Ningpo. It was there that Maria met Hudson Taylor, who was described as being "not idle, but aimless" and viewed by most who knew him as a bit eccentric with his Chinese robes and dyed hair and pigtail.[4]

Although Maria was described by Taylor as having a "very noticeable [and] decided cast in one of her eyes," it was a defect that apparently did not deter suitors. She had rejected marriage proposals from other young men, but in Taylor she found qualities she was looking for in a husband. He had a vision that few people possessed, and she was able to see beyond the rough edges into the future, when his vision would be enhanced through a husband-wife team ministry. Taylor described her as "a dear sweet creature," who "has all the good points of Miss S. [the young woman who had recently rejected his marriage proposal] and many more too. She is a precious treasure, one of sterling worth and possessed with an untiring zeal for the good of this poor people. She is a *lady* too." He was also impressed with her fluency in Chinese. Yet, he had reservations. She was a young woman of high social standing, at least in comparison with him, and that, he feared, would be an insurmountable obstacle.[5]

Maria's social position was truly an obstacle—not from her own perspective but from that of Miss Mary Ann Aldersey, the domineering "tiny little" sixty-year-old Englishwoman who ran the school where Maria and her sister served. Although she was not their legal guardian, she thought it fully within her domain to control their personal lives. She was adamantly opposed to Maria's interest in Taylor, and when he proposed, she demanded that Maria send an immediate letter of rejection. Taylor, however was not easily deterred, and Maria encouraged his determined effort to win her. After months of rankling between missionaries on both sides of the issue, Maria acquired the necessary permission from her legal guardian back in England and the marriage took place, but not without enduring bitterness from those who had fought so hard against it.[6]

From the beginning, the marriage of Hudson and Maria Taylor was a true partnership. Maria was actively involved in the decision-making aspects of their early work in China and in the formation of the China Inland Mission. As time passed, however, she became more burdened with the domestic concerns of family life. The constant trials of nursing little ones was an ever-present strain. She knew all too well the precarious nature of rearing children in the disease—infested areas of the interior, and on many occasions she frantically fought to subdue the angel of death, but not always with success. So it was in August of 1867. Eight-year-old Gracie had become ill. She was the oldest of the five Taylor children, an active and happy child who won the hearts of the Chinese nationals.[7]

Although Taylor had received medical training, he was unable to diagnose Gracie's illness. Apparently he did not think it serious enough to prevent him from going on a short business trip back to the mission house at Hangchow. While there he was called to another post to treat Jane McLean, one of his missionaries, who was said to be very ill. Her condition was not serious, but the added travel caused a delay in his return home. When he arrived, Gracie was in a coma, and soon after she died. Taylor's diagnosis was "water on the brain."[8]

The deep anguish Maria felt was compounded by anger—as is so often true in the death of a loved one. Deep down she believed the death could have been prevented—if only those involved had been more vigilant. Her inner rage was directed toward Jane McLean, but it was apparent that she felt some of the blame rested on her husband. In a hand-written note to Miss McLean that was probably never mailed she vented her frustrations. She spoke of the deep regret "which has occurred again and again—O how painfully at times—to one of the grief stricken parents—had the husband, the father returned at the expected time to the anxious mother and his stricken first born instead of giving the preference to the claims of a member of his mission whose life he feared was in danger." She would live the rest of her life with the unanswered question, "Might the early detection of the true nature of the child's disease have resulted in her recovery?" It was a question that was asked with the justifiable indignation a mother feels at the death of a child: "In other words," she wrote, "was the life of the child sacrificed to the life of the missionary? Perhaps not."[9]

If there was any consolation to be had in Gracie's death, it was that it served to reduce the dissension that was wreaking havoc with the newly formed China Inland Mission. But the terrible tension created by the concern for the health of little ones continued. The following year, in the summer of 1868, Maria traveled to Shanghai to have the baby vaccinated, "during which time she nursed it through a dangerous attack of measles and whooping cough." The following month, a year after Gracie's death, when she was back at the compound in Yangchow, the mission house was attacked by an angry mob. Again she feared for the lives of her children—and for the life of her unborn baby, her sixth, due in three months. In the mayhem, she jumped from an upper story and fled with the children to a neighbor's home. She managed to quiet the children de-

spite the pain and terror: "I was anxious not to let anyone know how much I was hurt," she wrote, "as I felt it would alarm them, and it seemed most important that all should keep calm."[10]

Less than two years after the Yangchow incident, Maria was on the threshold of another trial. She had survived the terrifying riot at the mission house, as had the baby boy she was carrying, but the ordeal that lay ahead was in some ways worse because she had to endure the months of dread that preceded it. Indeed, for a mother it was the cruelest form of torment: "Early in 1870 the Taylors realized that Bertie, nearly nine, and Freddie aged seven, should return to England before another hot season. Five year old Samuel was exceptionally delicate; he must go too, with little Maria as playmate, leaving only baby Charley in China." Emily Blatchley, a single missionary who had lived with the Taylors for most of five years, agreed to return with the children and serve as their "foster mother."[11]

Amidst the trauma of separation, tragedy struck again. "Fear of parting was too much for Sammy. He died on the Yangtze on February 4 and was buried at Chinkiang. . . . Six weeks later, on March 22, at Shanghai, Hudson and Maria wept their farewell to the children."[12]

By this time Maria was so physically and emotionally exhausted that she was in no shape to carry another child. But she was again pregnant, and the child was due in the hundred—degree temperatures of July. The baby boy that was born survived thirteen days. It was another deep sorrow for Maria, but this time the period of bereavement was short. She herself died three days later.[13]

## Rosalind Goforth

While mothers often grieved the most over the suffering and death of little ones, the fathers also suffered deeply at the loss of their children. But they sometimes viewed the deaths more philosophically than did their wives, and faithfulness in serving God in ministry was regarded a higher calling than protection of their children. This was evident in David Livingstone's comment, written after losing a child while on an exploratory expedition: "It is a venture to take wife and children into a country where fever—African fever—prevails. But who that believes in Jesus would refuse to make a venture for such a Captain."[14]

Jonathan Goforth had a similar philosophy of ministry. He and his wife Rosalind sailed for China in 1888. They developed a very effective evangelistic ministry with the Chinese—so much so that Goforth has been considered by many to be the greatest missionary evangelist ever to serve in the Far East. But his success was not achieved without exacting a high toll on the family. Five of their eleven children died in infancy or early childhood. The ministry involved a great deal of travel and, recognizing the value of his wife's joint ministry, Goforth wanted her to accompany him with the children— a life that proved disastrous to their health.[15]

Following the Boxer Rebellion, Jonathan returned to China to get back into the ministry while he awaited the arrival of Rosalind and the children. On their arrival he shared with her his new plan of evangelism:

My plan is to have one of my helpers rent a suitable place in a large centre for us to live in, and that we, as a family, stay a month in the centre, during which time we will carry on intensive evangelism. I will go with my men to villages or on the street in the daytime, while you receive and preach to the women in the courtyard. The evenings will be given to a joint meeting with you at the organ and with plenty of gospel hymns. Then at the end of a month, we will leave an evangelist behind to teach the new believers while we go on to another place to open it in the same way. When a number of places are opened, we will return once or twice a year.[16]

Rosalind Goforth, wife of Jonathan Goforth, missionary to China.

When Rosalind saw the excitement in his expression and listened to his scheme, her "heart went like lead." The concept itself was valid, but it was utterly unsuited to family life. Exposing their little ones to the infectious diseases that were so common in the villages of the interior involved risks she was unwilling to accept. She could not forget for a moment the "four little graves" they had already dug on Chinese soil. "My one and only reason," she wrote, "in opposing and refusing to go with my children, as my husband suggested, was because it seemed a risking of the children's lives."[17]

Jonathan was persistent and not about to be easily dissuaded, as Rosalind later related: "Oh, how my husband pleaded. . . . He assured me that the Lord would keep my children from harm. . . . He was *sure* God was calling me to take this step of faith." Finally, he went beyond the pleading, and intimated that God might punish her if she did not go along with his plan. "Rose, I am so sure this plan is of God, that I fear for the children if you refuse to obey His call. *The safest place for you and the children is the path of duty.* You think you can keep your children safe in your comfortable home at Changte, but God may have to show you cannot." Rosalind later conceded that "time proved he was right, but, as yet, I had not the faith nor the vision nor the courage to regard it in that light."[18]

It is interesting that Rosalind's recollection of Jonathan's conversation on the subject shows him at a distinct distance from the children: "He assured me that the Lord would keep *my* children from harm," and "the safest place for you and *your* children is the path of duty." It was an era when fathers could justify forsaking family for ministry, and Goforth demonstrated little apparent sympathy for the pain his wife had endured in losing so many little ones.

The struggle between Rosalind and Jonathan was played out over and over again between wives and husbands in the annals of missionary history. It was a struggle between the God-given instinct and instruction to protect and care for one's own flesh and blood and the God-given call and command to reach out with the gospel to those who were dying without Christ.

## Chapter 4

# Second-Class Citizens: Struggling With Sex Discrimination

For all their contributions to foreign missionary endeavors, women have rarely been treated as equals of their male counterparts. This has been largely due to the restrictions placed on women in Christian ministry in general, based on biblical admonitions and church traditions. In many instances, constraints on women were tighter than any biblical passage might have warranted, and this sometimes created dissension between the sexes.

Were women missionaries feminists, as R. Pierce Beaver would have us believe from the subtitle of his book, *American Protestant Women in World Mission: A History of the First Feminist Movement in North America*? This is an issue that has been debated in recent years. Some feminist historians have implied that because women eagerly accepted such daring roles as pioneer overseas missionaries and because other women at home supported them in these ventures, they, indeed, must have been reflecting a feminist position.

On the other side of the issue are those who would strongly deny *any* correlation between missionary women and feminism. Elisabeth Elliot is an example: "Today strident female voices are raised, shrilly and ad nauseam, to remind us that women are equal with men. But such a question has never even arisen in connection with the history of Christian missions. In fact, for many years, far from being excluded, women constituted the majority of foreign missionaries."[1]

Elliot assumes that because women were in the majority they never raised their voices for equality. Not only is the logic faulty, but so is the conclusion. Women did raise their voices for equality. The question is, were they motivated by feminism? The issue is not a simple one in that feminism is not an easy term to define, especially when it involves the historical perspective. Jane Hunter, who has studied women missionaries in China, however, argues that feminism was not a factor in motivating women missionaries. In her study of their correspondence and published articles she found that the vast majority of women missionaries were motivated by a deep sense of commitment to God far more than by any desire to attain personal recognition or power. "For feminism to have gained a foothold among the women's missionary community would have entailed the replacement of the underlying premise of women's mission work, self-denial, with its opposite, self-advocacy."[2]

While it is difficult to make a case that feminist instincts prompted women to enter missionary service, there can be no doubt that there was a strong proclivity for independence that characterized these women. Nancy Cott provides an astute analysis: "If the popular sales of the published memoirs of female missionaries are any guide, that model of religious commitment, which proposed a submission of self that was simultaneously a pronounced form of self-assertion, had wide appeal."[3]

Despite their independence, missionary women generally acknowledged the leadership of the male sex with little complaint, and in some cases they strongly protested any suggestion that they might be feminists. Sue McBeth, who planted churches and preached among the Nez Perce Indians, strongly objected to being categorized as a feminist. Speaking of herself, she wrote:

> Dr. Lowrie must not think for a moment that she is what is called a "Women's Rights Woman." (I am afraid she is not even among the strong minded.) She has no affinity for such. Has more "rights" now than she can make good use of—and aims to try to be with God's help a true woman.[4]

Women generally accepted the restrictions placed on them and sometimes even went above and beyond the call of duty to accommodate critics. Isabella Thoburn agreed to speak at a Sunday service after she had returned home on furlough only on the condition that she be permitted to answer questions from the front pew instead of "preaching" from the pulpit.[5]

Some women objected to the equality that was thrust upon them. They protested the conditions that required them to do what was typically considered men's work. Jeannie Dickson, who worked with the Dakota Mission, resented having "to take a man's position in everything" and of having to fill a work assignment that entailed all the duties required of a man but granted her none of the privileges. "The property must be looked after which is no light matter is this country," she wrote.

> Now this I am not complaining of. If it is my Father's will concerning me that I preach the Gospel or wash the dishes, I want to do it for His glory, but if I have a man's responsibility, why can I not also have a man's privilege in knowing something of the many matters in connection with this mission.[6]

Typical of the female response to male leadership was that of Mrs. Ethan Curtis, who assured the audience that listened to her read a paper at the Woman's Board of Missions in Brooklyn in 1891: "Nowhere do we oppose man. Our first object is to be his ready and willing assistant."[7]

If there is serious doubt about the assertion that women missionaries were feminists, there is no question as to the frequent opposition they faced. In many cases it was subtle opposition, as was true when Isabella Thoburn, at the request of her brother, Bishop James Thoburn, went to India to begin educational work for girls. During the early months after her arrival he kept her so busy with his personal secretarial duties that she had no time to devote to her educational work. She finally insisted that she be allowed to conduct her own work, and he acknowledged the injustice of his actions. Speaking of himself, he wrote: "He understood for the first time that 'a Christian woman sent out to the field was a Christian missionary, and that her time was as precious, her work as important, and her rights as sacred as those of the more conventional missionaries of the other sex.'"[8]

In other cases the prejudice against women was much more blatant. This was particularly true in the mid and late nineteenth century, when women missionaries were a novelty. Although married women often worked as hard as their husbands in the ministry and accomplished sometimes as much as their single sisters, in many cases they received no salary at all. Thus, Helen Holcomb, a Presbyterian missionary in India, complained of this to the mission board, telling of the difficult financial circumstances that compelled her to write in an effort to augment her husband's meager salary. Single women often fared little better. Adele Fielde received only half the salary that her unmarried male colleague was allotted.[9]

A more common complaint of women concerning sex discrimina-tion related to their lack of representation in board meetings and field council conferences. In 1899 Bertha Caldwell wrote an indignant letter to the Presbyterian Board of Foreign Missions secretary, explaining why she boycotted the annual meeting: "This year it was given out that the gentlemen did not wish the ladies at all in their sessions, and so the latter sat stupidly about, and gossiped or slept and wished Annual Meeting would be over." She then listed several women and their significant ministries and went on to protest that despite this active involvement in the mission the women "get no voice at all in the matter unless specially asked, and absolutely no vote. . . . I fear this Mission is much behind the times."[10]

The discrimination women encountered in missions continued well on into the twentieth century and sometimes became most caustic in nature. The outspoken opposition of John R. Rice is an example:

The deputation work of great missionary societies has suffered greatly at the hands of women missionaries. If godly, Spirit-filled men, manly men, should go to the churches with the appeal that those whom God has called for His work should come prepared for toil and sweat and blood and tears, it would do infinitely more for the mission cause than the prattle about dress and customs and food, with stereopticon slide pictures of quaint heathen groups presented so often by women missionaries, largely to groups of women and children. . . . It certainly violates the command of God for women to speak before mixed audiences of men and women and to take the pulpit in the churches. And we may be sure that the work of the gospel of Christ among the heathen is not prospered by this sin.[11]

There were women who raised their voices against such opposition and for greater equality in ministry. Perhaps the most vocal of these was Pearl S. Buck, the well-known author, who was raised in China by missionary parents. She was no friend of missions in later life, and she vehemently attacked the sexism that was so much part of the missionary lifestyle. Her reflections on her mother bear this out: "Since those days when I saw all her nature dimmed I have hated Saint Paul with all my heart and so must all true women hate him, I think, because of what he has done in the past to women like Carie, proud free-born women, yet damned by their very womanhood."[12] Mary Slessor also took issue with the Apostle Paul—though in a far more light-hearted spirit. In the margin of her Bible next to Ephesians 5:22, where Paul admonishes wives to submit to their husbands, she wrote, "Nay, nay, Paul, Laddie, that will not do."

In the vast majority of cases, however, when missionary women challenged restrictions placed on them because of their sex, the issue related to ministry. Women's rights was simply not an issue that gripped them. They had made extraordinary sacrifices for the cause of world evangelism, and it was a cause worth fighting for. It was on this basis then that women such as Lottie Moon fought for equal rights.

### Charlotte "Lottie" Moon

Charlotte Diggs "Lottie" Moon (1840–1912) has often been referred to as the "patron saint" of Southern Baptist missions because of the influence she had on missionary outreach and giving. She was raised on a Virginia plantation and after the Civil War pursued a teaching career in Georgia, but her heart was in foreign missions. She was motivated not only by her faith in Christ but also by her desire to move beyond the routine of life in the post–Civil War South. Other family members had "marched out to fight for the Stars and Bars" and had performed "splendid service" while she had remained home on the plantation. Now it was her opportunity to become involved in an exciting venture.[13]

In 1873 she sailed for China, where she initially taught in a children's school. Life was lonely and her job was unfulfilling. She was tempted to try to solve her problems by getting married, but she broke an engagement to a brilliant missionary—minded young man because he had adopted the Darwinian theory of evolution. He later became a professor at Harvard University, while she, in her own words, was left to "plod along in the same old way." Years later, when reflecting on the broken relationship, she said, "God had first claim on my life, and since the two conflicted, there could be no question about the result."[14]

With that decision to remain single came a determination to carve out for herself a more fulfilling ministry among the Chinese people. She was convinced that her talent was being wasted and could be better used in evangelism and church planting. She had come to China to "go out among the millions" as an evangelist, only to find herself chained to a school of forty "unstudious" children. Giving women such assignments, she argued was "the greatest folly of modern missions." She viewed herself as part of an oppressed class—single women missionaries—and her words were an appeal on behalf of all those who were facing similar frustration in their ministries. But the examples she used precisely fit her own situation. "Can we wonder at the mortal weariness and disgust, the sense of wasted powers and the conviction that her life is a failure, that comes over a woman when, instead of the ever broadening activities she had planned, she finds herself tied down to the petty work of teaching a few girls?"[15]

Lottie Moon's plea for her sex was always in the context of her ministry. Indeed, she was not pleading for women's rights as much as she was pleading for the right to best use God-given gifts in ministry: "What women want who come to China is free opportunity to do the largest possible work. . . . What women have a right to demand is perfect equality." It is interesting that one of her bitterest enemies on this issue was a woman—a not uncommon scenario in women's history. A Congregational missionary wife, Mrs. Arthur Smith, questioned Lottie's mental stability and denounced her "lawless prancing all over the mission lot." In her view the appropriate role of a woman missionary was to attend "with quivering lip" her own children.[16]

Lottie's insistence on doing evangelism and church planting was not readily endorsed by her field director. Indeed, she feared that he might seek to further limit the ministry opportunities for women in the mission. Despite some vocal opposition, women missionaries serving with the Southern Baptists were at least permitted to vote—a liberty not granted Presbyterian women missionaries. Fearing that that liberty might be rescinded, Lottie made her position very clear: "Simple justice demands that women should have equal rights with men in mission meetings and in the conduct of their work." And in reference to her field director's efforts to limit her ministry, she wrote, "If that be freedom, give me slavery."[17]

Lottie Moon, missionary to China. (From the Archives, Woman's Missionary Union, Auxiliary to Southern Baptist Convention.)

Despite her field director's initial opposition, she successfully conducted evangelistic work, and in 1889 her work in P'ing-tu was described as the "greatest evangelistic center" among the Southern Baptists "in all China." This remarkable success was in part due to her own personality and gifts. After working among the people for a time she wrote, "Surely there can be no deeper joy than that of saving souls." But there were other reasons as well, and her sex no doubt had as much to do with her success as did her own capability in this type of ministry. As an unordained woman, she was not qualified to lead the churches she planted. Thus it was imperative for her—more so than for her male counterparts—to train indigenous ministers as soon as possible. This worked in favor of a strong local church. Indeed, within two decades the Chinese pastor at P'ing-tu had baptized more than a thousand converts.[18]

In light of her own successful ministry, Lottie aggressively appealed to women at home to raise funds for China missions and to sponsor single women missionaries for the work. "What I hope to see," she wrote, "is a band of ardent, enthusiastic, and experienced Christian women occupying a line of stations extending from P'ing-tu on the north and from Chinkiang on the south, making a succession of stations uniting the two. . . . A mighty wave of enthusiasm for Women's Work for Women must be stirred." Her emphasis on recruiting women was based not only on the confidence she placed in female evangelists and church planters, but also on the stark reality that Southern Baptist men had virtually handed over the work of China missions to women by default. Earlier Lottie had written, "It is odd that a million Baptists of the South can furnish only three men for all China. Odd that with five hundred preachers in the state of Virginia, we must rely on a Presbyterian to fill a Baptist pulpit [here]. I wonder how these things look in heaven. They certainly look very queer in China."[19]

Lottie identified closely with the Chinese people, and when a time of great famine inflicted devastation on her Chinese friends, she gave her own food supplies to needy families. She was simply unable to eat when there were starving children at her door begging for food. As a result, she herself died in 1912 at the age of seventy-two from complications relating to malnutrition, and perhaps it was fitting that she died on Christmas Eve. She had initiated a Christmas offering from women at home for the China work, and her death served as a symbolic offering of the very life that stirred the conscience of the Southern Baptists. The Lottie Moon Christmas offering became a widely celebrated fund-raising tradition for missions among Southern Baptist women that in recent years has netted tens of millions of dollars annually.[20] For all that she did to promote women's involvement at home and in China, showing that women indeed could function on an equal level with men, Lottie Moon could not change the perception that some men would always have of women: in recognition of her singular work, the *Foreign Missions Journal* paid her its highest tribute by saying that she was "the best man among our missionaries."[21]

## Carie Sydenstricker

Carie Sydenstricker would have been lost in obscurity like so many other missionary women, had it not been for her biographer—her illustrious daughter, the Nobel and Pulitzer Prize winning novelist Pearl S. Buck. Biographers, like historians and scholars in other fields, always struggle with objectivity, and even more so when their subject is close to them. So with Carie it is important to remember that the biographical record of her life was written by one who loved her dearly and who identified with her closely.

The sex discrimination Carie struggled with was not the kind of prejudice that was evident in mission council meetings or in field assignments. It was a more subtle bias that was inherent in the marriage, and one that she would struggle with all her life. Many women simply accepted the restrictions placed upon them, but Carie could not. She lived by the rules, but inside she yearned for freedom.

Unlike Dorothy Carey, who was thrust into missions by marriage, and Mary Livingstone, who was thrust into missions by birth, Carie could claim a call of her own—if, indeed, it was a call. At the death of her mother she "vowed her life away." Prior to that she had listened to missionaries make their appeals in the village church, "but she had not herself sought to find a 'call.' . . . Now all that was changed. She must be—she was ready to go." Her preparation involved a course of study at Bellewood Seminary, a school for girls, and her marriage to Andrew Sydenstricker, a puritanical, pious, and single-minded missionary candidate whose life was committed to China. They were married in the summer of 1880 and set sail for China immediately thereafter. The departure was difficult for Carie. She had deep apprehensions about the decision she had made years

earlier. "She felt at that instant a hostility to this saint to whom she had married herself—nay more, a hostility, instantly repressed, to God Himself, who even at this hour of separation would not speak from the high heaven where He lived to tell her by any sign that she had done well."[22]

From the beginning of her ministry in China, Carie had mixed emotions about spending her life and raising her children in that faraway land. She ached with homesickness for the land she had left behind, and yet, as the years passed "she was bound also to China, bound by her very knowledge of it, bound by such souls as Wang Amah, bound by the three small bodies sleeping in that ancient earth and mingling at least their pale dust with its darkness." Losing little ones was the sorest trial the missionary calling could require of a missionary mother. With the death of each of them she was sure she could bear no more. "Underneath all the days and nights her heart was bleeding for her dead children. Andrew could go back to his work again, must go back, and she must be alone."[23]

"Throughout all my growing years, then" Pearl later wrote, "I was aware that my mother's real life remained in her own house across the sea. She made homes in China that were exquisite in taste. . . . There we found merriment, for my mother was of gay disposition, although she had certain moods which darkened the day for us and which we never understood."[24]

One of the trying aspects of Carie's missionary life that may have caused her dark moods were the differences and the distance between her and

Andrew. "Andrew was not a man who ever understood or loved children," wrote his daughter. "Not that he disliked them, but they did not exist for him in any real sense. His life was wrapped in a mystic union with God and with the souls of men—always their souls." His calling was a high calling. It was left to his wife to care for the children.

> Seven children never taught Andrew how to hold a baby or how to dress a child. He was born prophet and saint, a man far from the daily life of mankind. Even in his own home there was a quality of remoteness about him. No child of his thought of running to him to have a shoe tied or a button fastened. . . . To his children he was a figure always a little dim, living outside their world. . . . They preferred their mother's swift impetuosities, her sudden little tempers and warm instant apologies, her great close embraces and her little jokes and merry looks to all the cool goodness of their father.[25]

The children assumed their father was the way fathers were supposed to be. He was the only white man they knew. "White fathers, it seemed, rarely touched or caressed their children, or even their wives, and often seemed not to know they were there." Carie had some of the same reserve. Although she showed far greater warmth toward the children and more interest in their activities, she expressed very little physical affection. "Carie, apparently so benumbed by the lack of warmth in her marriage, never, in Pearl's memory, petted or hugged her children."[26]

It was not an easy marriage for Carie, but marriages in the nineteenth century—especially missionary marriages—were not made to be broken. "She belonged to an age when marriage, at least among respectable and certainly among religious people, was as irrevocable as death. She had pledged herself to a life with him and she would go on with it." But she would not be swallowed up in his life. That was evident when she insisted they move back to their home in Chinkiang, where the climate was more suited to survival. "Otherwise I go back to our own country," she informed him. "I have offered three children. I have no more children to give away to God now." Indeed, her children in many respects came first. "How rich I am in my children!," she wrote in her diary. And again, "My children have been my great romance." "Yet in justice to Carie it must be said that she never herself doubted the importance or the primacy of Andrew's mission," wrote her daughter. "She felt secretly that there was in his mysticism something too high for her and for us to understand, and we must just follow behind."[27]

There were other problems between Carie and Andrew as well, not the least of which were the "hot arguments sometimes over the conflict of Christian doctrine and the circumstances they found." As time passed, they drifted further and further apart. "Alone together in the house, alone on the junks, alone plodding side by side through the dusty country roads or along the crowded cobbled streets of cities, there was no talk to be made between them." Their personalities and manners of expressing themselves were entirely different. "Carie, whose cheerful, humorous, running conversation was a delight to so many others, found that to Andrew her racy comments on what she saw were often only a weariness and unwarranted audacities."[28]

Carie Sydenstriker with husband, the parents of Pearl S. Buck.

Although Carie carried on effective work among the women and was much loved by them, she struggled in her own spiritual life. "Deep down under all the fullness of her life, Carie felt at times still the inadequacy of her relation to God. She planned sometimes for a period when she would withdraw and really seek to find what she needed. She planned to read her Bible more and pray more and try to be 'good.'" Her faith was graphically compared with her husband's by a story that comes out of Pearl Buck's own experience when she asked her mother one morning

after breakfast, "What makes the red marks on Father's forehead?"

"They are marks from his fingers where he leans his head on his hand to pray," Carie answered soberly. "Your father prays for a whole hour every morning when he gets up."

Such holiness was awe-inspiring. The children looked for like marks of it on their mother's forehead, and one asked, "why don't you pray, too, Mother?"

Carie answered—was it with a trifle of sharpness?—"If I did, who would dress you all and get breakfast and clean house and teach you your lessons? Some have to work, I suppose, while some pray."

Andrew came out of his habitual abstraction long enough to overhear this, and to remark gently, "If you took a little more time for prayer, Carie, perhaps the work would go better."

To which Carie replied with considerable obstinacy, "There isn't but so much time and the Lord will just have to understand that a mother with little children has to condense her prayers."

The truth of it was that Carie was not very good at long prayers. She prayed hard and swiftly at times, but she prayed as she worked, and she was always perhaps a little conscious against her will that her voice seemed to go up and come back to her without surety of reply.[29]

Part of the inner struggle Carie endured in her spiritual life and ministry related to Andrew's view of women. "He was imbued . . . with the Pauline doctrine of the subjection of the women to the man and to him it was enough if she kept his house and bore his children and waited on his needs." Of course, she was permitted

45

to teach the Chinese women, "but he must have the final examination in the faith and knowledge of all and his must be the final decision, as priest of God, whether or not they were to come into the congregation." Unlike so many missionary women, who passively accepted their condition, Carie resented her station in life:

When Carie perceived his mind, all her swift, rebel blood boiled. It seemed to her that for the first time she saw this saint of hers that she had married for his goodness, as he really was—for all his goodness toward her he was narrow and selfish and arrogant. What—was she not to go to God direct because she was born a woman? Was not her brain swifter, keener, clearer than the brains of most men? Why—was God like that, Andrew's God? It was as though she had come bearing in her two hands her rich gifts of brain and body, giving them freely and as touchingly sure of appreciation as a child—and her gifts had been thrown back at her as useless. It was her first real and acknowledged contact with Andrew's mind.[30]

As much as Carie struggled in her spiritual life and her missionary life in China, it was she who remained in China during her last years while her husband returned to America to take care of business matters and enroll their youngest daughter in school. She died not long after he returned, after serving most of three and a half decades in her adopted land of China. For all she had sacrificed, she had very little sense of accomplishment. "I suppose she would have considered her life a failure if she had judged it by the measure of what she had meant it to be," wrote her daughter. "Certainly if at the beginning she could have seen the end she would have called it failure. . . . She was one of those who, having visited the sick and those in prison and cared for the widowed and fatherless and fed the hungry . . . reproached herself that she had not chosen a better part."[31]

## J. Hudson Taylor

Although missionary women faced opposition from mission leaders and from their husbands in their efforts to enjoy a fulfilling ministry, it is important to remember that missions offered women opportunities no other area of church ministry did. This was largely because of outspoken male leaders who recognized the value of women in ministry and were willing to risk their reputation in their defense of the "weaker sex." The success experienced by women like Lottie Moon in China did not go unrecognized by J. Hudson Taylor and other great mission leaders.

One of the greatest missionary statesmen of the modern era was J. Hudson Taylor, the founder and long-time director of the China Inland Mission. He is regarded by some as the founder of the Faith Missionary Movement because of his insistence that missionaries who were part of his organization not be salaried or solicit funds. His recruits were largely unordained lay persons—including large numbers of single women. In fact, in the first CIM mission party that sailed to China, seven of the fifteen new recruits were single women (the remainder being married couples). On the field single women were often stationed far in the interior and were responsible for evangelism and church planting in large regions, with no immediate male supervision.

A fascinating sketch relating to Hudson Taylor's attitude toward women in the China Inland Mission appeared in the *Missionary Review of the World* in 1898. Here Julius Richter, reflecting the attitude of many mainline churchmen, criticized Taylor's philosophy and practice regarding women: "Hudson Taylor makes extraordinarily ample use of the services of unmarried ladies; whole districts of the Chinese mission field are exclusively under the management of mission sisters. I took the liberty of suggesting how unbecoming and repellent to our German ideas was this free employment of single mission sisters in the midst of entirely heathen districts." Taylor had a ready reply, suggesting that Richter's problem was that he viewed the situation through "German or European eyes" instead of from a Chinese standpoint. He argued that single women were secure because they were required to be accompanied by a "married Chinese catechist." But more significantly, he emphasized the distinct advantage there was in relying on women for the work of cross-cultural evangelism:

The native catechist never comes to true inward independence at a station where he works under a European missionary; he feels himself to be only the dependent journeyman of the other, and is hardly noticed by the Chinese in presence of the overwhelming superiority of the European. It is quite otherwise when he is associated with a missionary-sister; then the whole work of teaching and preaching and representing the mission to outsiders devolves upon him; he counts as the head of the mission, and must act independently. But at the same time he is under the control of the mission sister, who is with him to advise and instruct him, and to report about him. The sister herself has a sufficient sphere of activity in the female part of the heathen population and the Christian Church, and if sometimes men also listen to her Bible-lessons, no offense is given. Of course, a great deal of tact is necessary for the sister and the catechist to maintain their mutual position.[32]

Taylor not only eagerly recruited single women to "man" the stations in China, but he also expected married women to do their share of mission work. To a male recruit he wrote, "Unless you intend your wife to be a true missionary, not merely a wife, home-maker, and friend, *do not join us.*"[33] Jennie, his second wife, certainly fit the description of a "true" missionary. In 1878, when Taylor was ill in England, she agreed to leave him and her young children behind in order to return to China with a famine relief team.[34]

There were many other mission leaders of the nineteenth and twentieth centuries who were equally committed to opening doors for women in mission, and their influence has paved the way for women in various other areas of church ministry.

# Chapter 5

# Sin in the Camp: Internal Dissension and Discord

The problem that has hampered modern missions perhaps more than any other has been that of divisiveness among missionaries—missionaries who sacrifice so much to take the gospel to inhospitable regions and yet cannot get along with each other, often to the dismay of the very people they are seeking to convert. It has sometimes been a matter of jest among male missionaries that the "single ladies" bicker among themselves and create problems for the mission. Certainly single women were not immune to the problem of divisiveness, but men and married women have also been guilty of creating dissension in the missionary community. This was true of Mrs. Henry Nott, who served with her husband on the island of Tahiti.

Henry Nott was among the first party of missionaries sent to the South Sea Islands by the London Missionary Society. Like others in the group, he was single and plagued by the temptation of alluring island women. Nott was more restrained than one of his colleagues, who abandoned his duties and was said to be keeping a whole harem of women for a time. But he did take a woman as his wife—for a time. Under pressure from the mission authorities he abandoned her, or in more acceptable terms, the marriage was "annulled by common consent."[1]

To alleviate the problem with its single male missionaries, the London Missionary Society arranged for four "godly young women" to sail to the South Pacific and offer themselves as missionary wives. It may have seemed like the perfect solution, but Nott might have been far more content with his native wife. The "godly woman" who became his wife was apparently physically attractive, described as having a "perfect curvature," but she did not serve effectively as a missionary wife. "Her tong [sic] is daily employed in abusing her Husband in the most cruel manner and to slander others with the lest [sic] cause," wrote a fellow missionary. "Her feet of late are never directed to the place where prayer is wont to be made but daily she joins with those who are studious in their design to perplex and thwart us."[2]

Mrs. Nott was regarded by most of the missionaries as a disgrace to the cause of Christ and to the mission. Dr. Ross, a colleague of her husband's, deplored her divisiveness and lamented her drinking problem, claiming that "when intoxicated she is absolutely mad and cares not what she does or says." When she died some time later, he maintained that she "drank herself to death."[3]

Sometimes the dissension that disrupted the work of missions involved disputes between men and women. In one instance, according to Leecy Barnett, "fighting between the missionaries so gravely damaged the reputation of the mission station that it was never able to gain the respect of the Indians and eventually closed." The conflict in this case had flared up between a Rev. Murdock and two missionary teachers, Sarah and Mary Ann Conover, who had been assigned to work among the Otoe tribe in 1857. Initially the friction was confined to verbal attacks. The Conover sisters were critical of Murdock because he too frequently canceled church services, and he denounced them when they expressed opinions that differed from his in his Bible class. The accusations escalated, with the sisters claiming that Murdock exercised "a spirit of tyranny" over the school children and employed "truly insolent language and threats to horsewhip the children who ran off."[4]

"Finally the tension at the Otoe mission exploded into open hostility and violence." Murdock dismissed the Indian students and ordered the Conover sisters to leave. They refused, and utter chaos ensued. "Rev. Murdock then ordered the sisters out of the room. When they didn't obey, he struck Sarah several times. Mary tried to come to her sister's aid but in the struggle Murdock knocked her to the ground. After this incident the differences between the missionaries were beyond repair."[5] This ugly incident hidden in the annals of missionary history illustrates the deep dissension that sometimes wreaked havoc on Christian evangelism, and it shows the not-uncommon frustration single women endured in working with their male superiors.

Dissension between married women was not uncommon (and in many cases was aggravated by their husbands), while in other cases the dissension involved personality or procedural conflicts between the men that deeply affected the women. In such situations, women often had the most to lose. This was true of Narcissa Whitman and many other women who struggled to make a life in a new environment.

## Narcissa Whitman

Narcissa Whitman was a pioneer missionary to the Oregon Territory with her husband Marcus, a physician, who had learned his "trade" by "riding with a doctor." Although Oregon was not overseas, it was during the first half of the nineteenth century still considered a 'foreign' mission field. The Whitmans were commissioned by the American Board of Commissioners for Foreign Missions and began their missionary venture in the spring of 1835, traveling westward with the American Fur Company.

Narcissa, the daughter of Judge Stephen Prentiss, was a teacher before she met Marcus, but she was not fulfilled. She had heard the story of the Nez Perce Indians in the far West who had pleaded that someone be sent to bring them the "Book of Life," and she desired more than anything else to answer that plea. The American Board was actively seeking missionary volunteers—single men or married couples. Single women were not eligible. For Narcissa, marriage was the only answer to her dilemma. It was the gossip associated with her predicament that prompted Marcus Whitman to visit Narcissa. He, too, had a vision for missionary service in the Far West, and he had heard that Narcissa might make a suitable wife. With that in mind, he visited her to discuss Indian missions. He was planning a preliminary expedition to Oregon, and he agreed that if he determined the venture would be suitable for a wife, he would return and marry her. "He left with no promises. It was not a love affair nor an engagement. It was more of a business arrangement."[6]

Marcus did not venture all the way to Oregon as he had planned, but turned around before he had completed the crossing of the Rocky Mountains, and returned to New York to marry Narcissa. They were married in February of 1836, and the day after their wedding they left for Missouri to join the American Fur Company on their trip West. Accompanying them to Oregon were Henry and Eliza Spalding, who were also missionaries with the American Board. It was a difficult journey that

exhausted any patience and good will the men might have had for each other when they started. The original plan had called for a team enterprise, but after nearly five months of strained relationships and overt hostility, the men determined they would go their separate ways.[7]

Narcissa Whitman, wife of Dr. Marcus Whitman, missionary to the Oregon Territory.

For Narcissa and Eliza, who needed each other's company in that desolate wilderness—especially during the first winter—the decision was an unfortunate one. Narcissa was pregnant when they arrived, but there was no time for leisure or rest as she set up housekeeping in their makeshift lean-to. It was a difficult time for her. She suffered the pain of loneliness more than her husband

*51*

who was consumed with the work of establishing his mission. She craved the woman-to-woman companionship she might have enjoyed with Eliza, judging from a journal entry she made months before the separation: "Mrs. Spalding . . . possesses much fortitude. I like her very much. She wears well upon acquaintance. . . I think we shall get along very well together; we have so far."[8]

The problem of loneliness was unfortunately not solved by the additional recruits that arrived in 1838. The presence of the three new couples created further discord. There were personality conflicts and there seemed to be few issues on which the missionaries could agree. One of the wives described her reaction to a typical flare-up: "It came on so sharp that I was compelled to leave. . . . It is enough to make one sick to see what is the state of things in the mission."[9]

Many of the conflicts related to mission location and assignments for the men and their families, but some of the conflicts arose out of the difficult situation Narcissa faced in attempting to house such a large group of missionaries who needed a place to stay until they were settled in their permanent locations. This created tensions in the Whitman household, especially for Narcissa. The excitement of a cross-cultural ministry with the native American Indians of Oregon had begun to fade, and the drudgery of being hostess to uninvited guests brought on anger and discontent. These feelings could not be disguised when in the fall of 1838 William Gray brought the new missionaries to their home at Waiilatpu. "The Whitmans, not knowing how many would be in Gray's party or even whether he would return with any assistants, were wholly unprepared to receive so many. They were embarrassed by lack of room" in their "adobe house which measured 30 x 36 feet."[10]

It was in this setting that Narcissa's discontent was openly manifested. Mary Smith's diary gives glimpses of the tense situation. "Mr. Smith came to the pantry & found nothing but milk & melons. Didn't like it. Mrs. W[hitman] [made] cut[ting] remarks about milk, sugar &c. At supper Mr. S. said he was very hungry, had had no dinner. In forenoon Mr. Smith sent out to give a melon to some boys . . . . Mrs. W[hitman] countermanded." Two weeks later Mary's diary read, "Mrs. W[hitman] has said and done many things that do not suit Mrs. S[mith] today." The following week she wrote, "Mrs. Whitman quite out with Mr. Smith because he was unwilling to let her have Jack [a Hawaiian] help her." The following weeks brought no improvement in the situation. On November 17 she wrote, "After breakfast Mrs. W. went to her room & there remained through the day without concerning at all how or what was done. I know not, I am sure what she wishes or thinks. But I think her a strange house-keeper. It is hard to please when one cannot know what would please." Apparently much of the work fell on Narcissa; Mary noted several days later that she was doing the washing and "has less help from the other ladies than she ought."[11]

In addition to the household burden and the inability of the women to share in the work harmoniously, Narcissa was distressed by the conflict raging between the men. On December 3, Mary's diary entry reads: "Monthly concert in the evening after which Dr., his wife & Mr. E[ells] & wife, husband & self sit up till midnight talking about Mr. S[mith] & G[ray]. Mrs. W[hitman] gets to feeling very bad, goes to bed crying." The following day, Mary wrote, "Mrs. W. in a sad mood all day, did not present herself at the breakfast table. Went out doors, down by the river to cry."[12]

Throughout the cold winter that followed the little irritations were magnified by the close proximity of the guests in the small house. They often stood elbow to elbow in Narcissa's kitchen to keep warm by the stove, and among them was Elkanah Walker, whose habit of chewing tobacco greatly offended Narcissa. Speaking of all this intrusion into her life, she wrote to her sister the following spring, "Now how do you think I have lived with such folks right in my kitchen for the whole winter?"[13]

Unity did come during times of tragedy, but the price for such unity was a heavy one, as was true in the summer of 1839:

> Sympathy and sorrow healed the wounds of bitterness, as the Whitmans suffered the pain of a heart rending ordeal. It was a late June Sunday afternoon at Waiilatpu. . . . Marcus and Narcissa were engrossed in reading and little Alice was playing close by— or so they thought. When they suddenly realized she was missing, it was too late. The precious little two-year-old had wandered off and drowned in a nearby stream. The Spaldings came immediately to share the sorrow. . . . A year later a package arrived from back east with the little shoes and dresses

Narcissa had requested from her mother.[14]

Narcissa was a strong woman and she accepted her daughter's death as part of God's divine plan, but the years would bring further difficulty and disappointment. Missionary life was not how she had envisioned it. Indeed, had she been allowed to serve as a single women, she might have had a fulfilling ministry, as did so many other single women who came later, such as Kate and Sue McBeth and Jeanie Dickson. As it was, she was tied to her husband's mission station that also served as an immigrant inn. Her time was consumed with feeding and housing the dozens of travelers who were often in residence while they were establishing themselves in the untamed wilderness.

The mission at Waiilatpu was located in a lush green valley, and it attracted settlers by its very presence—an unsettling situation in the eyes of the nearby Cayuse Indians. It is not surprising, then, that they bitterly resented the incursion of the white man, and the Whitman mission compound was a symbol of this incursion. Although Dr. Whitman offered his healing ministry to the Indians, his assistance to white immigrants who were passing through was seen as giving aid to the enemy.

In 1847, less than twelve years after their work in Oregon was begun, their mission compound was attacked by a small group of Cayuse Indians, and fourteen residents were killed, including Marcus and Narcissa. The five Indians involved in the murders were hanged, and all the mission work in the region was sus-

Lammermuir party, the first missionaries of the China Inland Mission to sail to China. (Permission from Overseas Missionary Fellowship.)

pended on government orders for more than two decades. Narcissa's life was a tragic one in many respects, and the frustrations and dissension that filled her days were all too common in the missionary community.

## Jennie Faulding and Emily Blatchley

There were other forms of personality conflict and dissension that caused missionaries to be distracted from the ministry besides the open and overt dissension that Mrs. Mott created among the LMS missionaries in Tahiti and that which engulfed the Whitman mission in Oregon. In many cases the conflicts were more subtle, and sometimes conflicts and scandal were created by those who envied the success of others. This occurred during the early years of the China Inland Mission. Dissension marred the sea voyage, and after the party arrived in China, Hudson Taylor was accused of improprieties with two

single women, Jennie Faulding and Emily Blatchley. Their own feelings for him ran deep, and not without some highly charged emotional turmoil and conflict that developed between them.

They were among the first party of missionaries to sail on the *Lammermuir* with Taylor and the newly formed China Inland Mission in 1865. It was an eventful voyage that began with great excitement and a spiritual commitment that was difficult to maintain during the long months at sea. Although the card playing and cursing among the crew members had given way to Bible reading and hymn singing, all was not well among the missionaries themselves. The "germs of ill feeling and division" had crept in, and the once harmonious band was sounding dissonant chords before it reached its destination. "The feeling among us appears to have been worse than I could have formed any conception of," wrote Taylor. "One was jealous because another had too many new dresses, another because someone else had more attention. Some were wounded because of unkind controversial discussions, and so on."[15]

In many ways Emily and Jennie were opposites. "Emily . . . was highly strung and over-conscientious; she was also intelligent, dumpy and destined for a short unhappy life. Her bosom friend was Jennie Faulding, a financier's daughter, who was energetic, pretty and always singing." So light-hearted and enthusiastic was she that the Chinese referred to her as "Miss Happiness." That spirit served her well. "She lived long and eventually married the man Emily secretly worshiped."[16]

The ordeal that marred their friendship was brought on by the hostility of Lewis Nicol, who with his wife had sailed with the *Lammermuir* party. He was a major source of dissension on the sea voyage and immediately challenged Taylor on various issues once the party arrived at their mission in Hangchow. Although he had agreed beforehand to the CIM policy of wearing Chinese dress, he chafed under the regulation, convinced that his "Chinese gowns made him feel humiliated and vulnerable and . . . lowered his standing in the eyes of the natives and exposed him to the ridicule of other Westerners." He likewise balked at the idea of embracing Chinese eating and living habits. Taylor was not a man who easily backed down on such issues, and a clash was inevitable. To bolster his case against Taylor—especially to Anglican missionary George Moule—Nicol began making unfounded accusations against his leader. "Taylor, Nicol suggested, was not only a petty dictator

and a crank, but he had far too many unattached females about his household. Exactly what he said is unknown, but he plainly insinuated that Hudson was keeping a sort of Hangchow harem with at least two mistresses in addition to his wife."[17]

Moule, who did not approve of "young unmarried ladies" on the mission field in the first place, took Nicol at his word and wrote to friends back home that the CIM was a "sham and a delusion." He did not omit the stories of Taylor giving his young women a goodnight kiss every evening, and he sought to bolster his claims with good solid logic, interspersed with his own feelings and experience: "Consider I beg you what hazard your own soul runs in this connection. You are their physician and spiritual pastor and live in close proximity, with some of the restraints of social etiquette relaxed. . . . You would be more than human if you were not capable of being tempted." This was advice that came from the heart of a man who, by his own testimony, "for twenty years has known a plague in my own breast."[18]

It was a trying period for Emily and Jennie—and, of course, for the Taylors themselves. Indeed, so distressed was Taylor that, according to Emily, he asked one of his male missionaries "to receive from each of us ladies individually a statement as to Mr. Taylor's bearing towards us being nothing but that of a Christian and a gentleman." It was an unpleasant task. "I rebelled, revolted at his having to stoop so—as if his character were even on an impeachable level," wrote Emily, "but he thinks it better to condescend to unquestionable proof for the mission's sake and from each of us Mr. Williamson received the required testimony."[19]

This was not the first time that Taylor had been the center of a scandal that involved the opposite sex. He had created such a stir in the missionary community at Ningpo a decade earlier when he sought to court Maria that Maria was denied communion until she repented of the sin of entertaining his advances. He was accused of "offensive indecorum" by taking "advantage of her youth to induce her to trample on the prohibition which had been laid upon her" (that being the prohibition of spending time with him), and it was suggested by one of the local missionary leaders that he "ought to be horsewhipped."[20]

But Taylor had been determined that no amount of scandal would prevent him from pursuing the woman he loved. Through supportive friends he arranged to see Maria privately, at which time she consented to the marriage proposal of this much maligned and impulsive young man. Of this six-hour meeting he wrote, "I was not long engaged without trying to make up for the number of kisses I *ought* to have had these last few months." What appears like innocent lovers' mirth by today's standards was scandalous behavior for that day and age, especially in the conservative missionary community, but Taylor won the day, and some months later he and Maria were married.[21]

Few who knew Hudson Taylor a decade later could take seriously the charges that he was carrying on an illicit affair with two single women missionaries in the very household that was run by his wife. Maria was an astute woman who could not have been easily fooled. Yet many may have questioned his judgment in maintaining such a warm relationship with them—particularly in a society in which men and women remained separate and more than one unrelated woman in a household was a sure sign of polygamy. Despite the scandal, Emily and Jennie continued to live in the Taylor home. For himself, however, "Taylor kept a cooler distance from them and there were no more goodnight kisses." It was not an easy transition for the women—especially for Emily. "I am so lonely, so utterly alone," she penned in her journal. "And now my intercourse with them [the Taylors] must be straitened even yet more. But why should I cling so? Oh Christ, take hold of my hands. . . . I find such joy in being with the Taylors, but I must not let it intoxicate me. I must not revel in it."[22]

The tension that had developed between the young women and the Taylors also spilled over into their own relationship. Never would they be as close as they had been in the early days of the mission venture. What created the greatest tribulation in the relationship was the death of Maria. Prior to her death Emily had accompanied their children to England and had agreed to stay there and care for them. She had become a mother of sorts to the Taylor children, and it perhaps seemed natural to her that the widowed Taylor would remarry, and that he would remarry the "mother" of his children.

Undoubtedly Emily knew him better than Jennie did, having lived in his home for so long. The correspondence between them continued unabated, with his children in her care as a permanent link between them. Jennie, fully and happily engaged in her own work, had less cause to write to him, but from time to time she saw him when he came to Hangchow.[23]

But despite Emily's hopes, Taylor apparently did not have the same feelings for her that she had for him. Whether coincidentally or planned, he sailed back to England in 1872, on the same ship with Jennie, and by the time they arrived home they were engaged to be married. "Tongues must have wagged in the heads of some who remembered Moule's accusations about those good night kisses in Hangchow," but Taylor had no apologies to make.[24]

The one who most needed apologies was Emily, but all the apologies Taylor could have formulated would not have sufficed. "I feel sure from what I know of my own nature that I should, if I had had the chance, have been Mrs." she painfully wrote in her journal. "And so it is in love and mercy my God cut off my flowing stream at which He perhaps saw I should drink too deeply. Such a sweet sweet stream, such a painful weaning! Therefore such a great blessing must await me for Jesus to bear to see me have so much pain." Her depression was severe and may have affected her immune system and resistance to disease. She died of tuberculosis not long after Taylor's marriage.[25]

Jennie surely could have derived no satisfaction from her friend's pain and emotional distress. But she, too, loved Hudson Taylor, and she was eager to fill an emptiness in his life that only Maria had filled. She went

on to serve for more than thirty years as the first lady of the China Inland Mission, and she agreed on one occasion to leave her family behind and return to China alone to lead a party into the interior when her husband was too ill to go himself. With her optimistic spirit and good health she was the kind of wife Taylor needed as he continued the immense task of conducting the affairs of the China Inland Mission.[26]

## Martha Crawford

The dissension that flared up between missionary women (or men), single or married, has been documented often and well in letters— both personal letters and formal letters to the mission board. Indeed, it is depressing to read the accounts of dissension in various parts of the world and of the resulting problems and misunderstandings that were brought on the national churches. An area of conflict that has been less frequently documented has been that involving marital discord. For various reasons missionaries were less candid in divulging such problems. Then, as now, marital conflict among missionaries was presumed not to exist, and rarely did husbands or wives dare to admit that their marriage was filled with strife.

Martha Foster Crawford served for many years in China with her husband, T. P. Crawford, during the last half of the nineteenth century. At the age of nineteen, soon after recovering from a serious illness, she attended a revival and there felt "the finger of God" calling her "to a heathen world." To heed this calling, she needed a husband. She was a Baptist from Alabama, and the idea of sending single women abroad had not yet come of age. She had had several suitors, two of whom had proposed to her, but at twenty-one she was still single with no single missionary men in prospect.

> Terrified by the repugnant possibility of winding up an old maid, and much enjoying hugging, kissing, and romantic conversation, she yet feared further sexual intimacy ("a serpent, a fiend intruding upon me"). She also deeply resented the role that both her religion and her society would thrust upon her as any man's wife ("To be called inferior! Inferior! In what?").[27]

It was not until her pastor sent word to the Foreign Mission Board that Martha was seeking a missionary husband that her prospects brightened. T. P. Crawford had recently accepted an appointment to China, and he was looking for a wife. He promptly traveled to Alabama, and three weeks after they met they were married. Within months they were on their way to China, optimistic about their future ministry together. Not long after their arrival, however, marital tensions arose. T. P. agonized in his efforts to learn the language, and "he could not suppress a feeling of resentment at the swifter progress of his young wife Martha." For her, the situation was unexpected and stressful, as she confessed in her diary:

> He said ... the contrast would be observed always unfavorable to him. It would be bitter that he [be] in any respect inferior to his wife. It would be a continual trial. This was unexpected to me. I had prayed long and earnestly that God would make me willing to see my husband daily outstripping me ... But O I was not prepared for this.[28]

T. P. did learn Chinese well enough to converse freely with the people, and his fears of being outstripped by his wife in that area were never publicly realized. But the strain that developed over language was only the beginning of their many problems related to ministry and personality. Martha was childless (although she reared two Chinese children) and thus had considerable time to devote to her ministry of teaching. She had established a successful school and T. P. resented the amount of time and energy this ministry consumed. He wanted her to be more heavily involved in direct evangelism and insisted that she abandon the school. She "was distraught over the choice—husband or school—that she was being asked to make. Of her husband's demand that she close the school she wrote, 'I should deplore this. The very thought of it seemed like amputating all my limbs. I hardly think it necessary.' "[29]

There were other problems in their marriage as well. T. P. had great difficulties getting along with other missionaries and with the Chinese Christians, and this caused Martha to be "beside [her] self with grief and anxiety" to the point that she confessed it was "more than my nerves can stand." Nor was T. P. above severe emotional stress. Other missionaries had observed his instability and he himself had admitted that he had "trouble with his brain of years standing," a problem that was complicated by a neurological difficulty that resulted in numbness and partial paralysis. In the summer of 1878 he suddenly left the mission compound, going, in the words of Martha, "he knows not where."[30]

It was not until months later that Martha heard that her husband was in San Francisco. From there he traveled throughout the United States and finally returned to China more than a year after he had left, "so much fleshier and more cheerful," wrote Martha, "than I had seen [him] for years." His cheerfulness, however, was short-lived. In his absence, Martha's school had grown and she was having greater success than ever before—a fact that sorely vexed her husband. She made concessions by cutting back on her teaching and medical work and by joining him in his rural evangelism, but even that did not please him. The relationship became more tense, and she feared for her own well-being. "She had been highly conscious since her early Shanghai days—when she watched the icy-hearted Issachar Roberts turn his wife into a suicidal 'raving maniac'—of the absolute emotional interdependence cf the foreign husband and wife in China." She desperately needed to get away, and in 1881 "she left Tengchow as precipitately as her husband had in 1878."[31]

Before she returned in 1883, T. P. received a letter from Martha stating that she was determined to "come back to China to be a good wife, and cooperate with him." This gave him "inexpressible delight," but it did not solve their marital problems. "In winning his wife away from her schoolboys Crawford in a sense lost her himself. In her articles and public statements she certainly supported him; but in pursuing her new country work she spent up to five days a week away from home, and he saw less of her than ever." Complicating the situation were his persistent personality conflicts with missionary colleagues and Chinese nationals. He had strong views about how the work should be carried out—views not supported by others, thus the work under him in Tengchow "remained notably unsuccessful." In 1888, without warning, he once again departed alone for America. Irwin Hyatt writes that he "never came to terms with the life he had chosen for himself. The Chinese did not measure up to his designs on them, so he wound up despising the Chinese and hunting witches among well-meaning fellow Americans."[32]

The story of the Crawfords is tragic. Martha was a strong, talented woman, an apparent threat to her husband (as were, indeed, most other people he worked with). Their marital problems were severe and colored every aspect of her life and ministry. "From jealousy and from a terrible kind of dependence," T. P. insisted that she "exchange work that she loved for a life of practicing what he preached; she became certainly a better and more useful person than he, but only at what her best friends described as great psychic cost and disappointing concrete achievement." What was his legacy? According to Hyatt, "other than some strong negative impressions, Crawford left nothing."[33]

Historians will never know how many other missionary marriages there were that experienced similar stress. These are the hidden family afflictions that are too painful to be shared. The stories of women who suffered silently, unable to express themselves as Martha Crawford did, are forever hidden in the padlocked closets of history.

# PART II

# MINISTRY OPPORTUNITIES

While opportunities for women in meaningful ministry were often very limited on the home front, precisely the opposite was true on the mission field. Practically every area of ministry imaginable was wide open to them. There was criticism when they overstepped the bounds of what was considered to be the "woman's sphere," but the criticism was muffled by the overwhelming needs of the missionary enterprise as well as by the fact that women on the mission field quickly proved to be more than equal to the tasks before them. This was the position of J. S. Woodside, a missionary to India for some sixty years, who wrote to the Presbyterian Board of Foreign Missions in 1881 to defend the active ministry of women:

> My honest opinion is that many of the Ladies I have known have been superior to many of our male workers in [all] that goes to constituting the true missionary. Their intense earnestness, their love to the people, their zeal, their untiring energy, and their long-suffering patience have been far greater than in the men.

He went on to mention some of these women by name, and concluded: "The example of these women testifies that no better agents could possibly be sent to this country. There is a mighty work to be done by Ladies in India and I only wish we had hundreds more like those I have named."[1]

But even before women went abroad in missionary service, they found tremendous opportunities to be involved in support efforts at home. Mary Webb inspired a generation and more of women to save their "mites" for missions, and Mary Lyon dedicated her talent as an educator to preparing women for foreign missionary service. This was considered the proper place for women in missionary involvement, but not all women were willing to accept such limitations. Anne Marie Javouhey and Eliza Davis George founded and directed their own mission societies. Other women, who were less eager to penetrate what would be considered a man's world, were content to remain on the home front—to answer the call to urban ministries—and in doing so had no less fulfillment in their desire to serve God than their sisters who went abroad.

For those women who went abroad—married and single—opportunities abounded. Mary Slessor and Mildred Cable were among the many women who gave their lives to exploration and pioneer work. For those who were more inclined to settle down, church-planting and preaching were options, as testified to by Sue McBeth, Eleanor Macomber, and Malla Moe. But as more and more women joined in the missionary enterprise, the needs on the home front increased. Women like Annie Armstrong and Helen Barrett Montgomery worked tirelessly to mobilize lay women to support them.

Women, like men, often tended to specialize in ministry overseas. A frequent choice of women was working with women, and missionaries such as Adele Fielde and Margaret King were very successful in this specialty. The needs of children also captured the hearts of women missionaries, as is seen in the lives of Amy Carmichael and Lillian Trasher. Closely related was the ministry of female education; here Isabella Thoburn and Pandita Ramabai stand out. Humanitarian and health ministries could not be ignored, and women, like their male counterparts, often gave up lucrative careers in their homelands to serve in needier areas of the world. The stories of Eleanor Chestnut, Ida Scudder, and Lillian Hammer are stories of sacrifice and love. Another specialization that caught the imagination of women was that of Bible translation, and during the twentieth century women such as Eunice Pike and Marianna Slocum made remarkable contributions in this field of ministry.

## Chapter 6

# A Woman's Place: Support Efforts Behind the Scenes

Without mission support organizations, the American missionary movement would have been severely disadvantaged—especially during the early decades of the nineteenth century. Throughout the nineteenth century evangelical women provided the support base for foreign missions. It was the women's "mite societies" that sent out the first missionaries from American shores, and after these missionaries arrived on the field they wrote back to their churches imploring women to do even more.

Before women rallied behind the cause, potential missionaries had no support base in America. Indeed, in 1810 Adoniram Judson and his colleagues, aware of the difficulty in raising support among the New England Congregationalists, had contemplated going to England to seek financial support. He realized the potential value of women's fundraising, and later he "enjoined American women to forsake 'the demon vanity' for the amelioration of their sisters in the East," and he suggested they form "Plain Dress Societies." Church publications supporting missions made similar requests of the women in their denominations. "American Christian women were perceived as having a special responsibility to practice 'proper economy' within the home and in terms of their personal attire. The mites they saved by eschewing necklaces, ear ornaments, and the seductions of creative millinery were to be set aside for their heathen sisters."[1]

Even before Judson's appeal, however, women had begun organizing support systems to help meet the need for missionary endeavors. In 1800, Mary Webb organized the Boston Female Society for Missionary Purposes, "the first woman's missionary society in the world."[2]

Two years later in that same city, the Cent Society was born—a concept that quickly spread down the Eastern seaboard. It all began at a dinner party at the home of Mehitable Simpkins and her husband John, who was the treasurer of the Massachusetts Missionary Society. As they were eating, the conversation drifted to the subject of missions and the funding that was needed for missionary support. One of the guests commented about the cost of a glass of wine—only a penny—and suggested that if that amount were given by families to missions each week it could go a long way toward meeting the pressing financial needs. Mrs. Simpkins took up the challenge and was soon "deluged by pennies." The idea was particularly inviting because "one cent a week was about the sum almost any woman might be able to give if she denied herself some little thing. It appealed also to the widow's two mites of Jesus' parable, and the vision of the collective purchasing power of thousands of pennies made each single cent seem significant."[3]

The "mite society" concept was not only passed along from church to church in America, but it soon spread to churches abroad. In 1806, the *London Evangelical Magazine* reported on the Cent Societies in Boston and elsewhere in the United States and suggested that if a similar plan were adopted in England "among the female members of all religious congregations, and devoted by a committee of each society to the missionary cause, or to any other institution intended to promote the good of souls, what a vast sum might be accumulated without inconvenience to individuals."[4] It was an idea whose time had come—and it was set in motion by Mary Webb who, in spite of being physically handicapped, paved the way for women to take up the cause of mission support. It was hardly a revolutionary endeavor, and yet such activity was unprecedented in many religious circles of the day.

## Mary Webb

Mary Webb was an unusual woman in an era when physically handicapped people were often viewed as a disgrace to the family and a burden to society. Due to a crippling disease at the age of five, she was confined to a wheelchair for the rest of her life. Although she was determined that she would not allow her handicap to incapacitate her, she did at times shrink from the public arena. Baptism in particular became a hurdle for her. As a Baptist, she was expected to submit herself to a public baptism by immersion as an outward confirmation of faith in Christ, but she was too embarrassed to do so and delayed the dreaded ordeal until she was nineteen.[5]

In 1800, at the age of twenty-one, Mary organized with thirteen other women the Boston Female Society for Missionary Purposes. Even though this society consisted of women only, it was a revolutionary step for a woman to assume leadership of a religious organization. According to her biographer, "She was blazing a path, perilous for a young woman, through an unbroken wilderness," but he is quick to point out that "she had no spirit of revolt against the prevalent views among Christians concerning the sphere of woman."[6]

Though Mary was the chief organizer of the society and its impetus for continued outreach and expansion, she did not serve as president. She left that role to others while she carried out the duties of secretary and treasurer for more than forty years. In this capacity she exerted great influence. Through her encouragement, "members skimped their household allowances. . . . Farmers' wives scratched together a few dimes by keeping extra chickens and selling the eggs. Townswomen knit stockings and sold the product. A servant girl bequeathed to the cause the slender savings of a lifetime."[7]

Like so many other female mission activists who would follow her, she was not denominationally restrictive. Of the thirteen women in the group, seven were Baptists and six were Congregationalists. Most churchmen of the day would have shunned such ecumenical activity, but for a lay woman it seemed only natural to cooperate in the task of world evangelism. Mode of baptism was less important than bringing souls to Christ. But such idealism was not to continue. Missionaries were sent out by denominations, and denominations were headed by churchmen who found cooperating with other denominations difficult. In 1829, after working together for nearly three decades, the women separated in order to support their own separate denominations.[8]

The split in this first mission support organization had a positive repercussion in that the number of organizations was increased by one. Indeed, Mary Webb's enthusiasm for missions spawned several other, similar organizations during her more than fifty years of active service. She sought to maintain a network between the various groups, and by 1817 she had corresponded with representatives from more than two hundred other women's missionary societies in an effort to promote cooperation and communication between the various organizations.[9]

In addition to encouraging the formation of new organizations by women in other denominations and in other areas of the country, Mary sought to expand her own organization into other areas of service. According to Leon McBeth, she had an amazing ability to influence others to become involved in humanitarian ministry:

> Several societies were spin-offs from the parent group, such as the Female Cent Society in 1803; the Children's Cent Society, first recorded as a society in 1811; the Corban Society, 1811, to raise money to help educate young ministers; the Fragment Society, 1812, to provide clothing and bedding for needy children; the Children's Friend Society, to provide day care for young children of working mothers; and a Penitent Females' Refuge, to help rescue and rehabilitate "those poor unhappy females who have wandered into the paths of vice and folly." She also founded societies to minister to immigrants, blacks, and Jews. No wonder Mary Webb was described as a "society within herself."[10]

It was entirely fitting that Mary Webb be the first woman to publicly organize women in support of missions. As non-controversial as that activity may seem in the modern age, it was scandalous to many of her contemporaries, and there was vocal opposition to what she and her female colleagues were doing. Women had their place in the home, but outside activity was to be severely restricted—especially that which entailed leadership responsibilities that might infringe on the male domain.

But as a single woman who was handicapped and much admired for her spunk, Mary was able to make inroads where few other women would have dared venture. Also, she "knew her place" and was careful to concede that she was a mere woman, "destined by the Parent of nature to fill more retired stations in life than our brethren."[11]

It is important to keep in mind that Mary Webb was involved strictly in a support ministry and that the recipients of the support were by and large male missionaries. When the city mission work began, two ministers (a Mr. Davis and Mr. Rossiter) were employed to do the work, and a five-year review of the work in 1821 showed that six men in addition to Andover seminary students had been employed to carry out the ministry. Mary worked within the prevailing confines of the religious attitudes of her day. She did not hurl bold challenges at the accepted sex role standards, and yet, through her activism she contributed significantly to a changing mind set that would slowly open the doors for women in missionary service. She died at the age of eighty-two of breast cancer.[12]

## Mary Lyon

A very significant support effort for the foreign missionary movement during the mid-nineteenth century was the work of Mary Lyon, the founder of Mount Holyoke Female Seminary. The idea of a school for women's higher education was not readily supported by her contemporaries. She was determined to "provide a college for young women on the same conditions as those for

men"—viewed by many as "a strange, extravagant and dangerous notion." Yet, she was no revolutionary. She had no desire to offer women an education that would prepare them for pastoral ministry or other professions. Rather, she wanted to give them an education that would make them better teachers and better wives—roles that were suited to a woman's nature.[13]

Mary Lyon, founder of Mount Holyoke Female Seminary.

Mary was a popular, self-sacrificing teacher, which lent credibility to her publicity campaign for the school of her dreams, but fund-raising was not easy in the 1830s as she traveled through the small towns of New England. "I wander about without a home," she wrote in a letter to her mother, "and scarcely know one week where I shall be the next." Her health declined, but she refused to quit. "Our personal comforts are delightful, but not essential. Mount Holyoke means more than meat and sleep. Had I a thousand lives, I would sacrifice them all in suffering and hardship for its sake." Friends pleaded with her to wait until economic times were better, but she was convinced that God's timing did not necessarily correspond with the nation's economy.[14]

Mary's itinerant publicity work for Mount Holyoke was not an altogether new endeavor for her. Her interest in missions had begun in her childhood when she first heard of Samuel Mills and William Carey. She was intensely interested in the development of the newly formed American Board of Commissioners for Foreign Missions and organized the first mission society in her hometown of Buckland, Massachusetts. She visited all the families in the area, seeking members and materials for the work. In addition to women, some sixty children were recruited to help.[15]

She founded Mount Holyoke in 1837, with the express purpose "to cultivate the missionary spirit among its pupils; the feeling that they should live for God, and do something as teachers, or in such other ways as Providence may direct." Her emphasis in training teachers was to have them serve as home missionaries of sorts. They were to go to the cities and to the rural areas, and even to the remote Indian schools on the frontier, and train a generation of children to study Scripture and rev-

erence God. She defended her strategy with clear logic and strong rhetoric:

> Fill the country with ministers, and they could no more conquer the whole land and secure their victories, without the aid of many times their number of self-denying female teachers, than the latter could complete the work without the former. . . . This work of supplying teachers is a great work, and it must be done, or our country is lost, and the world will remain unconverted.[16]

The result of Mary Lyon's commitment to establishing a female seminary was that many women did serve as Christian teachers with a mission to convert their young students. But equally important was the fact that the seminary offered a ready supply of wives to the male missionary force of the mid-nineteenth century. During the first twelve years after the school opened its doors, twelve of the students went out as missionary teachers to the American Indians, and by the time of Mary Lyon's death, seventy students had become foreign missionaries. Though not regarded as missionaries in their own right, these women were a powerful asset to the foreign missionary endeavor.[17]

Although Mary Webb and Mary Lyon accepted the restrictions that were generally imposed on women during the early part of the nineteenth century, they nevertheless greatly contributed to the progress that women would enjoy in the generations that followed.

## Chapter 7

# High Level Leadership: Founding and Directing a Mission Society

The nineteenth century was a great age of voluntary mission societies. The Baptist Missionary Society, the London Missionary Society, and the Church Missionary Society were formed in the last decade of the eighteenth century, and dozens more organizations like them sprang up in the nineteenth century. These societies are generally thought to have been Protestant and male dominated, but that was not necessarily the case. Catholic religious orders that focused on overseas missionary work already had had a long history and, as was true of Protestant mission societies, they were headed by men—with a few notable exceptions. One of these exceptions was a Catholic mission society, the Sisters of St. Joseph, founded by Anne-Marie (Nanette) Javouhey in the early nineteenth century.

Catholic women actually began their foreign missionary endeavors more than two centuries before single Protestant women became involved. The first were those who went from Spain to Mexico to establish convents in the sixteenth century. Later, during the seventeenth century, Ursuline nuns from France sailed to Canada to teach Indian girls and establish convents.[1]

## Anne Marie Javouhey

Despite the enormous impact of Anne Marie Javouhey's work on the spread of Catholicism, she has been given scant recognition by historians. In his book *A History of Christian Missions*, Stephen Neill concedes that "Roman Catholic historians attribute the first renewal of African missions in the nineteenth century to the faith and enterprise" of this remarkable woman, but he himself devotes only one sentence to her in his entire text.[2]

Javouhey grew up in the French countryside during the turbulent era of the French Revolution. She demonstrated leadership abilities at a young age, and her father was convinced she was more capable of carrying out the family business than her brothers, but early on her interests turned to spiritual matters. She was determined to become a nun, and in 1800, soon after entering a convent, she received a visionary call to be a missionary. She later testified that she awoke from sleep hearing voices and seeing her room strangely illuminated. She looked around and saw children from different races and cultures. In the midst of them was a nun who spoke directly to her: "These are the children God has given you. He wishes you to form a new congregation to take care of them. I am Teresa. I will be your protectress." With those words the vision was finished and Javouhey was left to contemplate the implications for her future.[3]

Without papal authority, but with the impetus of this powerful "call," she began making plans to take her mission overseas. With the assurance that God was leading her she founded the Sisters of St. Joseph and commissioned her first missionary nuns to serve on an island in the Indian Ocean. In 1822, after the sisterhood was firmly established, she herself became a missionary to Africa. There she found the work and the people much to her liking: "I love the black peoples very much. They are good simple folk. Their only malice they get from us."[4]

Javouhey was a humanitarian and an activist. Hospitals, educational institutions, and agricultural colonies were all part of her expanding ministries. The agricultural colonies were formed to help overcome the injustice she witnessed in the colonists' treatment of blacks. She prohibited any form of race discrimination, and

she was eager to establish a native clergy, which was her rationale for founding a seminary for Africans in France. Nor did she limit her activities to Africa. She soon had her blue-robed sisters stationed all over the world. She personally supervised the work and was referred to by a sea captain as "my most seasoned sailor." King Louis Philippe paid her his highest tribute by saying, "She is a great man."[5]

Javouhey was popular with her nuns and there was never any question as to who was in charge. There had been personality conflicts at times, but she maintained her authority and did not permit dissention in the ranks. She claimed her authority directly from God, and "merely said, when announcing two or three important decisions during her lifetime, that 'God has made known to me in a particular way what He wants me to do.' This, of course, precluded any arguments," wrote her biographer. "The atheist might frown, the doubter might smile, the wayward might shrug, the faithful might quietly co-operate; none of them could know the truth—only Nanette. The measure of truth could only be in Nanette's results, and her results were great."[6]

Not everyone accepted Javouhey's claim to authority. Most notable among those who rejected her claim was her own Bishop in France, Bishop d'Hericourt. Although she had founded the Sisters of St. Joseph and had repeatedly been elected Superior General by her nuns, the Bishop, though himself still in his thirties, argued that because the motherhouse was in his diocese, he was rightfully the Superior General. At age twenty he entered the French Army but, according to Glenn Kittler, "he found in the Church the power he never earned in the army and he was carried away by it." His struggle to gain control over the Sisters of St. Joseph would last for eighteen years and would consume valuable time and energy that Javouhey needed for the affairs of her religious order. It created inner conflict for her as well. She had demanded obedience in her nuns, and now she was being accused of disobedience by her own bishop. Her argument was that though she personally was under his authority, the order was not, and in her official capacity of Superior General she was not obligated to obedience.[7]

Bishop d'Hericourt refused to relent. Despite her great success (or perhaps because of it) his resistance over the years grew stronger and stronger. Finally he took the ultimate action and excommunicated her. She was in Guiana at the time and was denied communion by the presiding priest: "With anguish she watched her girls, her sister nuns approach the communion table from which she was excluded."[8] It was a difficult time that lasted two years. She attended Mass, but did not go to the Communion rail, for "she saw no reason for providing a continuous cause for scandal to the people."[9]

The controversy raged on for years, with d'Hericourt seeking to take whatever measures he could to counteract her leadership and ministry. In 1850 he wrote a letter to Archbishop Sibour, the new prelate of Paris, in which he laid out his position clearly:

Permit me to draw your attention to a matter which has, for a long time, been of concern to me. Madame Javouhey, Superior General of the Sisters of St. Joseph, whose motherhouse is at Cluny, in my diocese, has—in defiance of all rules—set up a novitiate in Paris. Her aim, as it has always been, is to extricate herself from episcopal authority. She refuses to recognize any Superior; the choice and distribution of her membership is made without any discretion; her powers as Superior General expired several years ago, and things have come to such a pass that one cannot even be sure she has renewed her vows. Her business affairs are in total disorder; she cannot tolerate any control in their regard. . . . If, Your Grace, you wish to have reliable information as to the intrigue and behavior of Madame Javouhey, you could ask the bishop of Besancon, who is now in Paris. He is full acquainted with this melancholy story.[10]

Archbishop Sibour was not unfamiliar with the controversy. He had heard good reports of Javouhey's work, but he was well aware that not all churchmen agreed with the free rein she had been given in her ministry. At his request, she was asked to respond to d'Hericourt's charges. True to character, she was strong in her reply: "I am not only the Superior General of the Congregation of St. Joseph of Cluny; I did not merely cooperate in the foundation of that Order; I am its sole and solitary foundress. I am its Mother General as God is its Father, since it is I who created and have developed it . . . ."[11]

After gathering what evidence he could, Archbishop Sibour was left to decide who should control the Sisters. According to Kittler, he "substantiated Nanette's claim and exposed Bishop d'Hericourt for the power-grabber that he was. . . . D'Hericourt writhed in anger and frustration but there was nothing he could do."[12]

The long struggle had taken a physical toll on both Javouhey and d'Hericourt. Within a year after the Archbishop's decision both were dead. When Javouhey was close to death herself, she heard that her Bishop had died and responded to one of her nuns: "We almost met, he and I, on that very day, before the judgment seat of God. So he's gone in ahead of me, that good Bishop. Well, that is correct; that is how it should be. A Bishop should always enter first."[13] She died shortly afterward, leaving some nine hundred nuns scattered throughout the world.

## Eliza Davis George

It was not easy for a woman to establish her own mission society, especially if that society was not specifically a Catholic religious order or a Protestant "female agency." But complicating matters for Eliza George was the fact that she was a *black* woman. Merely obtaining a missionary appointment was a high enough hurdle for a black woman—black women before her had struggled against racism in their efforts to answer God's call to missionary work, and some had given up—but to found a mission society was a bold undertaking indeed.

Mary McLoad Bethune is an example of the difficulties faced by black women who wanted to go into missions. She was one of seventeen children born to an impoverished South Carolina farm family. Through

scholarships she received a secondary education and with the financial aid of a kindly Quaker woman was able to attend Moody Bible Institute. Here she prepared for missionary work in Africa with a Presbyterian mission board, but after graduating in the 1890s she was told that "there were no openings for black missionaries in Africa." Despite this rejection, she "accomplished remarkable things in her eighty years. She built a college and hospital for blacks in Daytona Beach, Florida. She mothered the influential National Council of Negro Women." She "advised presidents, had a hand in shaping the Charter of the United Nations, and worked for voting rights for all American women." Only missionary work to Africa was denied her.[14]

For Eliza George, the obstacles were similar. She grew up in Texas in the late-nineteenth century. Soon after she completed her course of study at Central Texas College, during the heyday of the Student Volunteer Movement, she dedicated her life to foreign missions at a prayer meeting at her alma mater, where she had been asked to stay on as a teacher and matron. During a lengthy prayer, while the leader was "all the way around the world and halfway back again," praying "for India, China, Japan, and Africa Eliza's heart was suddenly filled with an overwhelming desire to see her brothers and sisters in Africa. . . . As clearly as if she were there, she saw black people from Africa passing before the judgment seat of Christ, weeping and moaning, 'But no one ever told us You died for us.' "[15]

The immediate response to Eliza's disclosure that she had been called to be a missionary was, "You don't have to go over there to be a missionary—we have enough Africa over here." That was only the beginning of the opposition she faced. When she applied to her church, the Southern Baptist Convention, she found no support. Never before had a black woman from Texas become a foreign missionary, and the church leaders "did not believe she was able to take on such pioneering work." Finally, however, she was permitted to present her case at a special meeting, where she gripped the hearts of those obstinate men:

Eliza sat down, realizing that she had never once even looked at the notes clenched in her hand. Then, startled, she heard the board members applauding. Dr. Strong stood up, cleared his throat to bring the members to attention, looked at Eliza, and said: "Miss Davis, your eloquence and sincerity have moved us deeply. I for one can no longer stand in the way of your fulfilling your life's ambition."[16]

Eliza arrived in Liberia in 1914 and began working with another single woman in the interior where they established a Bible Industrial Academy. Within two years the school had an enrollment of fifty boys who were housed in a bamboo building with a thatched roof. "Even more thrilling to Eliza was the response to the gospel among the tribal people. Within the year more than a thousand converts had accepted Christ in the villages." But news from home was not so optimistic. The Texas Baptist Convention had separated from the National Baptists, who were in charge of the work in Liberia. Since Eliza was

from Texas, her support and appointment were now in jeopardy.[17]

With an uncertain future, Eliza was more vulnerable than she might have been otherwise, and it was in that frame of mind that she made a critical decision that would haunt her for years to come. Her acquaintance with G. Thompson George, a native of British Guyana who was working in Liberia with a Portuguese company, prompted a marriage proposal from him, which she initially turned down. "I didn't come here to marry," she responded in a short note. "I came here to work for the salvation of the souls of these natives, and nothing will deter me from my course." But that was before she received the letter from the Convention, telling her that a Rev. and Mrs. Daniel Horton would be replacing her at the Bible Industrial Academy, the very school she had worked so hard to establish.[18]

With that devastating revelation still ringing in her ears, George's promise that he would leave his job and help her start a new mission suddenly became more appealing. "Though she didn't love this little man with his English accent and his vast experience, she did respect and admire him. . . . And he was offering her the only hope to remain in Africa." Initially they worked together as a team, George keeping his promise to forsake his worldly ventures for her ministry. Very quickly, however, problems began to develop. She "had not found the physical intimacies of marriage easy, but she attributed this to the fact that she had been an 'old maid' when she married. But to have her husband smell of liquor repulsed her."[19]

Despite their marital conflicts they continued to work together in the years that followed, often in the face of heavy financial difficulties. Yet, they continued to make progress in their work. They traveled around holding revivals in churches and in areas where there were no churches, and they trained more than fifty boarding students at the thatched-roofed, mud school they operated—many of the students being promising future leaders.[20]

In 1939, after more than twenty years of marriage, George died. Eliza's decision to marry had been a mistake. George had not been suited for ministry, and Eliza was simply not wife material. A friend who knew them both later assessed the marriage:

> She was very sad about that situation. I don't think it could have worked; in the light of her character, her gifts, and her calling, it would have been difficult to have found a suitable husband. She was too absorbed in working for people to give sufficient affection, attention, and time to her husband. He would have to have been exactly like her. But husbands want to take the lead and want the wife to give them a certain amount of time. It would have been hard for her unless he had changed.[21]

In the years after his death, Eliza witnessed the greatest growth and progress ever in her work. By 1943, her mission work included four sub-stations besides her mission center at Kelton, and the local churches were cooperating in the work. But once again she faced opposition from church leaders in America. She was sixty-five, and the National Baptist Convention (from which she had received support) was determined to retire her and replace her with one of Eliza's former students who had gone to America for a college education. The letter bearing this pronouncement indicated concern for her health, but Eliza knew that once again her work had been undermined. She determined that she would stay on and continue without any denominational support, and she sought to put the incident behind her. In her recorded memoirs she simply states the hard fact: "In 1945 the Foreign Mission Board of the National Baptist Convention of America saw fit to discontinue my services as a missionary."[22]

From that point on, Eliza worked "by faith," supported largely by "Eliza Davis George Clubs" in the United States. She continued her independent mission work in Liberia, which became known as the Elizabeth Native Interior Mission. The mission acquired thousands of acres of land in the years that followed, and by the 1960s there were twenty-seven churches in the Eliza George Baptist Association, which was closely associated with the mission. She continued to be actively involved in the work until she was past the age of ninety, and she lived on to be one hundred. When she died, the work was carried on by capable nationals who had worked beside her over the years.[23]

# Chapter 8

# Weeping Over the Cities: The Call of Urban Ministries

Women have had a long tradition of active involvement in humanitarian efforts of all kinds, but urban ministry is an area that particularly stands out. During the early decades of the nineteenth century, when they were barred from serving as missionaries in their own right overseas, many women initiated mission work close to home. Indeed, many of the inner-city slum missions were founded by middle-class or wealthy women who were seeking to give meaning to their religious faith.

One such woman was Phoebe Palmer, whose influential ministry among Methodists earned her the title "Mother of the Holiness Movement." As important as her efforts were in bringing mainline Methodists back to the perfectionist teachings of Wesley, her most enduring ministry was her active involvement in urban ministries. She was one of the most outstanding early leaders of inner-city mission work and, according to Timothy Smith, her "pioneer work in social welfare projects illustrates the part which urban evangelization played in the origins of the Christian social movement."[1]

She was actively involved in establishing the Hedding Church, a city mission work that represented the early beginnings of the later settlement houses. She also conducted personal evangelism in the streets and in prisons and founded the Five Points Mission. This was her "crowning achievement"—a mission project in New York that housed some twenty poor families and provided schooling and religious training as well. According to Smith, the beginnings of Protestant institutional work in the slums can be traced to this mission.[2]

The foremost female pioneer in urban missions in England was Catherine Booth, the wife of William Booth and the cofounder of the Salvation Army. Catherine personally worked in the urban slums, and she insisted that the Salvation Army offer women equal opportunity in ministry with men. From the earliest years,

"Hallelujah lassies" were on the front lines of the Army in its holy war against the misery in the slums. The work was soon expanded overseas, and here also women were in the forefront. Commissioner Railton was sent to open the work in the United States with the "the Splendid Seven," a team of seven young women. Work also was inaugurated in Asia and elsewhere throughout the world. So successful were these women that William Booth was prompted to say, "My best men are women."[3]

Sarah Doremus, founder of the Woman's Union Missionary Society.

### Sarah Doremus

One of the most effective organizers of urban mission work in the nineteenth century was Sarah Doremus, who is also remembered for her founding of the Woman's Union Missionary Society of America in 1861. Initially, however, her work was concentrated in New York City, where she was involved in a vast array of Christian endeavors to help the poor and needy. She was the wife of a prosperous New York businessman and was the mother of nine children (eight daughters and one son), but her warm heart and compassion extended far beyond the boundaries of her immediate family. She "was the guiding light of practically every benevolent project in New York City," writes Patricia Hill. "Prisons, hospitals, foundling and old-age homes, and industrial schools as well as individual families were the beneficiaries of her personal, meticulous care."[4]

Sarah herself had never known any other life than one of privilege. She was born into wealth and grew up in elegant surroundings, and her marriage further advanced her social prestige. She had every opportunity to circulate among the fashionable elite, but her Christian values came first. She and her husband were active in the South Reformed Church in New York City, and she had committed herself to reaching out to those in need, even as Christ had. "She gave up articles of personal adornment and bestowed the price upon schools and hospitals.... On her own feet she walked to hospitals, to city missions, to homes for aged women, to schools for Italo—Americans.... She held services in jails and inspired released prisoners to better living."[5]

Sarah's prison ministry began in the 1830s, when she started conducting Sunday services in the City Prison in New York. Her special focus was on female prisoners, and she served as the first director of the Women's Prison Association. She was associated with this ministry for more than thirty years. One aspect of that ministry to which Sarah was particularly devoted was the Home for Discharged Female Convicts. Through her prison work she realized that prevention of crime was the most effective means of helping troubled youth and adults in the inner city, and she began expanding her ministry into other fields. She maintained an even longer tenure with the City and Tract Mission Society, of which she was manager for thirty-six years. And if that was not enough to keep her busy, she served for twenty-eight years as the manager of the City Bible Society.[6]

"The list of enterprises in which she was involved, often as founder and/or first director, is astonishing," writes Carma Van Liere. "It includes the New York House and School of Industry, which provided work for poor women and schooling for their children; the Nursery and Child's Hospital, providing day and hospital care for children of the poor; the Presbyterian Home for Aged Women; the City Mission and Tract Society; the City Bible Society; and the Women's Hospital."[7]

Sarah's hospital work was far—sighted for her day. Her prison and ghetto work had brought her into contact with women with gynecological and social diseases, and she determined that she would devote special attention to this problem. She worked with a medical doctor who had similar concerns, and through her persistence was able to acquire a charter and a large monetary grant from the state of New York.[8]

It is her support of foreign missions for which Sarah is most remem-

bered. With the assistance of women from other denominations she founded the Woman's Union Missionary Society of America, and served as its president until her death sixteen years later in 1877. She had delayed the founding of this organization until the strong male opposition she had faced in earlier years subsided. It was the first mission society specifically designed to sponsor single women, and it led the way for dozens more that would emerge in the decades that followed. Even before this, however, she had provided outfits for out-going missionaries and hospitality to returning missionaries, and "she furthered missionary interest by inviting large gatherings of influential men and women to her home to hear of what was being done in foreign lands by missionaries who were home on furlough." And perhaps the highest tribute she received was that "she gave herself to brain work and to organization while to others she gave the outward honor."[9]

## Emma Whittemore

There was a varied focus to the city-mission ministries women were involved in, but one that had a particularly profound appeal was that of reaching out to "street girls"—young girls in most instances who had been taken advantage of because of poverty or family problems. This was the focus of Emma Whittemore's work, and in many ways she is representative of the vast army of women who penetrated the cities during the nineteenth and early twentieth centuries with the Bible in one hand and life-sustaining provisions in the other. It was not enough to simply preach the gospel. These young women, like so many other homeless victims of the cities, were trapped by their environment and they needed a refuge where they could turn their lives around.

Emma Whitemore, founder of the Door of Hope.

Emma Whittemore was a remarkable woman who founded Door of Hope missions in cities throughout the world. She founded her first mission home in New York City in 1890, and by the time of her death in 1931 there were nearly one hundred such homes in major cities in the United States, Canada, Western Europe, Africa, China, Japan, and New Zealand. By some accounts she was believed to be "instrumental in saving more fallen women than any other person."[10]

Emma grew up in wealth and married into wealth. "Dinners, receptions, dances and going to places of entertainment occupied a large part of her life," until a back injury turned her into an invalid. She became acquainted with A. B. Simpson and his missionary and healing ministry, but she ridiculed the idea of divine healing—until she herself was miraculously healed. After that experience her active preaching ministry and inner-city mission work began.[11]

Whittemore's work overseas was in many instances more desperately needed than her work in North America. In Shanghai, for example, the situation was pitiable. "Very few of the girls in the brothels of the eastern port were there through their own fault or choice," writes Phyllis Thompson. "Most of them had been bought or kidnapped, and brought to submission by intimidation, even torture. One method employed was to string them up by their thumbs until they were ready to give in. . . . They were then dressed up, their little faces painted and paraded on the streets of the red-light district." What hope did they have? "There was only one way of escape for them, and that was through a Christian Mission known as the Door of Hope."[12]

One of the striking aspects of the Door of Hope in China was that it was recognized by the government. "Any girl who was able to get away from a brothel and appeal for help was handed over to the Door of Hope until her case came up in the courts. If it could be proved that the girl had been illegally detained in the brothel, she could remain in the Christian mission." Margaret King, a missionary with the China Inland Mission, told of her evangelistic ministry at one such mission in Shanghai, where one hundred and eighty girls were housed:

> A number of new girls are in from Yangchow. I wish you could have seen their faces when I began to speak. Some cried, some laughed, and all leaned forward to listen. When I gave the invitation to those who wanted to come to Jesus and be saved, they just crowded up the aisle. I felt as if my heart would break. Patiently, all the rest of the day, I dealt with one and another, hearing their stories. Oh, what stories. . . .[13]

Emma saw remarkable success in her work, as did other women who worked with "fallen" girls. Some historians have suggested that urban ministries were not successful in terms of developing a strong church and that permanently changed lives of "converts" were hard to find. But personal testimonies of girls in China and elsewhere overseas, as well as of those in American urban ghettos, however, seem to tell a different story.

Seth Cook Rees, writing in 1907, cites many instances of changed lives in his book *Miracles in the Slums; or, Thrilling Stories of those Rescued from the Cesspools of Iniquity, and Touching Incidents in the Lives of the Unfortunate.* The following are only a few of the "trophies of slum missionaries": Orpha, who "fell prey to a professional procurer . . . became a slum missionary and an ordained deaconess." Little H, who "had been taken to men's rooms and forced to drink," was later "sanctified and went to Bible School in order to prepare to became a slum missionary." Miss M "was put in jail for grand larceny" and later "became a missionary in the New York City slums." Lucy "was ruined by her employer who turned out to be a bartender and was put in a Negro sporting house." After she was rescued, "she began teaching a Sunday School class of nineteen scholars." Dicie was "a drunkard, cigarette fiend, and user of morphine, cocaine, and other druges," later "became a slum missionary." Little Ella, who was "sold as a prostitute for $5.00," later "became a Quaker and started preaching." And Christine, a pregnant teenager who "was forever hopelessly ruined," was "called to be a slum missionary" and "went to Bible school for training."[14]

Chapter 9

# To The Regions Beyond: Exploration and Pioneer Work

The love for adventure and the unknown was a driving force that prompted certain women to join their male colleagues in the often dangerous and daring exploits of pioneer missionary work. In some cases they echoed the sentiments of these men—of David Livingstone, who described his Africa inland travel as "a prolonged system of picnicking," of Wilfred Grenfell, who advised prospective missionaries, "when two courses are open, follow the most venturesome," or of Nate Saint, who described Operation Auca as "high adventure as unreal as any successful novel."[1] They were intoxicated by the thrill of discovering what was beyond the next mountain range, what lay across the raging river, or whether they could find an elusive tribe in the dense jungle.

Narcissa Whitman's journal entries as she traveled overland in the 1830s to the Oregon territory illustrates this perspective. She enthusiastically described the "varied scenes" and "beautiful landscapes" and com-

plained, "I could have dwelt upon the scene still longer with pleasure, but Brother Spalding called us to prayers." She accepted the privations in stride and was grateful for the bounty the land provided. "I never saw anything like buffalo meat to satisfy hunger," she wrote, "so long as I have it I do not wish anything else." And months into the most difficult journey, she could still write, "Thus are blessings so mingled that it seems as if there is nothing else but mercy and blessing all the way."[2]

In other instances these women, like many men, had no love for adventure. They were timid souls who trembled at the unknown. Yet they sensed the call of God and felt that they had no other choice but to claim his protection. In some cases—and this was true especially of women—the call of God had come through their spouses. The husband was eager to enter unexplored tribal regions, while the wife, with no predilection for adventure, fearfully accompanied him. This was true of

Rosemary Cunningham, who had been married only a few weeks when she entered the Brazilian jungle for the first time to join her new husband in his pioneer work. There was little to calm her fears, especially when she thought of the three previous missionaries who had ventured into the region. "They had met with cruel death at the hands of the merciless Indians. They had been clubbed to death by the very ones to whom they had so sacrificingly gone to take the Message of Life."[3]

The Brazilian villagers whom they met on the way only contributed to her fears of the tribal Indians with whom they were to live. "They are devils! They are animals without any soul!," a well-meaning "expert" warned her. "I would to God that every one was drowned in the middle of the river. Kill them all—that's what you do! You talk of taming them? Never! We know them better than you do." The fact that Rosemary's husband had already lived for a time with the Indians and prepared a house for her was little consolation. "If one did not realize the changeable nature of these wild Indians," she wrote after living among them for some time, "we could have laughed at the idea of treachery from those whose good-will seemed to be assured. But the fact that those who had apparently eagerly served and supported the chief for years could in a moment turn and shoot him in the back . . . was only another example of their fickleness." There were many terrifying, sleepless nights, spent wondering if the rumored threats against them would be carried out. Yet, these people needed to hear the gospel, and this was the "uttermost part of the earth" to which her husband had been called.[4]

But while Rosemary Cunningham leaned on her husband for courage and support, other women, such as Mary Slessor and Mildred Cable, went alone. They felt called to pioneer work, despite the dangers, and they were determined to depend entirely on God for their security.

## Mary Slessor

Perhaps the most widely written-about female missionary explorer and pioneer has been Mary Slessor, a Presbyterian missionary who served for nearly forty years in Calabar, West Africa (present-day Nigeria). She ventured into an area that had taken the lives of missionary men who had preceded her, but this dauntless Scottish lass, who had grown up under the tyrannical threats and physical abuse of her drunken father, was prepared for whatever obstacles lay ahead.

Mary's concern for missions had evolved since childhood, when she had attended mission conferences and listened to the lurid tales of missionaries who had returned home from faraway, exotic places. But for Mary a missionary vocation seemed out of the question. She worked in the textile mills to support her family—her mother and younger siblings—after her father died, and there was little hope that she would ever move beyond those dismal factory walls. She did, however, conduct mission work in her own backyard, working with the Queen Street Mission, where she served as a part-time missionary in the blighted neighborhoods of Dundee.[5]

Mary's opportunity for foreign missionary work came in her late twenties, after the financial burden of supporting her family had diminished. There were two catalysts—two deaths—that provided the impetus: the death of her brother, who had longed to serve as a foreign missionary, and that of David Livingstone. Mary was determined that she would take her brother's place and follow in the footsteps of her hero, the illustrious Scottish missionary explorer, whose death would inspire a host of new missionary ventures to Africa. Having read of Livingstone's sacrifice and adventure, Mary arrived in Africa in 1876, with romantic ideals of missionary life. She was astounded, however, when she found the missionary community enjoying proper English tea parties and the niceties of life that were entirely foreign to the factory life from which she had come.[6]

It was this lifestyle among the Presbyterian missionaries of Calabar more than anything else that prompted Mary to move inland, where she could have her own ministry with the Africans. "She discarded the Victorian missionary's hat, gloves, boots, bustle, long curls, and sometimes even her outer dress," writes Miriam Adeney. "She spent time in African houses, sleeping beside big sweating bodies, eating native food, going barefoot, suffering local diseases—but awake, aware, curious, asking questions, categorizing information, applying it." Here she served as circuit preacher, teacher, nurse, and as nanny for the unwanted babies she took in.[7]

Despite her active and productive ministry, Mary was not content with the limitations of working in one area. Following her furlough in 1885, and after she received word of her mother's death, she determined that she could take the risk of exploring the interior. "Heaven is now nearer to me than Britain," she wrote, "and no one will be anxious about me if I go up-country." "Up-country" was an area that had not yet been explored by missionaries, and she initially faced strong opposition from her colleagues. It simply was not considered appropriate for a woman to carry out such a venture. She, however, argued that as a woman she would be less of a threat to native tribesmen than a male missionary would be, and therefore safer. Yet she was fully aware of the dangers: "I am going to a new tribe up-country, a fierce, cruel people, and every one tells me that they will kill me. But I don't fear any hurt—only to combat their savage customs will require courage and firmness on my part."[8]

Mary was not a fearless trailblazer, who recklessly wagered her life for the thrill of daring adventure. She and her "adopted" little ones were escorted into the interior by a missionary and some Africans, who would be leaving her to carry out her exploratory work by herself. Suddenly she felt terribly alone. As she "faced the forest, now dark and mysterious, and filled with the noises of night, a feeling of helplessness and fear came over her. . . . Her heart played the coward; she felt a desire to turn and flee. But she remembered that never in her life had God failed her. . . . Still the shrinking was there."[9]

For the next quarter of a century Mary would work alone in the region of Okoyong, never fully overcoming her fear of the people who were immersed in witchcraft and divided into warring factions. She served as an intermediary in tribal disputes and was widely recognized for her healing powers. In spite of her fears, Mary became one with the people in a way that few other missionaries were able to do. She was able to live in a mud hut with a dirt floor, caring little about hygiene and regular eating habits. Though not always healthy, she lived for more than two decades in an area where no other missionary had been able to survive. According to James Buchan, she lived "not only like an African, but like a poor African."[10]

Mary Slessor, pioneer missionary to Calabar, West Africa.

But despite her calling to do pioneer exploratory work, Mary was not happy living alone. She desperately wanted companionship—the one stipulation being that the individual would have to live and work with her. For a time, her hope centered on Charles Morrison, a man several years her junior, who served on the mission staff at the coast. They announced their engagement, assuming that he would join her in the interior, but the mission board denied the transfer on the basis of his poor health. When asked if she would transfer to Duke Town, she responded forcefully:

> It is out of the question. I would never take the idea into consideration. I could not leave my work for such a reason. To leave a field like Okoyong without a worker and go to one of ten or a dozen where the people have an open Bible and plenty of privilege! It is absurd. If God does not send him up here then he must do his work and I must do mine where we have been placed. If he does not come I must ask the Committee to give me some one, for it is impossible for me to work the station alone.[11]

Mary made her own appeal for workers to come out and join her in an area well suited for women if they were willing to make the sacrifice such work entailed. "I feel dreadfully lonely," she wrote, "and want a helper, and I have made up my mind to ask the Committee at next meeting for a companion." She outlined a detailed description of what she wanted:

> . . . Consecrated, affectionate women who are not afraid of work or of filth of any kind, moral or material. Women who can nurse a baby or teach a child to wash and comb as well as to read and write, women who can tactfully smooth over a roughness and for

Christ's sake bear a snub, and take any place which may open. Women who can take everything to Jesus and there get strength to smile and persevere and pull on under any circumstances. If they can play Beethoven and paint and draw and speak French and German so much the better, but we can want all these latter accomplishments if they have only a loving heart, willing hands, and common sense. . . . There are thousands of them in our churches, and our home churches have no monopoly of privilege in choosing to keep them. Spare us a few. Induce them to come forward.[12]

Mary was an independent woman and was not really suited for a partnership. Single women had tried to live and work with her, but the relationships had not worked out well. Though she missed conversation and companionship with white colleagues, she was most suited to the African way of life, and it was that life that brought her real happiness. Indeed, she herself testified that she was "a witness to the perfect joy and satisfaction of a single life."[13]

In 1904, after spending most of two decades in Okoyong, Mary moved on to Itu, another remote area that was still unreached with the gospel. It was a natural move: another woman missionary was able to fill her place at her station outpost, and other missionaries were following in her wake and establishing new stations in the region. As for Mary, she was ready to do more exploratory and pioneer work in areas that had not yet been charted by missionaries. As had been true in prior years, she was not entirely alone. With her were her seven adopted children, the oldest of whom had become an indispensable

help to Mary in the work. She died in 1915, nearly forty years after she had first come to the region known as the "white man's graveyard."[14]

## Mildred Cable

Although China, unlike Africa, is not associated with exploration, there were regions of that vast land that had not been visited by Westerners until the coming of the missionaries, and some of those missionaries were women. Indeed, some of the greatest traveling evangelists in China during the first decades of the China Inland Mission's work were women. Among these were Mildred Cable and Francesca and Evangeline French, who after twenty-one years of conducting routine missionary work shocked the missionary community when they insisted that God was calling them to the unevangelized areas of China's great Northwest. While on a holiday they had heard of the "great cities where the name of Christ was not even known," and when they returned to their station they "all went back to work, but the claims of that unevangelized land on the Trio could not be stifled."[15]

They initially told no one of their call except the appropriate mission authorities of the China Inland Mission, some of whom objected to women—middle-aged women at that—taking on such a difficult assignment. "Even though the correspondence was confidential, the secret leaked out and many people took strong sides, which only helped to confuse the issue. Some wrote, saying in more or less parliamentary language, that there were no fools like old fools."[16] Indeed, it was an unusual request for transfer, and there were those who were convinced that these women had misinterpreted the call of God in their lives.

To a good many people it had seemed just plain foolishness. Why leave this important and successful school work to go off on some harebrained scheme of roaming over vast deserts looking for a few isolated tent dwellers and remote villages, when there were literally tens of thousands of people near at hand, all needing to hear the Gospel?[17]

After a year of waiting and indecision they became more convinced than ever that their going was the appropriate course of action, and it was their insistence that they were following the call of God that weighted the decision in their favor—a decision they sometimes questioned in the midst of hardship and privation. The journey itself was arduous and filled with uncertainties. They traveled for months by cart, which "rumbled and jolted over the uneven, muddy, mountain roads." On one occasion, when they were stuck in three feet of mud, the "call of the Great Northwest," writes Phyllis Thompson, "was very faint."[18]

Despite their hardships, they realized more and more with each day they traveled that the needs of the vast, unreached desert area of the northwest provinces were more than they could have previously imagined. They were at times tempted to stop and settle into ministry in needy areas along the way, but they continued on to their destination, finally arriving at the last town before the China border. Along the way they had conducted Bible sessions for untrained Christians, but when they reached their final destination—the City of the Prodigals—their ministry was among some of the very worst elements of society. The actual name of the city was Suchow, but because it was so isolated—the last city inside the Great Wall—it attracted a large criminal element who had run as far as they could from the law, short of crossing the vast expanse of the Gobi Desert that lay beyond the border. "They dare not go on, and they fear to go back. So they settle down in the last city inside the Wall."[19]

But there were not only criminals. The city was also a temporary home for vast numbers of traders and merchants. Indeed, the city was ideally located on an important trade route, and the women were convinced that such a location was most suitable for their work:

Little by little the Trio came to realize the tremendous importance of this network of trade routes, by means of which the cities of Central Asia are kept in vital contact with each other. The native news-distributing system whose speed, accuracy and simplicity baffles Western understanding might surely be made a means of spreading the knowledge of the Gospel, so that men on the market/places should hear, not only the political happenings of Europe or Afghanistan, but also that "Christ Jesus came into the world to save sinners."[20]

The City of the Prodigals became their base of operations during the winter when the icebound Tibetan passes were closed and blizzards brought travel to a standstill. Here they began a small nucleus of a church, where they served as teachers and preachers. But the remaining eight months of the year were devoted to evangelism in the vast region beyond the city. Here there were scattered settlements in arable areas, and "travel was always timed to suit the festivals and fairs of the district." These fairs allowed them to contact far greater numbers of people, who eagerly accepted the Scriptures and tracts the women had to offer them.[21]

Even though they avoided winter travel, the women were sometimes caught in dangerous weather conditions. On one occasion they were caught in a blinding snowstorm, an incident that was further aggravated by a dreadful accident:

It was Easter time and spring weather had been particularly warm, but when the Trio started on a missionary journey to Mongolia, the Gobi brought up its big guns at the first halting/place and blew a terrible blizzard with driving snow. The sleeping tent was set up under great difficulties, and it took the genius of an old desert hand to get the dung fire burning and the pot boiling. When a hot-water bottle was filled, Evangeline, as senior, was allowed the first hug, but as it was passed to her, in the dark, she gave a piercing scream of pain, for the side of the bottle had burst and deluged her with boiling water. She was badly scalded on arm, back and leg, and the difficulty of rendering first aid in the tent swaying like a ship at sea, working in a whirl of mixed snow and manure dust, must be left to the imagination.[22]

In addition to bad weather, the women were hampered by bandits and desert wars. On occasion they were caught in the middle of fighting bands, and for a time they were held captive by the most feared brigand

leader in the entire region. Yet despite the dangers the women knew that they must continue the work as long as they were able to travel, so when spring came they were out again on their long missionary journey, with a sense of accomplishment when they returned in the late fall:

At last they came to the Great Wall and, passing through the massive gates, they stopped the cart, standing together to thank God for His guidance and protection through all their wanderings over the mighty desert. They had lived and preached in twelve towns and many hamlets, and wherever they had gone they had pasted up Christian posters on the wooden walls of homes and temples. They had left Christian books in temples and given away more tracts than they could keep count of. They had entered 2,700 homes to tend the sick and tell of a Saviour, had held 656 meetings, and sold 40,000 portions of Scripture. The highways over which they had traveled were no longer safe, and the storms that had been gathering over the Great Northwest were breaking fast. But in the lull before the storm they had sown seed which sooner or later would surely bear a harvest. Satisfied, they made their way back to their home in the City of Prodigals.[23]

Sometimes areas were cut off from them for years at a time because of the fighting. Indeed, for five years they had been unable to return to the City of the Sands, where they had initiated a fledgling effort among the people. On the first Sunday of their return, however, they were amazed at what they found. "It was hoped that a few people would meet for public worship, but to everyone's amazement the inn room was crowded to the doors and, after the service was over, one and another stood and asked to have his name enrolled on a list of inquirers." The Scriptures they had left on the previous visit had made an impact that none of them had dared expect, and during their stay they were inundated with people from the town and outlying farms wanting to know more about their message of hope.[24]

In their pioneering ministry the women had many contacts with other women, but their most frequent listeners were men. Whether at home in the City of Prodigals, out visiting in a remote desert town, or bumping along in their cart somewhere in between, along the vast network of trade routes, the first people to approach them were usually men. Men were both their chief opponents and their major supporters. It was a man's world, and little could be accomplished without recognizing that fact of life. The place of women in local society was low, except for the power some wives wielded over co-wives and daugh-

ters-in-law. The tragic child marriage of Patima illustrates this. Like other Muslim women, she was veiled on her wedding day and "instructed henceforth to cover her face at the approach of any man, unless he be her husband." But even from him there would be no respect. "Though but twelve years old he knew that a woman had no rights, and that her only purpose was for his pleasure." As for her part, "she must learn subservience, obedience and docility in the presence of her mother-in-law, as well as absolute yieldingness to every whim of her boy husband."[25]

Despite this low view of women, it was through the amazing pioneer work of these three single women that the Great Northwest was initially opened to the gospel. They viewed their mission as one of primary evangelism. They did not found great churches or theological learning centers. They simply obeyed the command of Christ to take the gospel to every creature.

# The World My Parish: Church Planting and Preaching

It is not surprising that women were particularly adept at church planting in overseas mission work. They were eager to establish indigenous church leaders, and as unordained members of the "weaker sex" they, unlike their male counterparts, did not pose a threat to nationals. Lottie Moon's ministry in China bears this out. Likewise, women often sensed a powerful and very specific call to the ministry of evangelism and church planting. Ruth Hitchcock, a missionary to China, tells in her autobiography how God first impressed upon her the need for missionary service when she was only ten years old. Horace Houlding, a missionary from China, was staying in her home, and he told a story she would never forget:

On the great plains near the Yellow River, the peasants sow their wheat at the beginning of winter and then wait for the snow to cover it. During those snowy winter months they are shut up in their houses, busy with indoor things such as shoe-making, spinning, weaving, and sewing. One winter a man came two days' journey by cart to the Houldings' mission station. He asked for a missionary to go back with him to his village during this quiet winter time to tell the people the good news which they had heard was available from these foreigners. Later on, the farmers would be too busy in their fields to listen, but now they were free. The missionaries thought this a wonderful opportunity. Who could return with the messenger? To their dismay, everyone was busy with the work they already had at the mission station. No one could be freed to go. Though the man begged them to find someone, he finally had to return alone with his cart to that village where they wanted to hear the Gospel. At the beginning of the next winter he appeared again—and again the bleak decision was reached. No one could go. The cart crept slowly back across the miles.

Ruth responded to the need so graphically portrayed: "In my heart the resolve grew: 'Lord, when I grow up, I'll go."[1]

There were other women who did not feel called or qualified to do the work of church planting and preaching—women who acquired their vocation by default. This was the case with the single women missionaries of the Dakota Mission who were forced to handle the religious services after the male minister left the region. "We will find it a hard task," wrote Mary Barnes, "to conduct the meetings and attend to the various duties of which he relieved us." Some who had not felt called to such work quickly discovered latent gifts and were able to perform ministries they never could have imagined doing. Beatrice Stocker, also working with the Dakota Mission, discovered that she could preach but remained terrified at other aspects of the ministry. "The preaching does not dismay me like the praying," she confessed. "I don't think I should mind preaching now to an American congregation of two or three hundred, but to lead in family prayer extempore is an ordeal that is travail of the soul."[2]

## Eleanor Macomber

During and after the late-nineteenth century (when the Women's Missionary Movement was well underway), it was not uncommon to hear stories of women on the mission field involved in ministries only proper for men. Opponents of such female activity lamented that this was the natural result of the founding of "female agencies" that sent women off to do a man's work. Those who defended such women usually did so by arguing that there were not enough men to carry out the ministry, so that women had to take up the slack. What is amazing, however, is that long before these "female agencies" were even conceived, there were women who were engaged in every aspect of church ministry overseas—with the exception of offering the sacraments. The willingness of these women to do pioneer work where men were unwilling or unavailable to serve allowed them to function in such capacities without outrage from churchmen. This was true of Eleanor Macomber, whose ministry spanned the decade of the 1830s.

The story of Macomber's missionary career was preserved by Daniel C. Eddy in his book *Heroines of the Missionary Enterprise*, written during the mid-nineteenth century. He could hardly have been termed a supporter of women's rights. He spoke of the "weak, defenceless woman" who was "weaker than man and unfit for public duties." Yet, his glowing account of Eleanor Macomber would seem to utterly defy his own description of the female sex. Macomber's missionary work began in 1830 when she was commissioned by a Baptist mission society to serve as a teacher among the Ojibwa Indians in the region of Sault Ste. Marie, Michigan. After four years she terminated that ministry due to failing health. Within two years, however, she was involved in an entire new missionary endeavor with the Karen mission of Burma.[3]

As a single woman, there was little choice for Macomber but to live and work alone. Had she moved into the residence of a married couple, the Burmese would have made the immediate assumption that it was a polygamous household. So, upon arrival, she was escorted to her mission outpost at Dong-Yahn. "Mr. Osgood, who accompanied Miss Macomber from Maulmain to her field of labour, and whose duty required him to leave her there, an unprotected stranger in the midst of a brutal, drunken community of heathen barbarians" stayed with her for two days until arrangements for her living quarters could be procured. He described his departure poignantly:

After selecting a place, and making the necessary preparations for building, I prepared to return to Maulmain. Until this time our dear sister Macomber had borne the trials of the journey, and the prospect of being left alone, without the least appearance of shrinking; but when the moment of separation came, the thought of being left, without a friend, in the midst of a drunken people, and even in the house of a man completely besotted with ardent spirits, and at a distance of thirty miles or more from any civilized society, with scarcely a sufficient knowledge of the language to make known her wants— was too much for the delicate feelings of a female to endure, and she could only give vent to the emotions of her heart by a flood of tears. She soon, however, recovered her self-possession, and resolved to cast herself upon the merciful protection of her heavenly Father, and to pursue what seemed to her to be the path of duty.[4]

Unlike the ministry of so many missionaries—including that of the great Adoniram Judson, who served for several years in Burma without a convert—Macomber witnessed results from her preaching within a matter of months. Indeed, according to Eddy, "In a few months the little church, planted through her instrumentality, numbered more than twenty persons, who continued faithful in the duties and practices of disciples." She wrote home about the progress she was making:

A number of these poor, dark heathen, who were then bound in Satan's double chain (idolatry and drunkenness,) have been liberated and brought into the glorious liberty of the gospel of Christ, and are now rejoicing in hope of the glory of God. Ten have been baptized, four men and six women, and a number of others, I trust, will ere long seek the blessed privilege. Many are still inquiring, and some, I trust, earnestly seeking. But many are opposing, reviling, and persecuting, and a few are indifferent and unconcerned.[5]

The fact that she encountered powerful resistance made her accomplishments all the more remarkable. She was opposed by Buddhist priests and local authorities, and her converts met with persecution. Yet, she would not be intimidated. She announced her public worship services and prayer meetings and formed a training school that attracted a dozen willing pupils. The public baptisms that occurred every few months always had to wait until "brother Osgood came up again," for although she could plant a church, conduct worship and prayer services, teach in her Bible school, and personally lead an enquirer to conversion, she could not carry out the simple act of baptism—a "sacrament" that church tradition deemed proper only for the male sex to administer.[6]

Although her many activities along with language learning were enough to keep her busy, she was not content to limit her ministry to Dong-Yahn. She began training and sending out converts to the nearby tribes.

When she herself went out she went in the company of one or two of her male converts, who served as protective escorts and carriers, while at the same time being trained for evangelistic ministry themselves. "I have made it my personal business to go with some of them," she wrote, "so that I have visited all the families within six or seven miles, once or twice. . . . I can speak but little of the language; but keeping a Karen with me, who is accustomed to my broken speeches, I give him ideas which he explains."[7]

Macomber's varied ministry included becoming involved in church discipline. "The native Christians," she wrote, "have appeared remarkably firm and steadfast, and although some cases have required discipline, yet not one has had the appearance of contemplated or wilful sin." Indeed, for the short length of her ministry, the converts gave evidence of a strong conscience and a clear sense of right and wrong.

> One poor old man alone, twelve or fifteen miles off, was overcome, by the long solicitation of a numerous family, and under peculiar circumstances, so as to eat in a feast made to appease evil spirits; but he immediately came down here, confessed, and appeared truly humbled; said he did not forget God any moment, or cease to love him; but to be at peace with friends, he ate. I directed him to return and prove his sincerity by a future upright walk, and when we all returned, at the close of the rains, we would consult together on his case. There have been some other similar cases in regard to drinking, an evil which I fear more than all others.[8]

It was in the midst of this very effective ministry in Burma that Macomber became ill. Nine days later, on April 16, 1840, at the age of thirty-nine, she was dead. Her brief tenure in Burma had demonstrated that women could serve in every capacity as effectively as their male counterparts—and in many respects perhaps more effectively. As a woman, she was not a personal threat to converts or outsiders, and yet her authority was highly regarded in both the church and the community.

## Sue McBeth

For women missionaries working among the Indians on the American frontier, preaching became a routine aspect of ministry. There were rarely enough male ministers to fill the needs, and thus women had little choice but to preach and plant churches, whether they particularly desired that ministry or not. Sue McBeth, who worked with her sister Kate, very ably conducted such ministries among the Nez Perce Indians following the death in 1874 of Henry Spalding, who had initiated the work among them in the Oregon Territory. Robert Speer referred to her as a woman of "apostolic zeal who . . . trained preachers, taught and preached." If she had misgivings about such ministry, she knew that her Presbyterian administrators or colleagues would not be inclined to criticize, since for a period of time there were no Presbyterian ministers within a hundred miles of her outpost. She herself was handicapped by a partial lower-limb paralysis, but she did not allow that to curtail her work.[9]

McBeth was deeply committed to her work with the Indians. She had sensed a very specific call that served to buttress her ministry through the years. "If the call had been to go to India or China, I would have thought less of it," she wrote in her diary,

but the American Indians, a race in whom I had always felt such a deep interest. How could I slight their claim? . . . How distinctly I remember . . . examining the hieroglyphics, traced, as was supposed, by the red men when their tribes possessed the land. I recalled the deep sympathy I felt for the vanished race and longed to be a woman that I might go to the handful that yet remained and tell them the story of Jesus.[10]

Because of the lack of ministers, McBeth made it her priority to train native American men for that role. She held classes in her own home and taught several students at a time on a daily basis for a four-to-five-year course. It was a slow, tedious process as they translated the Bible from English to Nez Perce and then studied in detail particular passages, but she was convinced that the effort was worth it. "I would rather have one thoroughly trained and tested and efficient Nez Perce minister and pastor," she wrote, "than half a dozen half taught and tested." By the 1890s, some two-thirds of the tribe had been converted—largely through the outreach of the pastors she trained.[11]

She was a very effective teacher who was able to stimulate her students, not in the last place through her own enthusiasm for her work. In a letter to the Secretary of the Presbyterian Mission Board she wrote:

I cannot close without telling . . . what great encouragement I have in my work with these Indian men. I do not think any one *could* have more *interested, earnest* and *diligent* pupils, or those who make more rapid progress—in like circumstances. I do not think that, altogether, they missed two hours last month. . . . They are all farmers—and busy ploughing and sowing nearly every day. But they are here every morning by 7 o'clock, often before it. . . . If there is pressing need, sometimes one or two of them go home as soon as they are through with their own lesson—but they usually study without intermission until 12, or later—then work their farms in the afternoon, and study at night.[12]

Unlike such women as Mary Slessor and Mildred Cable, McBeth was not doing pioneer evangelistic work. That work had begun nearly four decades earlier. It was left to her to develop an effective indigenous ministry, which was too often a weak point of nineteenth-century missionary work—especially among the native Americans. It was her aim, "to try—with God's help—to raise up a native ministry and trained elders . . . who will be the leaders in a Christian civilization."[13]

McBeth's vision reached beyond the tribal boundaries of the Nez Perce. She longed to see the day when her trained pastors would be reaching out to tribes beyond their borders, and in 1887 she wrote to the Presbyterian mission board to ask for financial assistance in sending native American missionaries to the Crow and Shoshone Indians. "I . . . could scarce be at rest," she wrote, "with those two tribes, at least, still without the gospel. . . . It was for them . . . that the ministers of their second class were trained as pioneer evangelists (not pastors for the more enlightened Nez Perce)."[14]

The success that McBeth witnessed among the Nez Perce was unusual. Missionary work to the American Indians was not noted for large numbers of conversions and a stable indigenous ministry. But despite the outward success, her work was flawed. Like so many missionaries of her generation, she was unable to properly differentiate between "Christianizing" and "Americanizing" the Indians. She was concerned that they build wood houses, live in nuclear families, and that men cut their long hair. When an Indian convert "relapsed into the occasional blanket" instead of his "civilized garments," she was distressed. She was determined that "her boys" (as she was prone to call her converts) would not only be Christians but also patriotic Americans—Americans who would properly celebrate the Fourth of July:

260 Kamians—dressed in citizens clothes, marched with banners & in the grove near the Church, where Robert read the Declaration of Independence and made an address—followed by other speeches, a big dinner, singing, etc. The Church there is so peaceful and united.[15]

In defense of McBeth, she was deeply concerned about the welfare of the Indians and feared that if they did not assimilate into American culture they would be destroyed—"would inevitably disappear before the superior white civilization." "Neither Sue McBeth nor her colleagues went to the Indians to pray over their graves," writes Michael Coleman,

"but to save them for this life too. And the only way they could be saved, these missionaries believed, was by forsaking their old ways, and taking up the new." This she expressed explicitly in a letter to the mission secretary: "Emigration is pouring rapidly into Idaho—filling up the valleys and prairies, in some places to the very edge of the Nez P. reservation—and greedy eyes are looking over the edge—putting the Nez Perces in fear for there homes." What was her solution to this problem? "It is vital for the interests of the Nez P. church (under God) (I think) as well as to their prosperity or ever continued existence as people, that the Nez Perce men be fitted to take their places as men among men, as speedily as possible."[16]

Of McBeth's dedication and commitment to missionary work there is no doubt. The verdict is still out, however, as to her long-term effectiveness in preparing the Nez Perce to carry on the Christian faith in future generations. When compared to her colleagues, her work was impressive, but she was a woman of her times and she failed to fully appreciate the native American culture.

## Malla Moe

One of the most effective church planters and preachers in modern times has been Malla Moe (1863–1953). She was a pioneer missionary who served in Swaziland in Southern Africa for fifty-four years with the Scandinavian Alliance Mission, founded by Fredrik Franson, a strong supporter of women in ministry. She immigrated to Chicago from Norway in the 1880s, and was soon thereafter recruited personally by Franson. She had previously met D. L. Moody and became convinced that she should take two years of training at Moody Bible Institute before launching into Christian ministry. Franson believed otherwise. "God says 'go,' and the heathen say 'come.' You must go now," he admonished her.[17]

It was a most difficult decision for Malla. How could she agree to such a drastic course of action when she had family responsibilities and no training or experience in ministry? Yet, she felt God's call, and she had no peace until she responded in the affirmative. Within days she enrolled in Franson's Bible school—a two-week course "filled with Bible study, exhortation, and practical suggestions." There were no educational requirements for the course, but there were spiritual prerequisites: to be "filled with the Spirit" and to "know how to trust God." The candidates, three men and five women, were given one week to set their affairs in order before leaving for New York for their commissioning, after which they were to sail to South Africa.[18]

From the beginning of Franson's work in South Africa, women were expected to carry heavy responsibilities. Three of the five early Scandinavian Alliance Mission stations in Swaziland were founded by women, one of them by Malla Moe. She established the Bethel station in the late 1890s, which became her base for the next half century. Her success was largely due to her dependence on Africans. One of her first converts was a Zulu, Johane Gamede, who became her "lifelong companion and invaluable help in bridging language and cultural differences between herself and the Swazis."[19]

Few missionaries surpassed Malla Moe's close identification with the Africans. She accepted their culture as her own and began living their lifestyle during her first year among them. In 1893 she wrote: "I felt so happy because I had taken this step to . . . live out in the native kraals." The following year she was able to say, "with respect to the food, I have now learned to eat several of their courses, and there are some that I really enjoy." Her close affinity with the Africans and their love for her was observed by a colleague in 1903, just prior to her first furlough. He told how she "had won the hearts of the people" and how difficult it was for them to let her go. "Grown men cried like children, over the entire room there was a deep heart rending cry as if the heart would break. Many were the prayers that were offered for her safety and her soon return to them."[20]

Moe did not build her ministry in Swaziland without assuming a strong parent-child relationship with the Africans in her region. In this sense she was like most Western missionaries of her era—though in many instances she went far beyond the bounds of the accepted paternalism of the day. She had a domineering personality that was manifested in her dealings not only with her converts but also with those who resisted her evangelistic appeals. Indeed, her unorthodox methods of evangelism often dismayed her own colleagues. The following account was written by a friend of hers:

Malla Moe and "The Gospel Wagon."

The day before she told him [a Swazi] she was going to pray till he got saved. She shouted to him to come back and grabbing him by the arm pulled him down into the grass and prayed mightily to God to save him from Satan and hell. It was more than he could stand. He wept and prayed and got saved.[21]

While some of her colleagues admired her style, others were highly critical, believing that she was carrying out her work too independently and without proper supervision. Some "were of the opinion that she was too domineering and demanding, and many were not eager for her return in 1932, following one of her rare furloughs." In the words of one historian, "she could be domineering, impatient, tactless, unsophisticated, and paternalistic." This was demonstrated time and again when she made decisions and dominated meetings even after the Swazi churches had fully capable African

pastors. "She would even interrupt a service being led by an African if she thought she could improve upon it."[22]

In many respects, Moe was not only audacious but also innovative in her evangelistic approach. She conducted a far-reaching evangelistic program that resulted in the formation of dozens of churches among the Swazis. In 1927, at the age of sixty-five, she began a new ministry of evangelism, traveling from place to place in her "gospel wagon." Accompanied by a band of native helpers, she maintained a hectic preaching schedule often in areas where the gospel had never before been heard.[23]

In addition to all her other activities, Moe did not forget women's work. She worked closely with Bible women in a concerted evangelistic effort. Speaking from a position of Western superiority that was characteristic of missionary community of the 1920s, she wrote: "Dorika, the Bible woman, has just returned from a trip where God used her to the salvation of souls. It is a wonder what God can do through these poor ignorant natives. This should be a challenge to young people at home to come over and help us in the work." Dorika worked alongside Malla for more than four decades, and her contribution to the growth of the Swazi church was great.[24]

Moe filled many roles during her several decades of ministry in Southern Africa, including that of evangelist, church planter, preacher, and bishop. She was not ordained and was never referred to as a bishop, but she functioned as one—assigning pastors to the churches she founded and overseeing their continued growth and development. Yet, despite this active role in missions that was supported by Christians on the home front, she faced obstacles in ministry when she was on furlough. In Norway, the home of her birth, she was not even permitted to speak in the chapels. "Officials of the State church reminded her to read Paul's instruction that 'women should keep silence in the church.' "[25]

### Fredrik Franson

Without the almost fanatical enthusiasm for missions of Fredrik Franson, many women such as Malla Moe would never have served abroad as missionaries. As the founder of the mission that later became known as TEAM (The Evangelical Alliance Mission), Fredrik Franson was a contemporary of Hudson Taylor and a man of similar enthusiasm for missions.

As with Taylor, the urgency of the task of reaching the lost was far more important than any quibbling over the precise role of women. He argued this point in a widely-distributed unpublished paper entitled "Prophesying Daughters." After quoting population statistics of various non-Western nations where the Gospel had not penetrated, he wrote:

Therefore, the fields of labor are large, and when we realize that nearly two-thirds of all converted people in the world are women, then the question of women's work in evangelization is of great importance. In China each day 30,000 people go into eternity without having heard the Gospel. There is no prohibition in the Bible against women's public work, and we face the circumstance that the devil, fortunately for him, has been able to exclude nearly two-thirds of the number of Christians from participation in the Lord's service through evangelization. The loss for God's cause is so great that it can hardly be described.[26]

It was the success of women like Moe that compelled Franson to speak out forcefully on the subject of women in missions.

It is amazing how one can get such a false idea as that not all God's children should use all their powers in all ways to save the lost world. There are, so to speak, many people in the water about to drown. A few men are trying to save them, and that is considered well and good. But look, over there a few women have untied a boat also to be of help in the rescue, and immediately a few men cry out; standing there idly looking on and therefore having plenty of time to cry out: 'No, no, women must not help, rather let the people drown.' What stupidity![27]

The church planting and preaching that women so effectively accomplished in missions was often criticized by churchmen at home who were passively enjoying their acknowledged positions of denominational leadership. The needs in mission work were far greater than the vast majority of ordained male ministers appeared to realize. It took courageous men like Fredrik Franson and Hudson Taylor to open the doors to such ministry to women.

## Chapter 11

# Mobilizing the Masses: Organization and Training on the Home Front

Some of the most noteworthy guardians of the great commission were those who stayed home and carried out organizational, educational, and fund-raising tasks, especially through the Women's Missionary Movement. This movement has been neglected by historians who have written at length about other, related movements such as the Student Volunteer Movement, the Faith Missionary Movement, and the Laymen's Missionary Movement. Yet the former sustained more than forty mission agencies, mobilized millions of women on the home front, and sent thousands of women overseas during the late nineteenth and early twentieth centuries.

The underlying impulse of the Women's Missionary Movement was the rejection of single women for missionary service by existing mission boards. The need for women to reach their "heathen" sisters was widely acknowledged, but missionary wives were generally too burdened with domestic duties to adequately meet the need. Nevertheless, the option of accepting women as missionaries in their own right was not one most mission boards were prepared to consider.

From the onset of the modern missionary movement women had served faithfully in foreign service as wives, but they had no authority or official ministry of their own, and thus were not felt to be in violation of the Apostle Paul's admonitions regarding women. On the home front, women were the backbone of mission support efforts involving prayer and finances, but there was a growing desire among many of them to become more personally involved. As we have seen in a previous chapter, many women found an outlet in urban ministries, and during the nineteenth and early twentieth centuries hundreds of inner-city mission endeavors were founded by women. But as early as the middle of the nineteenth century women were beginning to clamor for wider opportunities for service. Many single women felt the call of God as assuredly as did their male counterparts, but without a marriage partner of like commitment they were barred from answering that call.

It was this obstacle that prompted the groundswell of devotion that became the Women's Missionary Movement. Women banded together to form "female agencies" to send their sisters overseas. The first such organization was the Women's Union Missionary Society, founded in 1861 by Sarah Doremus. More than two decades earlier she had become aware of the need for women's work overseas through David Abeel, a missionary to China from her own denomination, the Reformed Church in America. He challenged her with a simple but stirring message from women in China: "O bring us some female men." Doremus was prepared to act immediately but her vision was dampened by Rufus Anderson, who was then foreign secretary of the American Board of Commissioners for Foreign Missions. His long-standing opposition to single women in missions was well known, and since she was actively involved in support efforts for that mission, she deferred to his wishes. But the needs of women in foreign lands continued to weigh on her conscience, and finally, in 1860, she called together women from various denominations, and together they launched their mission endeavor by sending Sarah Marston, a Baptist, to Burma. The interdenominational character of this mission stymied its growth—not because women themselves objected, but because their own denominations opposed such ecumenical efforts. Nevertheless, the mission grew and after

two decades had supported more than one hundred missionaries on twelve stations. More significant was the influence this female agency had on women's missions in general.

Inspired by the success of the Women's Union Missionary Society, other women's societies were quickly formed along denominational lines, the first of them among the Congregationalists of New England. Rufus Anderson of the American Board had retired, and the new foreign secretary, N. G. Clark, was supportive of single women missionaries. He encouraged the formation of the Women's Board of Missions, which was incorporated in 1869. Methodist women were next to organize, the Baptists followed in 1870, and in the decades that followed a new women's mission society was formed on an average of one each year.

Maintaining growth and a sense of solidarity among members of these women's mission societies required active participation by members and often backbreaking work by officers, who often traveled extensively in an effort to stimulate the rank and file to more committed involvement. Mary Clarke Nind, who served as an officer with the Woman's Foreign Missionary Society of the Methodist Episcopal Church, is an example:

Much of her Branch was wilderness. The towns were few and far apart, the churches weak and struggling. . . . Her courage never faltered as by faith she laid the foundations of this great organization in Minnesota, the Dakotas, Montana, Idaho, Washington, and Oregon, traveling over the unbroken prairie and through the wilderness, in wagon, or cart, or sleigh, in summer and winter, by day and by night, by freight

Turn-of-the-century women's missionary magazines.

train or day coach (never in a Pullman, the Lord's money was too precious for such luxuries), compassing as many as 5,000 miles in a single year.[1]

Another important aspect of the work on the home front was educating women through the printed word. Missionary books written and published by women sold widely, and virtually every women's missionary society published its own magazine. These magazines kept women abreast of what was happening overseas in a more intimate and personal way than did many of the magazines published and edited by the male leaders of the denominational mission societies.[2]

This era of the women's missionary movement is significant not merely because of what was accomplished in the work of missions, but also because of the contributions made to missiology—the theory of missions. It was in a very real sense a heyday for women in missiology—except for the fact that women had a limited audience: other women. The most prominent leaders of the Women's Missionary Movement on the national scene were Lucy Peabody and Helen Barrett Montgomery. There were other women, however, who were not strictly a part of the women's missionary movement that sent single women overseas, but who nevertheless made great contributions in organizing the masses of women for missions involvement and in preparing candidates to go abroad. Annie Armstrong made tremendous headway among the Southern Baptists, despite the restrictions she encountered, and Henrietta Soltau dedicated her talents to preparing female candidates for the China Inland Mission. Although all of these women concentrated their efforts on the home front, their work was no less critical than that of those who went abroad.

## Annie Armstrong

One of the most powerful church women of the late nineteenth and early twentieth century was Annie Armstrong, corresponding secretary for the Women's Missionary Union of the Southern Baptist Convention. The power that she was able to wield in this position, and the manner in which she governed, illustrates the parallel between women's and men's work. There was very little difference between the actions of Annie Armstrong and the women she worked with and those of men in high positions. There were repeated struggles for control of funds and influence, and it was one of these conflicts that

undermined her authority and brought her seventeen-year reign to an end in 1906.

Annie was born in Baltimore in 1850. She grew up a Southern Baptist (a denomination formed in 1845, when it split from the Northern Baptists), but prior to her conversion in 1870 "she had often said . . . that she could be a Presbyterian or an Episcopalian but never a Baptist." Her conversion, however, was not only to Christianity but also to the Southern Baptist Convention, to which she became fiercely loyal from that moment on. Her interest in ministry developed naturally from her mother's active involvement in missions. Annie became active in the Maryland Women's Mission Organization and strongly advocated a national organization. By the 1887 Convention she had gained national visibility and began using her influence to bring the Women's Missionary Union into being the following year. With that accomplished, she "lost no time in assuming her role as an officer of the new organization."[3]

Annie was an imposing individual who did not fit the stereotype of the Southern belle of the Civil War era. "She was stately and erect and six feet tall." She dressed fashionably, according to the Victorian custom of the day. She was intelligent and never short of ideas for change and visions for the future. "She had a strong personality, was exacting, and never at a loss for words." But what sometimes made her a threat to the male establishment and an awesome force in the eyes of some of her female colleagues was her managerial expertise. She "was an organizational genius—highly skilled, able to manage large affairs, and with executive and business ability."[4]

Soon after Annie assumed her office as corresponding secretary she was confronted with the powerful male domination of the Southern Baptist Convention. At first she fully accepted the limited authority that the Women's Missionary Union was granted, but when the limitations affected her own work directly, she felt stymied. Throughout her years of ministry, and even as late as her farewell address in 1906, Annie had fully supported the three-fold purpose of the WMU—in her words, "knowing, praying, giving." Unlike many of the women's missionary societies that were organized during the last half of the nineteenth century, the Women's Missionary Union was not an independent agency that sent out women missionaries. It was an auxiliary organization—and a very restricted one at that.[5]

Yet, in 1890, when one of the male officials of the Foreign Mission Board, wrote to her that the best thing the women could do for missions was to "raise money for the Board and let the Board appropriate it," she found the advice frustrating. She was a woman of independent action, and she had her own ideas as to how the money should be spent. When she did request counsel from the Board on appropriating funds, she was on occasion ignored. In her efforts to support a chapel in Rio, she "felt the rug had been pulled out from under the WMU" after the appeal had already gone out. To the president of the Board she wrote: "Pardon me if I seem to be calling in question Dr. Tupper's judgment in this matter, but I do believe very thoroughly if our

work is to amount to anything, we must not be placed in a position where it would be very clearly seen that we do not know what we are about."[6]

Annie Armstrong, founder and first executive director of the Woman's Missionary Union of the Southern Baptist Convention. (From the Archives, Woman's Missionary Union, Auxiliary to Southern Baptist Convention.)

One of Annie's greatest conflicts during her seventeen-year tenure as the corresponding secretary for the WMU was with Fannie Heck, the president of the organization. The president of the WMU had served as little more than a figurehead at times, but Heck was determined that the president's position should be a strong one. Until her tenure in the late 1890s, "the executive committee controlled Union matters, and . . . Annie ran the committee." A clash was inevitable. Under Annie's rule, the WMU had given assistance not only to various mission endeavors but also to the Southern Baptist Sunday School Board. Heck strongly opposed money going for any other purpose than missions per se. The battle lines were drawn and the contest between two strong-willed women continued until Heck agreed not to run for president again in 1899.[7]

During her last years of service, Annie was involved in many issues that raised controversy. As a loyal Southern Baptist she was sharply critical of the Northern Baptists, whom she charged with infringing on Southern Baptist territory. She also had to deal with renegades in her own denomination—those who were following the convictions of T. P. Crawford (Martha Crawford's husband) that missionaries should be independently supported without the costly expenses of a large mission organization. For a time she feared that the Georgia WMU might split off from the national organization over this very issue, and she was forced to take strong action to prevent it.[8]

The issue of Annie's salary—or lack of salary—became another point of controversy that caused hard feelings in the WMU. Annie had prided herself in the fact that she worked tirelessly for years without receiving any salary—a sacrifice her male counterparts were not willing to match. Family finances had allowed her to continue, though by the early years of the twentieth century her funds were running low and expenses were increasing. There was sufficient support in the WMU to offer her a salary, which she wanted and needed, but in the end, fearing

criticism, she turned down the offer and continued to work without salary.[9]

The final conflict Annie was embroiled in and that "would lead ultimately to her downfall" related to the issue of religious training for women. Her particular concern was the training of female missionaries and missionary wives. Because she was deeply interested in this issue she wanted to bring the training under the control of the WMU, where she could personally play a powerful role in determining the location of the institution and its curriculum. Others in the Southern Baptist Convention, however, were equally determined to guide the future of women's education—not the least of whom were seminary administrators who felt that a women's program should be developed alongside the program for men.[10]

The battle raged for many months, and before it was over "Annie firmly believed she had been wronged, claiming she could have a number of persons prosecuted for libel if she chose to do so." Initially she had the support of the other women on the WMU executive committee, but with pressure from the opposing side they were swayed to support seminary training for women. So committed was Annie to the cause and so upset was she with the loss of support that she resigned her position.[11]

It is interesting that Annie's defense of her position was based on a very restrictive view of women. She argued that if women were permitted to take training in a seminary environment it would be the first step in educating them as preachers—a profession she argued the Bible did not permit. Those who supported the plan for women to be trained at the seminary were hardly feminists themselves and certainly did not advocate women preachers. They simply argued that such education would not lead to preaching. At least Annie's words were consistent with her actions. She herself would never speak in "mixed meetings."[12]

In her years of leadership in the WMU Annie made some significant contributions, particularly in the realm of home missions—more specifically, urban missions. She initiated the work with black women in Baltimore, and together with other women "started mothers' meetings for the black women and industrial schools for the girls." She was also active in helping the black women form an auxiliary to the National Baptist Convention and she often spoke at the women's meetings. After helping the black women in Cincinnati organize, one of the women paid her tribute:

> Miss Annie W. Armstrong—the trail blazer in Christian cooperation between white and Negro Baptist women of the South . . . guided us in the completion of the organization of the Woman's Convention. No woman in America has ever done more to encourage Negro Baptist women in their work. . . . It was she who offered the prayer for divine guidance at the close of our first day's session. Her presence was a benediction. She stayed with us, and took part. In the afternoon, she delivered one of the most inspiring addresses of the entire Convention.[13]

She was ahead of her time in her cooperation with black women, and for that she was criticized, as she was for her emphasis on home missions.

In fact, she took a trip to Mexico to observe mission work there in order to dispel the criticism about her emphasis on home missions. Her harshest critic was T. P. Bell, who did not hesitate to put in print his animosity toward Annie. In 1905, just after she resigned her post, he wrote a critical editorial about her in a Southern Baptist publication:

> For several years past, there has been a growing dissatisfaction in various parts of the South over some of the ways which have been adopted by the leaders of the Woman's Missionary Union. It has been felt that there was too much of a one-person power in the organization—a power that was wielded with too little considerations for the views, and even the feelings of other interested workers. At Kansas City, the matter culminated, with the result that the leader of the Union announced her determination to resign her position.[14]

In many ways it is difficult to evaluate the legacy of Annie Armstrong. There is no doubt that she made enormous contributions to Southern Baptist missions. She was an efficient administrator, and during her years at the helm the WMU made great progress. She was a domineering woman who wielded immense power—power that was unheard of for a woman in Southern Baptist circles—and yet she maintained that women had a subservient role that did not even permit them to speak at their own denominational conventions. To many she was an enigma.

## Helen Barrett Montgomery

The most noted female mission leader of the women's missionary movement was Helen Barrett Montgomery. She worked closely with Lucy Peabody—an influential team, described by R. Pierce Beaver as "dynamic officers of the Woman's American Baptist Foreign Mission Society and leaders in the interdenominational fellowship."[15] On the national level they encouraged ecumenical unity among the mission societies and made the movement a force to be reckoned with. The major purpose of their ecumenical organization was to educate lay women so that they would be more intelligently involved in missions. Montgomery summed up the view of many female missions leaders: "We have done very little original work. We have made very few demands upon the brains of the women in our missionary circles. And as a result, we have been given over to smallness of vision in our missionary life."[16] Indeed, the women's missionary movement made more demands on the brains of its adherents than any other missionary movement before or since.

Helen Barrett Montgomery was born in the early 1860s, at the very time the women's missionary movement was born. Her father was an educator who later went into the ministry—a man deeply concerned about his daughter's education. "My father had interesting ways of getting information into our heads," she later wrote. "We would creep into his bed in the morning and learn to count in Latin and would repeat the various declensions and conjugations. . . . so with the multiplication tables. And on walks we were shown the forms of trees and plants and told the names of rocks." It was her father who had the greatest influence on her life. Her

Helen Barrett Montgomery, missionary stateswoman.

deep devotion to him was unwavering:

> I loved both my parents with all the affection within me. But I am not quite sure that my mother's authority was completely successful. She was obeyed because she belonged. My father, on the other hand was adored. To this child God always looked like her father, and obedience to her father became the basis of submission to the will of God. There was reverence, there was fear, the right kind of fear, a dread of doing what was wrong in my father's sight.[17]

Helen had many other childhood experiences outside her family that would prepare her for the prominent role she would later play in missions and church work in general. When she was nine years old she joined a rhetoric class and was involved in public presentations. It was a suitable activity in an era before movies and other forms of public entertainment were widely accessible; besides, "in those towns where some kind of theatre managed to eke out its existence, it was tabu to Baptists." Helen's family were devoted Baptists, and that religious influence would have a powerful impact on her entire life.[18]

When she was fifteen, Helen's father graduated from seminary and became pastor of the Lake Avenue Baptist Church in Rochester, New York. "From that day onwards," wrote Helen, "this church became one of my reasons for existence." From the beginning she was very active in the work. She taught a young boys' Sunday school class each week after the morning worship service. On Sunday afternoons she taught a boys' class at the city mission, and on Sunday night she was involved in the youth meeting and was expected to attend the Sunday evening service.[19]

In 1880 Helen entered Wellesley College, which quickly enlarged her religious horizons far beyond her Baptist upbringing. Yet, she clung to her own traditions enough to refuse communion at the college. "Stiff little Baptist that I was," she wrote, "I used to walk to Natick and take communion in the church there." Other doctrinal issues came to the fore as well. She later confessed that "there were fierce altercations when I defended the practice of baptism by immersion." There was little time, however, for doctrinal debates or interaction of any kind. In a letter home she wrote of her tight daily schedule: "The law is that you *must* exercise one *hour* *every* day in the open air whether you know your lessons or not, and you must work one hour, and attend chapel twice, and Bible class once, and silent time twice, and spend one hour in elegant leisure at dinner, so you see very little time is left unclaimed."[20]

During her early student days at Wellesley she had written, "Oh, you don't know how it seems to *feel* that you are an *out* set, that you are regarded as narrow, bigoted," but as time went on she felt more at home and began to open up to new ideas. "I feel more and more that a teachable mood is to be desired above everything, for it becomes easier and easier to say sharp things and to pick flaws instead of seeing the beauties that are everywhere waiting, waiting to be seen. I can see the belittling effects of letting the mind dwell on the deformities rather than the excellencies of life."[21]

She lamented that she did not have the musical ability that her roommate enjoyed nor the brilliance of other students, but she did credit herself with expertise in certain areas. "The only parts of me that have been systematically used," she wrote, "are my thinking and arguing powers, and I find that there I can hold my own with any of them." Again, she wrote, "I enjoy the work of argumentation very much."[22]

After graduating from college Helen took a position teaching school, but more prestigious opportunities quickly came her way, including the possibility of filling the position of president at two women's colleges where there were vacancies. Her parents were anxious that she pursue a career, but her own inclination was toward marriage. William Montgomery, a businessman and a widower seven years her senior, had proposed to her, but, aware of her potential, suggested they put off their marriage for five years until she was well settled in a career. Though he himself lacked higher education, he was anxious that she make full use of her own. He was a deeply religious man, and during one of his visits prior to their marriage she writes, "he knelt down with me and together we consecrated our lives to God's work in the world, promising to make this work our first thought and asking for His strength to keep us unspotted from the world."[23]

Helen's commitment was expressed later on, after she had been in the company of a dogmatic Baptist who was convinced he was orthodox on every doctrinal point. In reflecting on him, she was philosophical about her own religion:

> I tell you this Christian faith of ours is all shop-worn being handled over the counter and mussed and creased and discussed. We want to get it off the counter and cut into coats to cover the naked. My own soul is sick with theory—I'm getting so I don't care how or when or where or whether the Pentateuch wrote Moses or Moses, the Pentateuch. There is good news, the gospel, the love of God, the life of Jesus, and here am I, sinful and selfish and blind as a bat—for the secret of the Lord is with them that fear him. I know enough things now to make me a saint if I lived 'em. I'm going to live more and talk less.[24]

Helen's commitment to serving God did not exclude civic involvement, and during the early years of her marriage she was very active in educational matters in Rochester.

She served for twenty years as president of the Women's Educational and Industrial Union and was elected to a seat on the school board. It was her church involvement, however, that was her first love. She took an active role in her father's parish, not only during his thirteen years of ministry, but also during the decades that followed. "During that period she was for forty-four years the teacher of the Barrett Memorial class, one of the most influential women's classes in the city of Rochester, the class which through her influence became a force not only in the church and the city, but throughout the world." The attendance at times exceeded two hundred and included some of the most influential women in the city.[25]

Helen was a licensed Baptist preacher, and it was not uncommon for her to fill the pulpit in her own church. She was well-known throughout the denomination, and in 1921 she was elected denominational president of the Northern Baptists. "It was the first time that any woman had held this position in any large Christian body, and when the name of Mrs. Montgomery was presented to the convention, the shouts made the rafters ring."[26] It was her missions involvement, however, that became the most consuming activity of her life.

Helen's organizational work on the national level began in 1900, the year of the Ecumenical Missionary Conference held in New York City. It was at that time that the Central Committee for the United Study of Foreign Missions was formed. Lucy Waterbury Peabody, a widowed missionary to India, headed up this organization

The Women's Missionary Jubilee Committee, with Helen Barrett Montgomery seated in the center.

while Helen helped with the organizational work of organizing summer school programs for women and taught some of the courses.[27]

In addition to her organizational work with the women's missionary movement, Helen was a prolific writer and a thought-provoking missiologist. Many of her works were published by the Central committee. The first of these was *Christus Redemptor: An Outline Study of the Island World of the Pacific*, which, unlike so many written by missionary enthusiasts, was a straightforward account of the problems wrought by western imperialism. A translator of the New Testament herself, Helen was deeply concerned that the Bible be translated for the non-English-speaking world and that the Bible be used effectively in promoting missions. These positions were enunciated in her books *The Bible and Missions* (1920) and *The Preaching Value of Missions* (1931). Although most of her writing was to a Western audience, she recognized the work and often superior methods of nationals. For example, she pointed to the ministries of Kagawa, Oneoto, and Kobayashi in Japan as examples of effective urban strategy.[28]

Both Montgomery and Peabody worked tirelessly to promote the Jubilee celebration in 1910, which recognized the five decades of women's missionary work. Meetings were held throughout the country: forty-eight two-day celebrations in major cities and many one-day meetings in smaller communities, some of which brought together as many as four thousand participants. More than a million dollars was collected in offerings.

One of the greatest contributions of the Jubilee celebration was Helen Barrett Montgomery's Jubilee book, *Western Women in Eastern Lands*. In that volume she summed up the accomplishments of the past fifty years: "It is indeed a wonderful story. . . . We began in weakness, we stand in power. In 1861 there was a single missionary in the field . . . in 1909, there were 4710 unmarried women." She went on to present the increase in numbers of women involved in missions—from a few hundred to two million—and the increase in financial giving—from two thousand to four million dollars. But the greatest cause for celebration was the results overseas. The gospel had reached many regions of the world where women had never before had opportunity to hear, and nationals were playing a prominent role in the ministry. There were nearly six thousand Bible women and native helpers in addition to some 800 teachers, 140 physicians, 79 nurses, and 380 evangelists.[29]

The unity that was developed during the Jubilee celebration prompted Helen and other national leaders to organize the Federation of Woman's Boards of Foreign Missions, and she became its first president in 1917. Her activities also included world travel. Her most extensive trip was a world tour of missions fields with Lucy Waterbury Peabody in 1913. Family responsibilities could have prevented Helen from going, but when Peabody inquired of Helen's husband about the prospects of her going, he was supportive: "When I married Helen Barrett I realized that she had ability and training to do what I could never do. I resolved, therefore, never to interfere with any call that might come to her. If Helen cares to go, I will help her in every possible way." They were gone several months and visited Egypt, India, China, Korea, Japan, Singapore, Malaysia, and other countries. It was a unique opportunity to gain a better understanding of women's work abroad, and they brought back new insights to the millions of women on the home front.[30]

In the decades following the 1910 Jubilee, the Women's Missionary Movement declined. There continued to be successful fundraising campaigns, but the movement as a whole weakened. Denominational boards had begun to accept single women missionaries, and there was considerable pressure for women's societies to merge with their "parent" boards. Many women fought against these mergers, fearing the loss of female participation if their work was taken over by male-dominated boards. Despite these protests the denominational boards prevailed, and, as was feared, the women lost their influence. The once-vibrant educational and publishing ventures of the Women's Missionary Movement were also absorbed into the general boards and eventually were abandoned altogether. Women continued to have a vital interest in missions, but their focus was turned more and more toward the new faith missions rather than the mainline denominational boards.[31]

Helen herself went on to achieve further triumphs. She was a Greek scholar and used her considerable ability to translate the New Testament—the first woman to do so. Her translation was published by the Judson Press in 1924. Over the years, through her writing and through money she had inherited, she became a wealthy woman, but the money was not used on herself. It is estimated that she contributed nearly a half-million dollars to missions and other charitable works during her lifetime and at the time of her death.[32]

### Henrietta Soltau

As important as doing organizational and public relations work on the home front was the work of screening and preparing candidates for overseas service. In some cases denominational and "faith" mission boards instituted a Women's Department to handle matters that specifically related to women, married or single. The Church Missionary Society is an example. Its Women's Department advised women on matters such as appropriate clothing to take along and assistance in acquiring it: "Through an arrangement made with a large wholesale firm, the Women's Department is able to procure for outgoing women missionaries woollen underclothing, *unshrinkable* and of beautiful quality, at more than 25 percent under ordinary prices." Among other items that were suggested were "2 cholera belts, woven and shaped" and "4 pairs canvas or other corsets."[33]

In many cases women were more attentive to the preparation and training of missionaries than were men, and separate preparatory institutions in the homeland for single women were seen as essential by some mission agencies, as were separate language schools for women once they reached their destination. By the late-nineteenth century, the importance of giving women special training was beginning to be recognized by some denominational and faith mission boards. Before that, it was only the women's missionary societies that had devoted their energies to special training and ministries for women missionaries involved in women's work.

Women who were sponsored by denominational mission boards had opportunities to develop unique ministries for women, but their efforts were generally individual ones in localized areas overseas for which they had no special training. The China Inland Mission, however, under the visionary leadership of J. Hudson Taylor, recognized the need for women missionaries to be uniquely prepared ministers in a variety of situations—especially to evangelize other women. The mission operated a training home for women in England, directed by Henrietta Soltau, that offered female candidates two years of specialized instruction, and then, after the women arrived on the field, they typically spent several months at the women's language school at Yangchow.[34]

Henrietta Soltau was born and raised in Plymouth, England, an area known for its religious dogmatism. It was the birthplace of the movement that became known as the Plymouth Brethren. Her family was deeply involved in the movement and its ideology followed Henrietta the rest of her life. It was among the Brethren that the need for foreign missions was impressed upon her. "There was constant talk in Brethren circles about the claim of heathen lands on the church. It was taught that the 'rapture of the saints' was to be looked for, yet it was always recognized that 'the Gospel must first be preached as a witness in all lands.' "35

But while the Brethren placed great emphasis on preaching the gospel to lost souls, they at the same time placed tight controls on women as to what type of preaching they could do—so much so that Henrietta's sister later left the movement. "The restrictions of Brethrenism lay irksomely on her, for although they allowed her to visit, to preach to individuals both men and women, and to teach the Bible to a large class of boys," if her "preaching was addressed to an audience, or teaching was directed to a congregation, she was under a ban which silenced her." Though their father held in theory to the restrictions on women that the Brethren held so strongly, it was he who initially thrust his daughters into open-air evangelism. "Yet, at first, neither of the girls ventured to break the habit of years and they only spoke under their father's immediate direction. Not until 1882 did Henrietta, to use her own words, 'launch out into a fuller life, publicly and freely preaching Christ.' "36

The most dramatic event that occurred in Henrietta's early adult life was her encounter with J. Hudson Taylor. His appeal for volunteers for China had an urgency she could not ignore, and at the close of the meeting "she offered herself for foreign service." Almost immediately, however, she became ill, and her plans to go to China were delayed. In the meantime she became involved in lay evangelism and Bible teaching. She organized a women's Bible class that grew to a membership of nearly two hundred. She and her sisters held religious services in the family home and "were tireless in following up the contacts . . . very soon they had access to most of the cottages and farms."37

Though she continued to have health problems, Henrietta never lost her vision for China. But it was when she was thirty-two, while visiting the Hudson Taylors in London, that her "long-cherished plan was finally vetoed." During the visit "she was prostrated by one of the worst attacks of headache she had had," and it was determined then that she would be unsuited for China. There was a ministry, however, that Taylor was deeply concerned about: the establishment of a home for missionary children. It is a somewhat amusing irony that he would select a woman who was prone to headaches for such a task, but she accepted the challenge and for the following decade and more carried out this task with loving dedication. During that time she had in her charge thirty-two children whose missionary parents were financially able to contribute only a small portion of their expenses. The home was established on a "faith" basis, which meant a precarious existence, often on the very edge of poverty. Indeed, there were many times when only through miraculous intervention she was able to feed the children adequately.38

Throughout her years of maintaining the children's home, Henrietta reflected back on her days of public preaching and personal evangelism and longed to once again become more actively involved in such ministry. It came as a welcome relief, then, when she was able to have enough leisure time to free herself from the children long enough to reach out into the surrounding community. Despite her busy schedule she eagerly accepted invitations to preach where she was invited. On one occasion when "one of the leading Brethren from the Plymouth meeting" failed to make his appearance at a hall where a large crowd had gathered, she was asked to speak on the spur of the moment. There was a rowdy gang of young men in the back, but she was not intimidated:

> I stepped forward, and fixing my eyes on the lads in the gallery gave out my text. I spoke, and as I did so the Spirit of God fell on the crowded congregation and many wept. The ringleader of the rough crew buried his head in his folded arms. An outburst of prayer followed my address and cries for salvation were heard. I asked my cousin to keep the congregation singing appropriate hymns while we moved among the audience and spoke to those who were anxious. I had led six to Christ before I reached the gallery stairs. I heard groans from thence. All helpers were busy, and even timid cousins who had been unwilling to speak were dealing with souls under conviction of sin. At last we reached the gallery, but not till eleven p.m. did light break upon his soul. He was gloriously saved. That Thursday evening was a night to be remembered. The Lord had set me free to be His witness.[39]

What Henrietta did was no less than shocking from a Brethren perspective, but the response to her preaching did challenge her to forsake the restrictions of her past and to enter more freely into whatever public ministry was available to her. Some time after this, in 1884 at the age of forty-one, she was invited to take charge of the evening meetings at the Railway Mission Hall. "There she quite simply followed the leadings of the Spirit and God set His seal upon her labours, for every service saw men and women yielding to Christ and every week the attendance grew." In addition to those services she conducted "midnight meetings for busmen," and held weekly prayer meetings in her house.[40]

Henrietta Eliza Soltau.

It was because of this ministry and her work with missionary children that Hudson Taylor approached her in 1889 to invite her to head up the newly formed women's department of the China Inland Mission. "As he unfolded his plan and she listened to what he had to say, every kind of difficulty loomed large in her mind. How could she handle candidates for a foreign field which she had never even seen?" The complete change in her ministry seemed, to her, unreasonable in light of her experience. "Was it reasonable to suppose that God would ask her to lay down the care of the children for which she felt she was fitted, and take up a career for which she knew her own training to be inadequate?" In the weeks of indecision that followed, the children, who had so completely depended on her, proved, one after another, no longer to be in need of her care. Some of the parents sent word that they were returning on furlough, and others wrote that they had decided that their children should join them on the field. It was an amazing turn of events, and Henrietta "was almost frightened to see the hand of God turning her into the path she wished to avoid."[41]

Henrietta felt she had no choice but to accept Taylor's request for her services, but she was not without misgivings. It was not easy to move to London with its "monotonous rows of houses which it seemed impossible to distinguish one from another" after having enjoyed the "variety and brightness of a sea-side town" where her children's home had been located. "The unutterable dreariness of the northern suburb lay like a pall on her spirit." Next to the house, "a dingy garden boasted some smutty shrubs," dirtied by the "constant trains" that ran by. The interiors of the two houses which would serve as headquarters for the Women Candidates' Department were equally dreary. Here was an unqualified woman in unsuitable quarters. How would the candidates react? "The surroundings could scarcely have been more gloomy, and as Miss Soltau sat there, waiting for the arrival of the first candidate, her loneliness knew no bounds. She had no idea how to begin with that young woman, how to prepare her for what lay ahead, or even how to judge of her fitness for missionary life."[42]

Though she herself was altogether insecure about her ability to take on the responsibilities of the Women's Candidate Department, Taylor had seen spiritual and leadership qualities in her that she herself was unaware she possessed. Her own experience in street evangelism, preaching, caring for missionary children, and dealing with individuals on every level of society gave her insight that many women—even women who had served abroad—did not possess, and Taylor valued these qualities more highly than actual missionary experience. But Taylor's confidence in her did little to raise her spirits. "Miss Soltau's own record of her first month in London is that every night she wept tears of loneliness and suffered torments of questioning and doubt."[43]

Once the candidates began arriving, the atmosphere changed dramatically, and Henrietta quickly realized the significance of the ministry she was involved in. Her responsibility was not to train the female candidates but rather to evaluate their qualifications for missionary service. It was her task to "receive all and sundry who were making application to the China Inland Mission, keep them for a limited period in her house and seek to form an estimate of their suitability for the work to which they believed themselves to be called." On Taylor's instructions, "each inmate should be given full opportunity for freedom of expression so as to reveal her natural characteristics, whereas in the Training School necessary discipline should exercise a salutary restraint on idiosyncrasies, it's very rules and regulations inducing a conformity which . . . must mask individualism."[44]

The candidate home operated continuously for twenty-six years until 1916, when due to the war-time emergency it was temporarily closed. During that time, 547 women whom Henrietta guided through the initial stages of candidacy went on to serve with the CIM in China and, in addition, a large number of women went on to serve in other areas of the world with other mission societies. Many of these women credited Henrietta with their eventual success in missionary work. The testimony of one woman was typical: "Miss Soltau must have seen at once what an unlikely subject I was to be favourable considered by the Council. Nevertheless I received nothing but encouragement from her, and she so helped me to steer my course that I was accepted for training and two years later sailed for China."[45]

Another woman wrote, "Had it not been for Miss Soltau and the help which she gave me, no Mission Board would have entertained the thought of accepting me for foreign service." By her own testimony, she was "noisy, assertive and loudly dressed"

and had no money to pay her board. Henrietta coached and counseled her for six months before she consented to her interview with the Council. "I was grievously disappointed in not being able to do so earlier," wrote the woman, "but before the end of that probation I saw the wisdom of the delay. By that time I had learned to speak and dress more quietly, and how to fit into the community life." Still another woman wrote how she was "torn in two" in her decision to become a missionary—her sense of call versus the "many voices" compelling her to stay home. She went to the Candidate Home with a "tortured heart," but through the loving counsel of Henrietta she decided to pursue her calling. "With her arms around me," she wrote, "I entered into peace."[46]

There were many cases in which Henrietta was not able to recommend a woman for foreign service. Despite her best efforts, they fell short of her standards, whether due to personal, health, or family reasons. Yet, she was convinced "that if this were the end of their service for the Mission Field something was seriously wrong; so she gave much thought and prayer as to how best she might link them on to the work, that their missionary zeal should not be wasted." Out of this concern developed the Helping Hands Association, a support organization that offered a variety of services to foreign missionaries. It was a time-consuming effort, but it provided a much-needed link with women in the homeland. She was in many ways a driven woman, eager to take on new responsibilities and "in constant requisition as a speaker" for women's meetings. But her first love was that of the Candidate Home, where intimate bonds were developed that she maintained the rest of her life.[47]

Henrietta's success in operating the Candidate Home was enhanced in 1897, when she took a thirteen-month tour of China, during which time she covered some six thousand miles and visited forty-four mission stations. She came back with the realization of "how the rigid or domineering attitude of a Senior might wreck the career of her Junior," and "the tragedy of unsuitable marriages . . . warped by the partnership of an ill-considered alliance."[48]

The counsel that Henrietta so freely gave to others regarding their personal relationships and submitting to the authority of others was not something that she easily dealt with in her own life. She was seventy-six in 1919 when the War ended and the Candidate Home was reopened. She had served with distinction, and the CIM officials deeply appreciated her years of sacrifice, but a new style of leadership was needed to meet the demands of the new era. The young postwar women were more independent and outspoken than their pre-war counterparts had been and it was feared that Henrietta's domineering individualism would present problems. For that reason, a much younger woman, Miss Edith Smith, who had returned from China for family reasons, was placed in charge of the work. For Henrietta the transition to retirement was turbulent. She had relished the control and authority she wielded over the Women's Department, and giving it up to someone else was an ordeal.

> As she saw the work on which she had concentrated all her powers removed from her and given to another, she became victim of the most lacerating self-reproach. She wept many bitter tears and endured endless questionings as to whether everything had been taken from her because of unfaithfulness on her part. For a time nothing availed to comfort her, and only gradually did she regain her calm. [49]

Henrietta lived thirteen more years, past the age of ninety. Through her many years of service with the CIM she exercised an authority on missions that few women of her era could match. Her screening of candidates and impact on prospective missionaries made her influence felt for decades in China and throughout the world.

Chapter 12

# Helping "Heathen" Sisters: Women's Work for Women

"Women's work for women" was the major justification for the Women's Missionary Movement, so it is natural that it became a primary ministry for women missionaries. It was widely believed by those involved in the women's missionary movement that women were the most potent force available to carry out the Great Commission. The rationale was simple: "A man's church will last for one generation. Mothers are the conservators of religion, bringing up their children in their own faith." Thus, the logical conclusion was that women reaching women was the most effective means of evangelism.[1]

Evangelism was the primary focus of women's work, but social issues were also a top priority. Women were treated shamefully in many cultures, and the Women's Missionary Movement sought desperately to raise the status of women abroad. In fact, most of the women mission leaders of this period were liberation theologians of sorts. Much of the missionary literature emphasized the oppression of women and how Christianity must be a liberating force. Jennie Fowler Willing was a strong proponent of this view. In 1869 she wrote:

> When we look at the domestic, civil and religious systems of Pagandom, we sicken at their rottenness. We feel greatly moved to give them the blessings of Christian civilization. . . . To Christianize the women, would be to capture their stronghold, and insure a better civilization. It would be getting a lever under their systems of wrong. With . . . God to apply the power, there would be a new order of things in those "habitations of cruelty," within a half a century.[2]

This statement shows the dual, seemingly paradoxical, theme in missionary women's literature. On the one hand, the focus is on the wretched condition in which "heathen" women found themselves. At the same time, many writers insisted that the only way to have a real influence on "heathen" culture was to reach the women, because they—

117

and they alone—had the influence to affect religious changes in the family and community. Reflecting on these "somewhat contradictory conclusions," Barbara Welter writes: "However degraded she might be, the pagan woman wielded great power, and these powerful women, because of local custom and taboos, were inaccessible to male missionaries."[3]

Despite such contradictions, it is a credit to women missionaries around the world that the influence of Christianity on the family and on the role of women in the home has had significant impact—especially in some non-Western cultures, where women have traditionally had a very low status in society. According to a Hindu observer in India some decades ago, the change was dramatic: "Before these people became Christians they bought and sold wives like we buy and sell buffalos. Now they choose one woman and remain faithful to her as long as she lives." This view was supported by Mrs. Graham Parker, a Presbyterian missionary who surveyed Indian women on the issue. To the question "Do Christian men treat their wives differently?" 143 responded in the affirmative, and only 20 responded negatively. To the follow-up question, "If so, how," there was a variety of answers: "They don't make us do what we know isn't right." "They let us have the money we earn." "They help wives in their work." "They don't fight." "They don't abuse us in words or actions." "They are kind and pray for us and our children." "They forgive us our faults." "They give their wives their rights." "In Christian homes husband and wife obey each other."[4]

One area of women's work for women that was widely written about in the nineteenth century was the zenana work in India. The zenana was the secluded women's quarter of the household—usually of upper-caste Hindus—and there were tight restrictions on the activities of women. Public activities were prohibited, as was participation in educational opportunities—unless they were offered in the homes. It was these women, then, that captured the attention and the prayers of thousands of women supporters at home and of many women who felt called to reach out to them in India. Yet, for all the energy that was expended on this area of ministry, its effectiveness was somewhat in doubt. Susan Janvier confessed that the work was often very discouraging:

> This is not an uncommon experience, to have one's heart all aglow with zeal, to pray for individual women with assurance of hope, to have the message to carry for that morning clearly grasped, and then only to find one sick, another absent from home, a third perfectly heedless, a fourth looking blankly as if she did not comprehend a single word, a fifth asking, "What is that cut on your hand?" Then does it seem that there are no promises to rest upon, and to speak to these souls is only to add to their condemnation.[5]

Few would doubt the positive influence that women missionaries had on women nationals, but it is possible to exaggerate the immediate effects of Christianity on long-held habits and patterns of living. Although women writers often gave glowing accounts of the dramatic change that accompanied conversion, such stories did not necessarily correspond to the actual circumstances. "In the flesh," writes Shirley Garrett in reference to Chinese women, "she was quite human, and some of her real characteristics were at odds with the cheerful picture the church presented to the public. She was superstitious, believing stubbornly in magic, native gods, and the spells and portents of wind and water and often sullenly resisting attempts to convert her." Even after she professed conversion, she was often slow in renouncing her old ways.[6]

Some women missionaries demonstrated strong negative attitudes toward the female nationals. The wife of Bishop Wilkinson in Zululand wrote about her domestic help, "The girls I have are the plague of my life, though they are very good girls on the whole; but if it were not for their own sakes I would not keep them an hour. I would have boys."[7]

Yet, even as more and more women flooded onto the foreign field, the task of reaching women remained overwhelming. The need was simply far too great for the relatively few volunteers to meet. What was the solution? From the very beginning, it seemed only logical to train native workers, and most of the women missionaries looked for capable converts to serve as assistants or, as they were commonly called, "Bible women." In most cases these women were trained privately, until the realization dawned in the late nineteenth century that a virtual army of Bible women was needed for the various ministries women missionaries were less than qualified to undertake. One of the first women to recognize this was Adele Fielde, who focused her

entire ministry on training Bible women.

## Adele Fielde

"But who shall teach the women of China?" The missionary—the ordained minister of the gospel who goes forth to preach, cannot gain access to the Daughters of the land. . . . Shall women then be there neglected?" This was the plaintive cry of Eliza Bridgeman, the wife of the first American missionary to China. In her book *Daughters of China* she appealed for women to come and teach Chinese women so that they could in turn teach each other.[8]

Adele Fielde (1839–1916), a spirited, independent woman whose personality and character defied any standard stereotype of a female missionary, was one of the many women who answered this call. She was born in East Rodman, New York, in 1839 and grew up as a Universalist. After graduating from college, she taught school—yearning, however, "to be a wife and mother." According to her biographer, "she was naturally domestic, and it was simply out of the question for her to conceive of a successful life for herself that was not based upon conjugal love, the care of a home, and the rearing of children."[9]

That compelling desire for marriage and the fact that she was approaching her late twenties prompted her to take a drastic step—a step that would have unanticipated consequences. After a whirlwind courtship with Cyrus Chilcot, a Baptist missionary candidate, she converted to the Baptist faith and agreed to devote her life to service half way around the world as a missionary wife. He left her behind with the agreement that she would join him in Siam some months later. When she arrived in 1865, the news was awaiting her that Cyrus had died. It was a devastating blow that would have caused most women in her circumstances to turn around and sail home to the comfort of family and friends. But Adele was an extraordinary woman. She stayed, determined to make her fiance's work her own. She was philosophical in a letter she wrote soon after she arrived: "I have journeyed seven weary months over tempestuous seas and in strange lands to meet my beloved and I have found his grave with the grass upon it seven months old. . . . Several of the Chinese members of the church have been to see me. . . . They feel their loss deeply. There is no doubt that I have something to do here."[10]

Fielde's hard work and commitment to ministry were not enough to endear her to the Baptist missionary community in Siam. She was outspoken and strongly protested the fact that her salary was only half that of her single male colleague. An additional complicating factor was that she was the only single woman missionary among them and was new to the rules and regulations of the straitlaced Baptists. When the humdrum of the daily routine became monotonous she began socializing with the business and diplomatic community, in ways that scandalized her colleagues. She enjoyed dancing and card-playing—both considered unbecoming to the Baptists. She even experimented with opium smoking. Though she was convinced that giving up dancing would be "a living death," she agreed to curtail her

activities for the sake of the mission, but her opponents were insistent that she was a hindrance to the work. The Baptist mission board dismissed her from her assignment and ordered her to leave her post.[11]

It was on her return trip to America that Fielde's commitment to missions became a deeply spiritual and motivating force in her life. She spent a short time in a China port city where she caught the vision for women's work and pleaded with her directors to be reinstated. In 1872 she was back in China where she began training native women. "Here she conceived a plan," wrote her biographer, "which, in a measure, revolutionized the missionary service in the Far East. This innovation is comprehensively described as the 'Biblewomen' plan and consisted in organizing, instructing and sending out native women to do the pioneer work of evangelism."[12]

Adele founded a school, wrote texts, taught classes, and conducted field training. During her twenty-year term of service she trained some five hundred women to evangelize and train their own people. Her methodology, according to Edward F. Merriam, a mission leader, was simple:

It was Miss Fielde's practice to gather Christian women for instruction and to teach them thoroughly one lesson from the Gospel. When they had learned it, she sent them out, two by two, into the country about to tell the lesson to the villagers. After a time they were gathered at Swatow and received another portion of the truth and having obtained a thorough grasp of it, went forth to carry the good news of salvation. By these methods Miss Fielde built up an organized corps of Biblewomen whose work, under her direction, has been a model for the work of Biblewomen throughout China.[13]

Unlike so many missionaries to China who bemoaned the difficulties in working with the Chinese people, Adele praised their work and apparently had an excellent working relationship with them: "The superintendence of the Biblewomen has become much less wearing to me than formerly, because the women have grown in grace and in knowledge of the truth, and I now rely much upon their helpful wisdom and patience in the management of all trying cases that arise. They are a perpetual joy to me."[14]

After she retired from active missionary service, she resigned from the Baptist mission board and began a career of scientific research that resulted in the publication of several articles. But her work in China did not end with the change of her career. Some forty years after she had first written gospel tracts in Chinese, "a great many of them" were still being used by missionaries in China. That fact provided tremendous gratification to her, as she confessed before she died: "Such experiences as that of knowing how long my work has continued to be useful is among the durable satisfactions of life."[15]

When she died in 1916, after devoting more than two decades to scientific study following her missionary work, the mission did not even publish her obituary in its official organ. Ten years later, however, the Baptist Foreign Mission Society eulogized her as the "mother of our Bible women and also the mother of our Bible schools".[16]

Adele's work with Bible women inspired many other women, especially in Asia, to carry out similar ventures. Indeed, during the last decades of the nineteenth century, the number of training schools for Bible women increased dramatically. By 1900 there were forty female training schools in China alone, and two of those, the Wesleyan Training School for Women at Canton and the Charlotte Duryee Training School at Amoy, had nearly fifty students each. In India there were more than thirty such schools, and in Japan and elsewhere in the Far East female seminaries could also be found.[17]

In Japan, Bible women were an indispensable part of the work. Almost all the Protestant mission societies established theological schools there early on, and many missions also opened schools for the specific purpose of training Bible women, such as the Kobe Training School. The programs at many of these schools had a strong academic emphasis. The curriculum at Kobe, for example, included not only biblical and theological courses, but also apologetics and church history as well as some secular courses.[18]

One of the most vocal supporters of Bible women in the twentieth century was Margaret Burton. She wrote in her book *Women Workers of the Orient*, published in 1918: "We need to train an army of Bible women. . . . Union Bible schools for women should be established in every province, or in every important centre." And these schools, she went on to say, must do more thorough and more advanced work than most Bible women's training schools have considered necessary in the past, "for the demands now made upon a Bible woman are very different from those of former years." There were new opportunities that required a higher level of education, "and the Bible women of today and tomorrow must not only have the desire to share the glad tidings, but the training which will enable them to adapt the message to the understanding of many types of hearers, to be able to answer many different kinds of questions, to appeal to the minds as well as the hearts of the newly awakened women of the East.[19]

Some women missionaries specialized in the task of training Bible women. Eliza Agnew is one example. She spent forty-three years in Ceylon ministering at the girls' seminary in Oodooville.

> She was called the "mother of a thousand daughters," for she had taken part in the training of three successive generations of Ceylonese girls; teaching the daughters and even granddaughters of her original scholars. When she laid down her work, it was found that not a single girl who had gone through the full course under this saintly teacher had gone back unconverted to a heathen home; and upwards of six hundred whom she had taught were penetrating with the light of the gospel the darkness of Indian zenanas.[20]

## Charlotte Tucker

India's zenanas—the secluded chambers reserved for women who were not permitted to be seen in public—became a rallying point for many nineteenth-century women who were anxious that the gospel be employed to free their sisters from "heathen" bondage. The Church of England Zenana Missionary Society focussed it's attention strictly on women in such bondage, but many other missions were involved as well. One of the women who served with distinction under the Church of England Zenana Missionary Society was Charlotte Tucker, a "popular author and woman of some means," who at the age of fifty-four was convinced God was calling her to India. Here she devoted the remaining eighteen years of her life to women's work.[21]

She began her language study before she sailed for India and was thus prepared to begin, though haltingly, to communicate the gospel. Zenana work was not easy, and more often then not the foreign women were rebuffed when they sought to enter the restricted domains. A reporter from the Pall Mall Gazette described her work:

> Undaunted by rebuff, she would wend her way to some more congenial house, well shaded from the rays of a tropical sun by a large white umbrella, padded in accordance with her own orders with a thick layer of cotton wool. When entrance was granted, a native charpoy (string-bed) was dusted for Miss Tucker to sit upon, and there, surrounded by a small crowd of women squatting on the floor, she was wont to show them Biblical pictures, talk a little, and end up with a hymn sung in Punjabi to a monotonous native melody easily caught up by her listeners.[22]

Miss Tucker did not easily give up when she thought there was hope in reaching a woman who had shown interest in her message. "There were houses where she was spit upon, or even rudely turned away by the master; but there were others where the women welcomed her as a friend and learned eagerly to anticipate her coming." On one occasion, when she was refused entrance to a zenana where a woman had previously shown interest, "she stood outside in the open lane and sang her hymn that haply some comfort might be carried to the prisoner within. Met with a torrent of invective by one Mohammedan mother, she was afterwards admitted to console that mother at the death of her son."[23]

Although Tucker was working for a mission that featured women's work as its specific focus, her ministry was also very effective among the male population. She worked closely with a boy's boarding school (and served for one year as its chief administrator), where she had a remarkable influence over many of the young men who later entered a profession or held government positions. "She became their friend and confidential adviser" and encouraged them to think for themselves on issues that were usually restricted to administrators and teachers. Perhaps even more importantly, she became a part of their social life. "She joined in their games" and "wrote school-songs for them." The eager responsiveness of the boys to her personality and her teaching efforts boosted her morale and thereby aided her in the much less rewarding zenana work, which she continued until her death in 1893.

## Margaret King

Working with Bible women and conducting "women's work" in general were inseparable activities for women missionaries of the late nineteenth and early twentieth centuries—especially for those who served in Asia. This is exemplified in the life and ministry of Margaret King, who was prepared to use her expertise during a crucial time in China's history. "The emancipation of women had hardly commenced when she first came to this land," wrote Geraldine Taylor; "but when the Youth Movement began and Chinese girls traveled as far in a single decade as their sisters of the West in two previous centuries, Margaret King saw its significance and realized that tremendous forces were being liberated for use in the service of God."[24]

Her ability to identify with Chinese women and to capitalize on the trends that were taking place in society gave her a ministry that has been equalled by few women in history. "An evangelist above all, first, last and always, she combined with her regular work frequent visits to schools and colleges and was much used by God in meeting the needs of young women in all stages of spiritual experience."[25]

Like so many of her female colleagues, Margaret worked closely with a Bible woman. Her description of this woman shows the depth of her appreciation for her and her ability to help develop the spiritual gifts of national women.

I wish you knew our dear Mrs. Sie, the Bible-woman. Not that she knows the meaning of the word "Bible-woman." She is just in the position of a servant, getting less than two dollars a month, out of which she provides her food and other necessaries. She is over forty years of age and one of the holiest people I ever knew. I wish I served the Lord with the singleness of purpose with which she does. She gives more than a tenth to the Lord month by month, and never misses an opportunity to witness for Him. She is a most faithful servant besides, and such a clever woman! We have many a laugh together on our trips out. I wish China had many such Christians. She literally takes everything to the Lord in prayer.[26]

Mrs. Sie was Margaret's close companion and associate for many years. Through her, Margaret learned to understand the Chinese female mind and to appreciate the potential that women had for influencing others for Christ. "Mrs. Sie was on fire for souls, and being in the position of a servant had the more liberty in preaching, as everybody knew she was not paid to do that work." She likewise proved to be "a most effective preacher ... earnest, eloquent, and filled with the constraining love of Christ."[27]

The ministry Margaret became best known for was her evangelistic work among school-age girls and young women. As the Youth Movement in China developed, more and more young women were inspired to question traditional beliefs and to think for themselves. This change among the Chinese correlated with a change in Margaret—a spiritual renewal that occurred in 1911, when she was attending meetings led by Jonathan Goforth, a Canadian Presbyterian missionary who had become the leading evangelist in China. "She went back to Yangchow with new power in her own preaching, which was manifested at the very first gathering at which she spoke." The meeting was an unpretentious Sunday afternoon study group at the girls school, where Margaret shared her reflections on the Goforth revivals. Almost without warning, a similar revival broke out among the girls, with "the same penitence, the tears and the confessions followed by the same sense of freedom and joy. A number of the older girls put their trust in Christ that afternoon, and the atmosphere of the whole school was changed."[28]

Margaret King, evangelist to China.

When news of that revival reached other missionaries, Margaret was invited to hold meetings at other schools, and "before long she became known as a very effective evangelist, especially among girls of the educated classes."[29] Margaret referred to her meetings at girls' schools as "missions," and she wrote to her sister about one of those experiences:

"Here I am, going home from a mission in a wonderful high school. . . . We have had lovely meetings. God richly blessed. All day, between times, and far into the night, I was dealing with anxious souls. How they clung to me! God has given me a special love for girls. . . ."[30]

While she worked in the schools with girls, Margaret continued her women's work. Following one series of meetings she wrote of some of the results: "Imagine my joy when a Mrs. Hsiao walked in with five women who had been in the meetings the day before, but had not decided. She brought them, as she said, for me to exhort them. Finally they all yielded to the Lord. We knelt down, they with their heads bowed right down to the floor, as they bow before their idols, and each one prayed." Although her evangelistic work was primarily focused on girls and women, men often made up a significant part of her audience. In 1929, she wrote of the meetings she was conducting in Yangchow:

We had a good time yesterday afternoon, and a still better at night, when crowds of men came and sat through a two hours' meeting. Is it not wonderful, after all the propaganda against the Lord and His people. Such awful things have been said against Him and against us! And still, men seek Jesus, and come where a full gospel of His precious, cleansing blood is preached.[31]

The success of Margaret's evangelism, especially with educated young women, had prompted her to establish a Bible seminary for those who desired further education for lay and professional ministry. It was not an easy task, however. The Youth Movement had strong opposition, and "in the midst of all the turmoil it proved no easy matter to establish anything so progressive as a Bible seminary for women."[32] The school became known as the Nanking Bible School, and by 1921 it was in full operation on a six acre plot with classroom and dormitory buildings. For a time, in 1927 and 1928, the school was closed due to heavy opposition, but it was later reopened and moved to even larger facilities. It was that school that maintained the legacy for which Margaret King had sacrificed. It lived on after her work in China was finished, preparing many young women to more effectively fulfill their call to Christian ministry.[33]

### Jessie Gregg

Jessie Gregg was one of the young women who benefited by the China Inland Mission's training for women. After her two years of training and six months at the women's language school at Yangchow, she was assigned to work with a missionary couple in Hwailu, a city in a northern province of China. But hardly had she become settled in her mission work when news came of widespread hostilities against foreigners. The Boxer Rebellion of 1900 had begun, and missionaries stationed in every direction from Hwailu had either been killed or forced to flee to safety. "The fact that Jessie and the Green family lived through the next few months," writes Phyllis Thompson, was due to a significant degree "to the amazing courage and loyalty of Chinese who befriended them." These five "foreign devils"—three adults and two small children—hid as fugitives for nearly four months from the terror of the Boxers:

> A friendly temple keeper provided them with refuge for six days, then when their whereabouts was reported they were smuggled into the isolated home of a farmer. They were there for a month, not daring to move out of their room until darkness had fallen, their servants coming from the city secretly to bring news and provisions. Then, knowing that once more the Boxers were on their track, they retreated into a damp little cave. . . . It was only a matter of minutes before they would be discovered. . . . Mr. Green was shot in the head [though not fatally], their spectacles, watches, rings were stripped from them, then they were pushed, dishevelled and bleeding, down the mountain, along the road, and back into the city.[34]

During the weeks that followed they were beaten, threatened, and imprisoned in various places. At one point "Jessie was dragged by the hair to a kneeling position, her head banged down on a table. . . . She was pushed down into the mud, and beaten again and again with the backs of swords and handles of spears." Yet, she was among the fortunate. More than one hundred other missionaries in China did not survive the fury of the Boxers. Following the ordeal, she returned to England for a furlough, but in 1901 she was back in China, ready to continue her ministry. On her return she became involved in itinerant evangelistic work, which would be her ministry in the decades that followed. "Off she would go with her woman servant, dressed in Chinese trousers and jacket, to some home in a village or town where a friendly invitation had been given to her to come and stay, and to 'preach the way.' Her single status was no disadvantage, for it placed her in Chinese minds in the special category of 'holy woman.' "[35]

Men were often as eager as women to hear Jessie preach, but "she made it plain to them that she had come to teach women." If they wanted to hear the word of God, she would call on a male missionary or evangelist to come to them, or she would send them to the city to seek one out. The women were tied to their homes and the villages, and her message was for them. Yet, she could not prevent men from listening to her, and as she evangelized she planted churches in six of the neighboring cities. She worked with nationals, but her own ministry attracted broad appeal. "She herself was developing into an outstandingly effective preacher. She was a born story-teller, with a sense of the dramatic and a simplicity of speech that was never cluttered with non-essentials." She was forthright in her manner, and yet she was not offensive. She more often moved her listeners to tears than to anger.[36]

What began as village work with small groups of women eventually developed into large-scale campaign work, which began when Jessie was invited to be guest speaker for a "five days' mission for women only, to which women from the outstations would be invited." The idea of a five-day metting for women seemed preposterous, because women rarely left their homes for extended periods of time, but to her amazement more than four hundred women came, and half of them made professions of faith before the "retreat" had ended. That initial "mission for women" established a pattern that she would continue to follow:

> For nearly fifteen years after that her life was one of almost ceaseless travel as she went from province to province holding evangelistic campaigns for women. The same sort of results were evident everywhere she went, with women flocking to hear her, and many of them confessing long-hidden sins, then receiving the forgiveness promised through faith in Christ Jesus.[37]

There were more invitations than Jessie could fit into her demanding schedule; all in all, she traveled some twenty thousand miles through fifteen of China's provinces. During these travels she conducted nearly two hundred "missions" or retreats for women and girls, more than five thousand of whom indicated that they wanted to become a follower of Christ.[38]

Women's work provided many opportunities for women missionaries abroad. Though some had entered this particular specialty because it was not so controversial as other ministries that were more directly the province of men, those who continued in the work rarely felt their time was wasted. Through the partnership of national women, they made remarkable gains in the church abroad.

## Chapter 13

# Rescuing the Unwanted: Orphanages and Children's Work

Women were peculiarly susceptible to the often heart-rending involvement in children's work. In many respects this ministry was an entanglement of sorts, because in most instances these women were not assigned to do children's work, and their involvement developed spontaneously out of desperate situations. Unwanted children were abandoned or sold by their parents, and there was no one else willing to care for them. Not infrequently the missionaries who took these children in were single women who had repressed their motherly instincts and were subconsciously eager to substitute unwanted children for the children of their own they were denied. There are countless cases of single missionary women "adopting" native children. Mary Slessor, Mildred Cable, and Gladys Aylward are examples. Their primary activity was not children's work, but they were encumbered with the care of children who became part of their households.

The case of Mildred Cable and her partners demonstrates the sacrificial nature of these single women who opened their hearts to unwanted children. In her case the object of love and pity was Gwa-Gwa, a little deaf and dumb beggar girl, who was ordered by her guardian to go out into the streets each morning to spend the day begging and collecting from garbage heaps whatever she could find that might be of value. She was scorned by passers-by and bitten by dogs, but it was all part of a day's work—until she was spotted by Mildred who "only saw a little girl with tousled hair and a dirty face, her legs and feet bare and her thin little body showing through the gaps in her ragged clothes." She became a daily visitor at the mission house where she knew she could get a warm meal and a loving smile from "the first person she had ever known to be kind to her."[1]

Gwa-Gwa needed more than a warm meal and a little kindness, but how to respond to her needs was a difficult decision.

> Willingly would Mildred have settled down to be mother of an orphanage in the City of Prodigals, for Gwa-Gwa was but one of a large number of beggar children there. How their pinched faces touched her heart as she saw the sad little creatures wandering slowly from courtyard to courtyard, stick in hand to ward off dogs, whining, "Pity me! Pity me! Give me a little to eat!" When winter came, she knew she must do something, and a large barn was furnished with huge bundles of soft, clean straw, where children who had no home at all could come and sleep each night, and get a bowl of steaming hot rice-porridge before going out in the morning.

> But as she talked to Evangeline and Francesca [her partners] about it, and as they prayed together that God would make it clear what He wanted them to do, they all realized that they could not stay any longer in the City of Prodigals. . . . There were men and women living in tents and temples and oases along those old trade routes.[2]

Gwa-Gwa was fortunate because Mildred later made arrangements with her cruel guardian to "adopt" her, and from then on she traveled with the women as they went out for months at a time doing evangelistic work. For Mildred and her partners, the call to do pioneer evangelistic work was stronger than the call to do children's work. This was not true for many women. Their compassion for the desperately needy little ones made all other types of ministry almost trivial by comparison.

## Amy Carmichael

Amy Carmichael, through her many years of service in India and her numerous books, is one of the most widely known missionaries of the twentieth century. She was raised in Northern Ireland and enjoyed a carefree childhood until her father died when she was a teenager, leaving the family in debt and uncertain about the future. Soon after that, in 1886, during a spiritual-life conference in England, Amy experienced a deep encounter with God that changed her entire outlook on life. She now focused on spiritual values and she discovered that her expensive taste in food and clothing had suddenly vanished. Her first realization of the change that had taken place in her came when she was invited out to a restaurant by a friend and was served very poorly prepared mutton chops. Such an incident would have previously upset the well-brought-up young woman, but she realized that she no longer cared about such trivial things.

> If mutton chops didn't matter anymore, neither did clothes. When Amy got back to Belfast, the long mourning period for her father was over and it was time, her mother said, to purchase a few pretty dresses—among them, of course, an evening dress for parties. They went to the shop. The shopman displayed his loveliest things. Suddenly Amy decided she could not have them. She was now, in the language of the apostle Paul, "dead to the world." To Amy, the "world" meant fashion, finery, luxury of any sort. She would follow Him who had no home, no earthly possessions beyond the bare minimum. She would be "dead to the world and its applause, to all its customs,

fashions, laws." For Amy, with her eye for beauty, it was the measure of her commitment that she did not hesitate to relinquish all that seemed to her inimical to the true life of discipleship.[3]

It was this commitment that paved the way for her effective ministry to children, a ministry that called for sacrificial giving and a renunciation of her own ambitions.

Amy Carmichael, known for her many years of children's work in India, is an example of a woman who found herself drawn into children's work not by design but by the compelling need that spontaneously thrust itself upon her. She had initially gone to Japan to serve as a missionary but did not find the conditions suitable. Insisting that God had given her specific instructions to go elsewhere, she dismayed her family and friends back home when they learned that she had sailed for Ceylon. When challenged about making such an impulsive decision after only fifteen months of service, she replied, "I simply say that I left Japan for rest and change, that when at Shanghai I believed the Lord told me to follow Him down to Ceylon, and so I came."[4]

In addition to the "call" of God, there were other factors that influenced Amy's departure from Japan. Like so many other missionaries, she found the language unusually difficult. She was, likewise, disillusioned with the missionary community. To her mother she confided, "We are here just what we are at home—not one bit better—and the devil is awfully busy. . . . There are missionary shipwrecks of once fair vessels." But the most pressing reason for her inability to function in Japan involved her own emotional instability. She had written to her mother that "the climate is dreadful upon the brain," and she later confessed in a letter to another missionary that she had "broken down from nervous prostration during the very first year of . . . service, suffering, as some foreigners do, from what was called Japanese head."[5]

Amy Carmichael, missionary to India. (Courtesy of Donhavur Fellowship.)

Despite her "call" to Ceylon, Amy did not remain there long. She was implored by a sickly friend to return home, and when she sailed back to Asia less than a year later, she settled in India. Still, Amy was struggling to find a place in mission work. Five years after she had heeded the call "Go Ye," she was still unsettled, following as it were, in the words of her biographer, a "pillar of cloud." She lacked direction in ministry and became discouraged by the "complete absence of converts among the Muslims of Bangalore" and "confessed her ignorance of the tremendous power of Islam—and of caste among Hindus." The apathetic attitudes of other missionaries further distressed her. "I began to feel like a fish out of water," she wrote, "and such a fish is a discouraged creature."[6]

As she was striving to find her place in India, Amy came to the realization that she had a powerful appeal to children. One day while she was involved in team evangelism, an eleven-year-old girl became the object of Amy's attention. A relationship developed between them much to the chagrin of the girl's parents. Indeed, they feared their daughter had been bewitched, and they sent her away to live with an uncle. There were other children who were captivated by Amy, and some of the Indian nationals began to suspect that Amy "used some mysterious powder which drugged their children and made them long to be near her."[7]

It was not until after a decade of missionary work that Amy took in her first temple child—the work for which she became known. Her concern for temple children had developed some years earlier, but the Hindu practice of taking young children as temple prostitutes was one of India's most closely guarded secrets. Government officials were aware of what was happening, as a census report in 1901 indicates: "The servants of the gods, who subsist by dancing and music and the practice of 'the oldest profession in the world' are partly recruited by admissions and even purchases from other classes." It was a practice that was simply accepted by many segments of society:

> As a meritorious act, the parents give or sell the child to the temple while it is a babe. When eight or nine years of age, it is taken to the temple and married to the god before the idol. The child's "husband" is at first one of the temple priests. She is early taught sensuous poetry, singing, and dancing, to make her more attractive to her future wide clientele than the illiterate Hindu housewives are to their husbands.[8]

It was in 1901, when Amy first had contact with a temple child who had escaped. From her she learned the horrors of what these children endured, but she could not find solid evidence to back the stories up. "For three years it was a vain search," she wrote. "We could not find the source from which the children, who were trained to be Temple children, were drawn. It was a bitter time. There were days when the sky turned black for me because of what I heard and knew was true. . . . Many missionaries told me it was pure imagination."[9] As had been true during the first decade of her missionary experience, she was viewed as an eccentric woman who avoided any ministry that would fit into a job description.

From the beginning of her efforts to reach out to children there were setbacks that amounted to tragic losses for Amy while providing further evidence to discredit her in the eyes of the missionary community. Not all the children she attempted to "rescue" were temple children, and the rage rightfully felt by the parents was seen by many missionaries as a deterrent to genuine evangelism. One such instance is related by Amy's biographer:

A real tragedy occurred . . . when a girl from a village near Dohnavur decided at all costs to follow Christ, and sought refuge at the bungalow. But there was no upper room, as at Pannaivilai, and no door that would lock. Amma [Amy] took her up to the tower of the village church close by, and there they slept that night. But in the morning the church was surrounded by a clamorous crowd. At last the women from the girl's village promised . . . that if they saw her and she refused to come with them, they would be content. So Amma brought the girl down to the vestry. They crowded round, and one of them rubbed her arm. It was an aunt, one who seemed to have a mysterious power over her. Her resistance broke down, and murmuring, "I come, my aunt," she followed her out of the church. No one ever saw her again.[10]

By 1904, Amy was responsible for seventeen children, including six temple children who had been rescued. This was the work that would become known as Dohnavur Fellowship, and it was finally gaining respect among the missionary community. In addition to the children, there were several national women who began associating with Amy in the work. One of those was Devai. "She proved to be God's special gift for the task of discovering children who were in danger, pleading with their relatives or guardians, and bringing them triumphantly to Dohnavur." Her commitment to the cause was remarkable. "For her no journey was too long or arduous. She would arrive exhausted after missing one or two nights' sleep, and leave again in

an hour or two if word was brought of another child in danger. She was often disappointed, and followed many false trails, but she never lost heart." Many of the young girls who were rescued also manifested a deep faith and commitment to Christian ministry. "I am greatly struck by the simple childlike faith of some of these dear convert girls," wrote Amy in 1906. "I do so often wish my friends at home could see these dear children."[11]

The success of Amy's work depended heavily on national women and the Dohnavur alumnae that remained with the fellowship to devote their lives to the ministry. Devoted, single-minded service is what Amy required of her associates. In fact, she formed a religious order of sorts to accommodate these women: Sisters of the Common Life. The women were not compelled to take vows, but if they married they automatically lost their position in the sisterhood. Amy herself had committed her life to celibacy, and she expected those who lived and worked with her to do the same. Accepting singleness had not come easily for her. Years earlier, when she was still in Japan, she had confronted the issue, and she later shared the incident with one of her "children," whom she was advising to follow the same course:

On this day many years ago I went away alone to a cave in the mountain called Arima. I had feelings of fear about the future. That was why I went there—to be alone with God. The devil kept on whispering, "It's all right now, but what about afterwards? You are going to be very lonely." And he painted pictures of loneliness—I can see them still. And I turned to my God in a kind of desperation and said, "Lord, what can I do? How can I go on to the end?" And He said, "None of them that trust in Me shall be desolate." That word has been with me ever since. It has been fulfilled to me. It will be fulfilled to you.[12]

Although it took Amy a decade to "find herself" on the mission field, she made up quickly for lost time. Once she had settled down and her ministry was clearly defined, there were no bounds to her vision and her capacity for accomplishing the impossible. By 1923, two decades after her children's work began, "there were thirty nurseries in Dohnavur, and throughout this decade there was never a time when new buildings of one sort or another were not in course of erection."[13]

By 1945, after four decades of ministry, the work had expanded beyond anything Amy could have ever hoped for. Sherwood Eddy, a missionary statesman who was visiting her in that year, described the amazing Christian outreach that was centered at Dohnavur:

The number of children about to be dedicated [to Hindu gods] who were rescued by Miss Carmichael now runs into several thousands. . . . There are now, in 1945, over eight hundred children in her three homes. Each institution is at once a Christian home, a school, and a center for character building. . . .

Thirty of Miss Carmichael's lads are now in the Indian army, navy, and air force. Many of the girls have become earnest Christian workers. Hundreds of them are wives and mothers in good Christian homes. There is a fine medical work . . . which reaches people from distant places. The hospital is thoroughly evangelistic and has yielded spiritual fruit.[14]

Despite her great success, Amy confronted opposition—from the missionary community, from Hindus, and from within the Dohnavur Fellowship itself. Initially, fellow missionaries had been skeptical about Amy's work, some insinuating that the temple children were a figment of her imagination. Once her concerns were verified and the work got underway, there were other points of criticism. Some suggested that she had become too involved in humanitarian efforts. To those critics, she retorted: "One cannot save and then pitchfork souls into heaven. . . . Souls are more or less securely fastened to bodies. . . and as you cannot get the souls out and deal with them separately, you have to take them both together."[15]

But the most serious opposition Amy was confronted with in her work was from Hindu nationals themselves. More than once she was brought into court for criminal charges of kidnapping, and threats of physical violence were commonplace. But of greater concern to her than her own safety was the safety of her children. And this is where she experienced tragedy in her work, as Sherwood Eddy related when he visited her: "Miss Carmichael has just lost another child, spirited away or kidnapped—a ten-day-old baby girl."[16]

The most paradoxical opposition Amy had to deal with was probably that which came from within the Dohnavur Fellowship. The Sisters of the Common Life were committed to serving God and to carrying out Amy's vision, but such dedication did not result in a harmonious, trouble-free community. Indeed, Dohnavur was not the idyllic utopia that some supporters had described it to be. There was often dissention among the workers—a problem that caused Amy recurring bouts of anxiety and tension, especially in her later years.[17]

Throughout her life time, Amy's work was becoming internationally acclaimed in Christian circles. This was largely a result of her writing. Before she died at Dohnavur in 1951, at the age of eighty-three, she had written some thirty-five books detailing her more than a half century in India. These books were primarily personal or biographical—telling the story of a rescued child—and they served to challenge the Christian world to the needs of children in India.

### Lillian Trasher

"In 1910 I was a young, happy girl of not quite 23, full of dreams. . . . The most important was the 12 children I hoped to have. I wonder how I would have felt had the curtain been lifted and I had seen myself this morning, 50 years later. Here I am—a tired, old, gray-haired woman looking out my window and seeing not 12 children but 1200." Those were the words of Lillian Trasher in 1960, after a half century in Egypt, ministering to unwanted children.[18]

Lillian had intended to be a pastor's wife. Her fiance was a minister, and their wedding date was less that two weeks away when, after hearing a missionary speaker, she was convinced that God was calling her to be a missionary to Africa. She broke the engagement, and within months was on a ship bound for Egypt, with no mission board backing her and without any promise of financial support.[19]

On her arrival she made arrangements to live with a missionary family and engage in language study, but within months she was on her own. Her approach to ministry was simply not acceptable to the other missionaries. "I wanted to look after every neglected child that I saw," she later confessed, and when she brought her first orphan infant home, the other missionaries were disturbed and told her to take it back. She had found the infant when she had visited the squalid hovel of the dying mother. The baby's only nourishment was "a tin of milk that was stringy and green with age." She could not take the child back. The mother had died, and there was no one else to care for it. With no other alternative, she rented a house and began the orphanage work that distinguished her ministry for the decades that followed.[20]

The obstacles were many during those first years, but by 1916, after five years of disappointments and hardships, Lillian had fifty children under her care. With the support of those who believed in her ministry she was able to purchase property, and as the number of children grew new buildings were constructed. In 1919, during an outbreak against British rule, Lillian and her dozens of children hid for three days in an abandoned brick kiln to escape the terror in the streets. Other buildings in the neighborhood were destroyed, but the orphanage was left untouched—a marvelous credit to the reputation of Lillian and her sacrificial work. It was

Lillian Trasher, missionary to Egypt.

in that same year that Lillian received official sponsorship from back home. The Assemblies of God, a denomination founded only five years earlier, accepted her as one of their own missionaries.[21]

The school continued to grow, and by 1923 there were some three hundred children under the care of Lillian and her co-workers, some of whom were local women, while others had come from America. An educational program had been developed, and despite her lack of formal language training, Lillian herself taught classes and wrote textbooks. Yet, there were few spiritual victories during the first sixteen years. That changed suddenly, however, in 1927: "I have witnessed the greatest revival I have ever seen," she wrote. "Scores have been saved. Many have been filled with the Holy Spirit. I sent for the big boys who have left the orphanage and are living nearby. We prayed together and all 25 dedicated their lives to God."[22]

During the decades that followed there were as many disappointing setbacks in the work as there were miraculous victories. In 1933, Muslim authorities removed seventy of the Muslim children from the home, and Lillian had no choice but to see them torn away from the only home many of them had ever known. At times funds were so low that she rode on a donkey from town to town, pleading for help, while at other times food and supplies came that were never requested. During World War II, when the orphanage was in dire circumstances, a much needed supply of clothing, bedding, and food came from a Red Cross shipment on its way to Greece, unexpectedly diverted to Egypt.[23]

By 1961, the year of Lillian's death, there were some fourteen hundred children and widows living at the orphanage. Her distinguished ministry had reached out to more than eight thousand orphans, and her self-sacrificing life had touched many thousands more, as was evident at the time of her death. "As the gilded horse-drawn hearse carried Lillian Trasher's earthly remains through Assiout to the cemetery, people everywhere wept. In every window, every balcony the procession passed, people stood remembering this great woman who had loved so deeply and given so much."[24]

*Chapter 14*

# Quickening Minds for Christ: Educational Ministries

One of the most important aspects of women's and children's ministries overseas was educational work. If women and girls were properly educated, the reasoning went, they could read the Scriptures and would be motivated to change their lives in both spiritual and social matters. In many instances it was religious oppression that prevented women from learning to read and write, and thus Christianity had an appeal by offering education. Indeed, in many parts of the world Christian education was the only education offered to the female population. Enlightened, progressive parents had no choice but to send their daughters to the mission schools if they wanted them to acquire the rudiments of an education.

It was for this reason, then, that women missionaries often were more influential than men in the area of education. Women missionaries eagerly took advantage of the opportunities to work in education, and by the turn of the twentieth century there were hundreds of female edu-cational institutions all over the world, and the numbers continued to grow rapidly in the decades that followed. Some of these schools offered a broad Western education, while others focused on teaching students to read and write in their own language and to prepare them for Christian service among their own people. In either case, generations of women and girls were brought into the faith through the dedication of missionary women educators.

Educational work was not without controversy, however. Some argued that it served as a bribe to nationals who could not otherwise afford education for their children, and they argued that direct evangelism brought more souls into the kingdom with fewer man-hours expended. There were also conflicts with nationals about the philosophy of education. This was true in Japan in the late nineteenth and early twentieth centuries. Western education was generally welcomed by middle-class families who were eager to modernize their country—but not to the point that their daughters would begin acting like Western women. "On the surface the aims of female missionary educators seemed modest, little calculated to arouse strong feelings in the societies to which they went. But with Western missionary women in charge of the schools, the clash of cultures was inevitable."[1]

Lizzie Pourbaugh, the founder of the Reformed Church School for girls in Sendai, encountered opposition along these lines. The Japanese head of the boys' school "complained that missionaries did not teach gentleness and manners. The lively and expressive style they encouraged seemed mere rowdiness to him. To Lizzie Pourbaugh Japanese girls already seemed gentle to the point of subservience." The conflict was not easily solved. "Since the Japanese wanted to groom the girls in a short-term finishing school and the missionary women wanted to transform their behavior and status, the battle lines were drawn." In this instance, the Japanese triumphed. "After an acrimonious dispute . . . Miss Pourbaugh realized that her values would not prevail, and she eventually fled to America after suffering a loss of faith in the meaning of her work as a whole."[2]

Most missionary women experienced far greater success in their educational work than did Lizzie Pourbaugh. Eliza Agnew served as the principal of a Presbyterian girls' boarding school in Ceylon from 1839 until 1879. After her students graduated she continued to visit them and to encourage them in their faith. "She was a spiritual mother to a host of women and girls," according to

R. Pierce Beaver, "and the cumulative effect of her influence was unequaled in the pioneer period. In contrast to the schools for boys in Ceylon and India at the time, which had few converts, more than six hundred of Miss Agnew's pupils became Christians."[3]

Another very effective nineteenth-century missionary educator was Fidelia Fiske, who served for some fifteen years in Iran, where she was the director of a female boarding seminary. Several revivals occurred under her leadership, and district women's assemblies were organized that carried the work far beyond the school itself. Rufus Anderson, who had strongly opposed single women missionaries, wrote of her work, "I should certainly find it hard to name one, among the thousands and more who have gone forth into the missions of the board during my official life, who has a brighter record of missionary service."[4]

A shining example of a young woman converted through mission school education is Christiana Tsai, who grew up in China during the early years of the twentieth century. She was the daughter of the wealthy vice-governor of the Province of Kiangsu, and grew up in a home with dozens of servants. Her earliest education was under the tutelage of private Buddhist instructors, but she was eager to go beyond what they had to offer her. As was typically the case, mission schooling was all that was available for further female education. She had vowed she would never convert to Christianity, and she deeply resented the religious services she was required to attend. "This only increased my resistance," she later wrote, "and I made up my mind that I was not going to 'eat' their Christianity, so I used to take a Chinese novel with me to chapel and read it as I knelt at the bench. I did not like the preaching. I thought it was unpleasant and openly opposed it."[5]

So upset was Christiana with her teachers and required religious training that she collaborated with another high-born girl to "write a book denouncing all Christian teaching, insisting that Confucius and Buddha were our teachers and that we did not want Christ." What she did want, however, was to perfect her skills in the English language so that she could quench her insatiable thirst for knowledge. To do that she joined an optional English Bible class, and, by her own testimony, "God used my love for English to draw me to Himself." It was through reading Scripture that she was converted—an experience that created anger and despair among her family members. One of her brothers tore up her Bible and hymnbook, and her mother openly grieved that her daughter would care so little about her that she would deny her future homage through ancestral worship.[6]

Eventually, however, Christiana's testimony and changed life began to have an effect on her family, and one by one they converted to Christianity. Her influence also spread far beyond her family. After graduating from the mission school she began teaching at a government school, where she talked personally with students about her faith in Christ and opened her home to Bible studies. So effective was her witness that more than seventy of the two hundred students professed faith in Christ. Opposition, however, was intense. A newspaper article indicates the hostility she created: "The Government normal school has employed a music teacher and gotten a Christian evangelist instead, who is teaching all the girls to cry, 'God! God!' and making Christians of them. The parents are up in arms!" The dean of the school confiscated all New Testaments found in the dormitory and threatened the girls that they would be expelled if they continued to attend the Bible studies. It was a futile effort. Their faith was infectious, and the dean herself was soon converted.[7]

Christiana's influence in China continued for generations, and her autobiography, *Queen of the Dark Chamber*, influenced countless people in the Western world—and all as the result of a mission-school education. She later summarized the effect of that education on her family:

> So the brother who tore up my Bible and persecuted me in the early days at last confessed my Lord. In all, fifty-five of my relatives, adults and children, have become God's children and expressed their faith in Jesus. I have never been to college, or theological seminary, and I am not a Bible teacher; I have only been God's "hunting dog." I simply followed at the heels of my Master, and brought to His feet the quarry He sent me after.[8]

## Isabella Thoburn

The woman whose name is often associated with the pioneering of mission girls' schools overseas is Isabella Thoburn, the sister of the well-known Methodist Bishop in India, James Thoburn. In the region where

Bishop Thoburn initially served in Northern India, "there was not one woman who could read or write, and there was bitter prejudice on the part of the Hindus against the education of women." This deficiency led to the founding of the Woman's Foreign Missionary Society of the Methodist Church, which functioned in behalf of women missionaries and national workers for generations to follow. The first two missionaries sent out by the Society included Isabella, ready to begin her educational work, and Dr. Clara Swain, who was to begin a medical outreach among India's millions of unattended women.[9]

Isabella served for more than thirty years in Lucknow, India. Her ministry there, according to R. Pierce Beaver, "illustrates how education for girls could develop naturally and extensively under a woman who was an inspiring teacher, a true friend to her students, and an able administrator." She began with "six little Christian girls, and a man with a club outside the door to protect them." The school grew to twenty-five in the months that followed, and the following year the mission purchased a nine-acre estate for a combined boarding and day school.[10]

One of the greatest obstacles in pioneering female education in India, particularly when it involved boarding school accommodations, was the issue of caste. Unless special allowances were made for each girl, it was virtually impossible for them to maintain caste rules and restrictions. Some Indian nationals, including Pandita Ramabai, criticized missionaries for being insensitive to caste. As for Isabella, she was very conscious of caste differences and, like most missionaries, was utterly perplexed when faced with the controversies they raised. Should low-caste or outcast girls receive the same privileges as high-caste girls? In his biography of his sister, Bishop Thoburn addressed this problem:

Many differences, some of them petty and some of them painful, grew out of this question of race from time to time, and it is probable that Miss Thoburn at times suffered more acutely in her feelings on this account than from any other one cause during her whole life in India. She believed that in a country like India, where the very atmosphere seemed surcharged with caste and class feeling, it would be impossible to plant a pure and aggressive Christianity, unless the problem of raising up a people "of one mind and one heart" could be practically solved. She knew well that this problem could never be solved by artificial adaptations. The highest could not all be brought down to the level of the lowest, nor the lowest all elevated to the plane of the highest. There could be no uniformity of salary, of occupation, of dress, of style, of taste, or of position. And yet there could be, and there must be, a blessed unity which would bind all hearts in a common family relationship. . . .[11]

Isabella's success in establishing a girls' school for elementary and secondary education led her in the 1880s to plead for the cause of a women's college in India. Some of the girls who were soon to graduate wanted to go on to higher education and enter a profession, but their options were limited. It was for this reason that Isabella forcefully put the need before her constituents when she returned to America on her second furlough. She wrote articles and spoke out for the cause. In one widely distributed leaflet she wrote: "There are over one hundred colleges in India for young men, but only one for young women, and that not Christian. Think what efforts we would make if there were only one college for women in America, and, in some measure, let us recognize the universal sisterhood, and make like efforts for the women of India."[12]

Isabella Thoburn, missionary to India.

In 1887 the Isabella Thoburn College was opened, the first Christian college for women in India and in all of Asia. It was not an easy task. Indeed, some had suggested that the idea was preposterous. Alexander Duff, who had founded the first Christian college for men, had said decades earlier that "you might as well try to scale a wall fifty feet high as to educate the women of India." But Isabella was determined to succeed, and her achievement is clearly attested by the students who graduated from her school.[13] One of her most celebrated students was the brilliant Lilavati Singh, who later became a teacher at the college. She traveled with Isabella to America, where she enthralled her audiences with her insight into Scripture and other academic disciplines. When President Harrison heard her speak in 1900 at the Ecumenical Missionary Conference in New York City, he reportedly said, "If I had given a million dollars to foreign missions, and was assured that no result had come from it all except the evolution of one such woman as that, I should feel amply repaid for my expenditure."[14]

Lilavati Singh's own recollections of her famous missionary teacher portray the dedication Isabella displayed in her work:

> She taught us our literature, and I can never forget how her enthusiasm for heroes and poets kindled a like enthusiasm in us. . . . When I first came to school, I did not know the name of a single flower. . . . What a new world was opened to me the day she gave us our first baby lesson in botany! . . . I shall never forget her Sunday afternoon prayer-meetings with us. How clearly she explained the laws of the spiritual kingdom. . . . Another thing that Miss Thoburn trained us in particularly was voluntary Christian work. . . . Sunday after Sunday, two by two, bands of Christian girls and teachers from Lal Bagh still go out to the native part of the city to teach the little girls in the zenana of the blessed Savior.[15]

## Pandita Ramabai

Some of the most outstanding female educators who reached out with the gospel in the non-Western world were nationals. Pandita Ramabai stands out among them. She was an out-spoken and controversial woman, but her contribution to the Christian church in India through female education was enormous.

Ramabai was the daughter of a wandering Hindu guru, who spent his adult life in a religious pilgrimage of visiting temples and shrines and other holy places with his family. It was a difficult life for her, but she enjoyed one advantage that few Indian girls shared: "I am a child of a man who had to suffer a great deal on account of advocating Female Education," she wrote. "I consider it my duty, to the very end of my life, to maintain this cause, and to advocate the proper position of women in this land."[16]

The position of Ramabai's father illustrates the fact that Christians were not the only ones advocating female education in India. Indeed, Ramabai might have become simply another Hindu reformer had she not also taken up her father's intense search for God. After her parents died she began a wider search for true religion, which included an in-depth study of Hindu scriptures and a comparison with Christianity. One significant difference, she discovered, was the attitude toward women. Hindu belief, though inconsistent on most subjects, said "that women of high and low caste, as a class, were bad, very bad, worse than demons, as unholy as untruth, and that they could not get *Moksha* as men." Ramabai further claimed that in Hinduism, "the only hope of their getting this much-desired liberation from Karma and its results . . . was the worship of their husbands. The husband is said to be the woman's god; there is no other god for her."[17]

Ramabai's initial response to her search through Hindu scriptures was to become a reformer and seek to uplift the place of women in Indian society. She was particularly concerned about the plight of widows, many of whom were young girls, relegated to a life of utter degradation in their widowhood. This concern became more personal after the death of her own husband, less than two years after she was married. As a Hindu reformer, however, she continued her search for truth, and it was in that context that she became acquainted with some Anglican sisters while she was visiting England.[18]

Ramabai had vowed before going to England that she would never convert to Christianity, but she found herself irresistibly drawn to biblical teachings—especially when she compared them to Hindu scriptures. With the encouragement of Sister Geraldine, she confessed faith in Christ. She was not always a properly compliant convert, however. She was independent and determined that she would study the Bible on her own rather than assume that all truth could be found in the Church of England—a denominational name that was inappropriate and offensive to a woman such as herself. She insisted that her new faith was not a betrayal of her cultural heritage, as was evident in some of her very forthright letters to Sister Geraldine:

I am, it is true, a member of the Church of Christ, but I am not bound to accept every word that falls down from the lips of priests or bishops. . . . I have just with great efforts freed myself from the yoke of the Indian priestly tribe, so I am not at present willing to place myself under another similar yoke by accepting everything which comes from the priests as authorized command of the Most High.[19]

It is apparent from her correspondence that she was creating discord by her questioning of Anglican doctrine. "I regret that I have been the cause of making you feel yourself wrong for the part you acted in my baptism," she wrote to Sister Geraldine. "I wish I knew that your Church required a person to be quite perfect in faith, doubting nothing in the Athanasian Creed, so that he had left nothing to be learnt and inquired into the Bible after his baptism." When Sister Geraldine suggested that by refusing to eat puddings made from eggs she was still "clinging to caste prejudice which ought to have been thrown to the winds" when she embraced Christianity, Ramabai had a stinging response:

> You may, if you like trace my pride in pies and puddings. . . . I confess I am not free from all my caste prejudices, as you are pleased to call them. . . . How would an Englishwoman like being called proud and prejudiced if she were to go and live among the Hindus for a time but did not think it necessary to alter her customs when they were not hurtful or necessary to her neighbors?[20]

It was this confidence in her ability to study the Bible and think for herself that often set Ramabai at odds with the missionary community. Much to the chagrin of her Christian friends, she insisted that she was a "Hindu Christian" (a term that was not necessarily contradictory, since the word "Hindu" means Indian). She maintained close ties with her Hindu friends and continued to lecture at

Hindu functions and to preach in Hindu temples. She did not regard it a conflict of interest when she read from Hindu scriptures and shared her Christian testimony at the same assembly. She, likewise, fashioned her own concepts of female education, which did not correspond with traditional mission-school philosophy. In response to all the criticism she generated, she wrote, "I am having a right good time in the storm of public indignation that is raging over my head."[21]

Pandita Ramabai, Christian educator in India.

Ramabai's first school for child widows at Poona allowed the girls to maintain the caste rules and to study the Hindu scriptures if they so wished. The Bible was also available, but the curriculum was essentially secular. This created controversy among missionaries, especially since she was being supported by Christians from the West. The harshest condemnation, however, came from Hindus—particularly after word spread that several of her students had requested Christian baptism. Hindu reformers denounced her for having misrepresented her supposedly neutral stance on religious matters, and some of the parents removed their girls from the school. In 1898, Ramabai abandoned her secular policy and openly introduced Christian teachings, but she did so in a way that respected Hindu customs and caste regulations.[22]

In 1896, during a period of severe drought, Ramabai expanded her ministry to included famine relief. She established facilities in various locations to accommodate the hundreds of desperate women and children. The largest of these settlements became known as Mukti, meaning Salvation—an appropriate name, considering the hundreds of young girls who professed faith in Christ in the great revivals that occurred around the turn of the century. These professions of faith came as a result of Ramabai's teachings and as a result of divine miracles that she reported with enthusiasm. In 1900, during one of these severe droughts, she wrote:

Two of our large wells were quite dried up, and very little water left in our other two wells. Many of our friends were praying that God would give us water—and so He did. Although there was none for cultivating the vegetable garden, God gave water for all our people. More than 1900 people, besides over one hundred cattle and the buildings that are fast going up, required a great deal of water. Each of the two wells had all its contents used up every day; every evening one could see the bottom of the wells, and would wonder where the water would come from for tomorrow! But there came a fresh supply in the morning in each well, and it lasted all day.[23]

As important as relief work had become, Ramabai was an educator at heart and education with a Christian emphasis continued to be a primary thrust of her work. She herself studied in America and completed her degree at Bombay so that she met the qualifications to serve as the principal of her Mukti high school. Although her focus was education, she also sought to meet the needs of the uneducated. She was an accomplished linguist and took it upon herself to produce a simplified revision of the hundred-year-old translation of the Bible in the Marathi language. It was her goal "to put the Scriptures into the simplest form of Marathi speech, so that the women of the country with . . . a limited vocabulary could easily understand it." She devoted much of her time for fourteen years on that project.[24]

Ramabai's educational and relief work was closely tied in with evangelism. At Mukti she trained women and girls to share their faith and then sent them out in "Gospel Bands" with "the vision of the evangelization of India." Eventually she developed a "force of four hundred women ready for service, filled with the Holy Spirit, available to publish the good news of salvation among the heathen."[25]

Maintaining a dynamic spiritual level in her schools was paramount to Ramabai, and her intense desire for revival came to fruition during the early years of the twentieth century.

I was led by the Lord to start a special prayer circle at the beginning of 1905. There were about seventy of us who met together each morning and prayed for the true conversion of all the Indian Christians, including ourselves, and for special outpouring of the Holy Spirit. . . . In six months from the time we began to pray in this manner, the Lord graciously sent a glorious Holy Ghost Revival among us, and also in many schools and churches in this country.[26]

Her prayer for the "true conversion" of all Indian Christians might have seemed peculiar to some missionaries, but based on her own experience, Ramabai believed such a petition was appropriate. "I came to know, after eight years," she wrote, "that I had found the Christian religion, which was good enough for me; but I had not found Christ, which is the Life of the religion and the Light of every man that cometh into the world."[27]

Ramabai's educational work in India was far-reaching, and she did not limit her educational facilities to women and girls. Boys' programs were developed over the years, partly because of her concern that boys as well as girls be offered a Christian education, but also because of her concern for her girls. Indeed, she had an ulterior motive. She found that the boys who took her training "make good husbands and fathers."[28] To simply house and train girls with no Christian boys as potential husbands was running the risk of losing her girls to Hindu husbands. For her, Christian education was a broad means of helping individuals cope with all aspects of life.

Over the years the Mukti Mission grew to include several normal schools, farms, emergency famine relief, a home for unwed mothers, and an industrial arts school. The Mukti church that was part of the main complex could seat some two thousand people and it also functioned as a relief center. All of this was operated on a "faith" mission basis, with money coming, not from Europe and the United States, but from India. And not only that, but offerings were collected at the Mukti church to be used in other missions in India and to the China Inland Mission. Through these endeavors and through the impact of her students, Ramabai's influence in India and around the world has continued for generations.[29]

## Chapter 15

# Angels of Mercy: Health and Humanitarian Services

Medical missionaries, as is still true, often had opportunities to reach certain individuals that might have been out of range for an ordinary evangelist or church planter. The healing of a young child or a wounded warrior could turn the heart of a tribal chieftain from hostility to gratitude and pave the way for the acceptance of the Christian faith among the people. In more sophisticated societies it might be a high-ranking government official who would plead with the missionary doctor to bring medicine to his dying wife. Medical work was very closely tied to evangelism, and medical missionaries were well aware of the status that was conferred on them when they performed their services well.

The first woman physician to serve overseas as a missionary was Clara Swain. She began her work in India in 1870, under the sponsorship of the newly formed Woman's Missionary Society of the Methodist Episcopal Church. During her first year she treated some fifteen hundred patients—not a high number for a missionary doctor. Indian women were hesitant at first to seek her out. Within a decade, however, she was treating some seven thousand patients a year. Yet, she considered herself primarily an evangelist and focused her attention on sharing the gospel with the women she treated.[1]

After fifteen years of ministry, Clara was asked by the Rajah of Khetri, a native Muslim prince, to become the palace physician for women. She accepted the offer and found a new field of ministry awaiting her there.

We brought a quantity of religious books, parts of the Bible, and our hymn books, all in the Hindustani language, and as we have opportunity we distribute them. I suppose there are more than thirty persons singing our hymns here already, for we have taught them to every one who would learn. Some of them take wonderfully, and the singing women in the palace sing them to her highness every evening.

Clara Swain, America's first female missionary doctor.

The rajah and his wife have only one child, a little girl two years and a half old, and she has learned to sing parts of several hymns, and sings them sweetly. Her highness says our songs are much purer than theirs and she likes them better. What an opportunity for good this is! For some of their songs are very vulgar, and we would not think of listening to them. Our hymns reach every woman in the palace, and they are sometimes sung to his highness. We often find that we can sing Christianity to these people when we cannot preach it. This is an opportunity such as no one of our missionaries has had before, of carrying the Gospel into the very heart of native royalty.[2]

The opportunity to minister to people in high places was also enjoyed by Lillias Underwood, a pioneer Presbyterian missionary who ministered with her husband in Korea. They were married in Seoul in 1889, soon after Protestant missionaries had first entered that country. Lillias had come to Korea in 1888 with a degree in medicine and nursing experience from a Chicago hospital. "The most illustrious of Lillias' patients was the Korean queen, to whom she was officially appointed medical attendant." Her initial reaction to her appointment was one of apprehension. How could she properly attend the queen's health needs without breaking some time-honored customs and forever alienating her majesty?[3]

Although Lillias was handicapped by cultural and language barriers, they were minor compared to the sex barriers that had previously separated the queen from her Korean medical attendants. Korean etiquette did not permit male doctors to be in the same room with their queen, "so they 'felt' her pulse by means of a long cord fastened round her wrist and carried into the next room, and looked at her tongue when she protruded it through a slit in a screen." Lillias discovered that there were some tight restrictions for her as well. When she "found that the queen had a small tumor or boil she innocently proposed to lance it. The mere suggestion of approaching the sacred person with a surgical instrument, however, caused a storm of indignation and horror from the queen's attendants, and the slight operation was absolutely forbidden by the king." Lillias prescribed an alternative course of treatment and left the queen's presence in good standing.[4]

Over the years Lillias "became such a familiar figure at court" that "she was able to dispense with the formality of an interpreter when she was talking with the queen," and "she often forgot that she was not chatting with an intimate friend." Yet, despite their intimacy, Lillias, conscious of Korean etiquette, was reluctant to initiate a forthright presentation of the gospel. She knew the timing must be right, and she pleaded with her fellow missionaries that they join her in praying for an opportune situation. That occasion arose one Christmas Eve, when the queen sent for her and inquired about the origin of this Christian holiday. It was the very opportunity Lillias had prayed for and she was able to present the message of salvation to this great woman.[5]

The hopes that Lillias had in reaching the queen with the gospel were dashed in 1895, when, following the Chino-Japanese war, the Japanese began a period of oppressive rule in Korea. They viewed the queen as an enemy to their cause, "and on the eighth of October, 1895, Japanese cutthroats, under the eyes of the Japanese army officers, rushed the palace guard and murdered her." It was a painful loss to Lillias, but she continued her medical work in Korea without her friend the queen.[6]

Much of the medical work Lillias performed was far more demanding than taking care of the queen, as was certainly true of medical missionaries in general. Their days were exhausting, and the work was never done no matter how much of their lives they poured into their sacrificial service of healing. Sometimes they buckled under the strain, as did Clara Eddy, who served with the Creek Mission to the American Indians. During a measles outbreak in one of the mission schools, she was taxed to the limit. "I could not even count the nights I have been up all night," she wrote. The physical exhaustion soon affected her spiritual vitality:

> The fatigue consequent upon the close confinement to the sick room has caused me to suffer much with depression of spirits. I have been led to ask the question why I was here, nursing these sick babies, performing actually more menial labor than any slaves on the place. I have often felt that God had hid his face from me, that his loving kindness had completely withdrawn.[7]

In addition to those women missionaries who were involved strictly in medical work, there were many who were involved in various other forms of humanitarian services. Some of these were not missionaries *per se*, but they functioned as missionaries. An example would be those women who served abroad under the auspices of the YWCA (Young Women's Christian Association). "Between 1895 and 1970 over eight hundred American YWCA women—teachers, administrators, and social workers—served overseas in over thirty countries."[8]

These women formed an army of humanitarian workers who were prepared to serve in virtually any situation. They were "posted in refugee camps in Poland, in the slums of Buenos Aires and Istanbul, and in villages in rural China." Although many of them insisted "we are not missionaries," most of these young women considered themselves "emissaries of Christ." Ada Grabill insisted that her "sole motive in China is to show Christ"—an outlook common among YWCA women who went abroad. Their work was humanitarian, but their purpose was to demonstrate the compassion of Christ.[9]

## Eleanor Chestnut

Dr. Eleanor Chestnut went to China in 1893 as a Presbyterian medical missionary, after a difficult childhood and youth in England. Her father abandoned her mother at the time of Eleanor's birth, and three years later her mother died. Eleanor was taken in by a impoverished neighbor family, but "she was unhappy and lonely, hating control and longing for the sympathy of a mother's love." At the age of twelve she was sent to live with relatives in Missouri in "an ignorant backwoods country community where school privileges were of the most primitive character, and the struggle for life in the home was too strenuous to leave anything for the expense of education." It was in this new environment, however, that she learned of Park College, where students could earn their way through both the academy and the college. She was happy to have found the opportunity for an education, but she struggled in dealing with her impoverished situation. Her clothing consisted of second-hand items that were donated to the school, "a charity which she never could receive in any spirit of gratitude, but which she accepted of necessity and with bitter resentment."[10]

Despite her inner struggles, Eleanor's life was affected by the Christian atmosphere of the school. She joined the Presbyterian church and decided that she would be a foreign missionary. In 1888 she left Park College to pursue her first love, medicine. She entered Woman's Medical

College in Chicago. Again, she faced impoverished circumstances. "She lived in an attic, cooked her own meals, and almost starved." To complicate matters, she was convinced that she needed nurse's training as well, and thus at the end of her first year of medical school she took on a double load. After completing her training in Chicago she served as a resident physician in Massachusetts and then returned to Chicago to attend Moody Bible Institute.[11]

When Eleanor applied for missionary service in 1893, she was a well qualified candidate:

> She had made her own way through college, medical school, and nurse's training-school, while she worked as a nurse in summer vacations, having nursed Dr. Oliver Wendell Holmes in his last illness. She had also taken hospital training, including a good deal of pharmaceutical work, and she had sought to make up for what she regarded as her shortcomings in the knowledge of the Bible and spiritual experience by going to the Bible Institute. . . . She was appointed without hesitation as a medical missionary on August 7, 1893, was assigned to South China, and sailed in the fall of 1894.[12]

On arriving in China, Eleanor began language study, but the medical needs around her were so great that she felt compelled to spend the greatest share of her time in medical work. It was a difficult decision, and she paid a price for it. Of one patient she wrote: "Am afraid she will not recover, though I do hope for her sake and for the work's sake she will. Every patient that I lose counts so much against the work here. I really do labor at a disadvantage. Being able to talk so little, I do not get as clear a

Eleanor Chestnut, missionary doctor to India.

history as I might at home." Another language-related handicap involved dispensing drugs. Only limited varieties were available, and even when the proper drug was available, she wrote, "sometimes I can't find it because many of the bottles are labeled in Chinese."[13]

In 1898, after having served in an area with other missionary doctors, Eleanor was transferred to Lien-chou. For a time she served alone there, responsible for all the outpatients and as many as thirty in-patients at a time. Complicating the situation was the fact that most of the in-patients were government officials who expected more care than ordinary citizens would have. In the absence of an operating room, she performed all surgeries in her bathroom. One such operation involved the amputation of a coolie's leg. Complications arose and skin grafts were needed. When asked about the scars on her own leg, she brushed the question aside, but a nurse later revealed that a skin graft for the "good-for-nothing coolie" had come from the doctor's own leg.[14]

Some of her patients were easier to

treat than others—the opium addicts were among the most trying. Yet, she took personal responsibility for their well-being. Of one she wrote: "Tonight I have a case of dementia on hand, a Lien-chou official who has ruined himself with opium. . . . He thinks he is continually pursued by demons. I had no place for him but my study. He is sometimes violent and has to be carefully watched. So I am sitting here on guard now."[15]

Despite painful operations and difficult patients, Eleanor maintained her sense of humor. To a friend at home she wrote:

> The other night the druggist gave me a prescription which you may find useful, though the ingredients are more difficult to procure in America than in China. You must catch some little rats whose eyes are not yet open, pound them to a jelly, and add lime and peanut oil. Warranted to cure any kind of an ulcer.[16]

With additional medical help at Lien-chou in 1900, Eleanor was able to spend more time with women patients and to build a hospital specifically for them. Some money for the work was provided by supporters; the rest came from her own funds. "She lived on $1.50 a month so that the rest of her salary could be used to buy bricks. Her board learned what she was spending on bricks and insisted on repaying her. She refused the sum offered, saying, 'It will spoil all my fun.'"[17]

Dr. Chestnut survived the terror of the Boxer Rebellion of 1900, but more riots erupted in 1905. Prior to this she had been offered a position as head of a woman's hospital in Hu-nan, but she declined saying, "It would be a mistake for me to leave Lien-chou. I am acquainted with the people there, their dialect, diseases, faults, virtues, and other points. Then I am so fond of them. I do not believe I could *ever* have *quite the same* feeling of affection for any other people." Yet, those who took her life came from among these very people.[18]

The day of infamy was October 29, 1905, the Chinese celebration of Ta Tsin. It might have been an uneventful day, but Dr. Machle, one of Eleanor's colleagues insisted that a mat shed, connected with the "idolatrous ceremonies" of the celebration be removed from the mission property. It was duly removed by some of the local officials—but much to the objection of some of the citizens, who came armed with weapons. Dr. Machle and some of the other missionaries sought to flee the mob, but to no avail. Eleanor had time to alert authorities and could have escaped, but she returned to help rescue her colleagues. It was too late for her slain colleagues, but there were others who needed help. Her final act of service was to rip a piece of material from her dress to bandage an injured child.[19]

She had given her life for the people she loved—and perhaps needlessly. Had her colleague identified with the feelings of the local citizens and their need to feel they still had control of their land, in spite of the presence of the "foreign devils," this terrible atrocity might never have occurred. The very people who killed her were ones for whom Christ died, whom Eleanor had come to serve, but her life was cut short and the missionary outreach in Lien-chou was suspended.

## Ida Scudder

Ida Scudder (1870–1960) was one of a long line of Scudder medical missionaries to India who served under the Reformed Church in America. Her grandfather, Dr. John Scudder, was the first American missionary doctor. He had seven sons, all of whom became missionaries to India, including Dr. John Scudder, Jr., Ida's father. "In subsequent years forty-three members of the Scudder family gave over 1,100 years to missionary service." It was an illustrious family, but from her youth Ida was determined not to follow family tradition. She had known the deprivation of living and serving in India, and her dream was to have a better life—one that included luxuries and pleasure, and one that allowed families to stay together without the agony of long separations.[20]

Ida had known the pain of parting and of family separations. When she was a girl, her family had returned to the United States for furlough, and then her father went back to India alone. Two years later, her mother left to join him, leaving Ida in Chicago with relatives. It was a traumatic experience for both mother and daughter, as Ida's biographer relates:

> The memory of that night could still bring a stabbing pain. The rain outside had been as wild as her own fourteen-year-old helpless grief. She had not even been allowed to go to the station to see her mother off for India. When her clinging arms had been finally, regretfully, unloosed, she had rushed upstairs and sobbed all night into her mother's empty pillow. . . . with the passing weeks and months the aching loneliness had never ceased, merely subsided.[21]

Ida remained in America for the next several years and graduated from Northfield Seminary in Massachusetts before returning to India. Her mother had been ill, and she wanted to spend time with her. During that visit she helped with the ministry, but she still was repelled by the idea of sacrificing her life for the work. Her attitude changed, however, when the need for women's medical work was forcefully brought home to her one evening as she sat by a lamp writing letters—an episode in her Christian pilgrimage that has been referred to as "three knocks in the night." Three Indian men—a Brahmin, another high-caste Hindu, and a Muslim—knocked on her door in the course of one night, pleading for medical help for their wives who all were having severe difficulties in childbirth. Ida's father would have gone, but custom would not permit such contact with the opposite sex. Ida later reflected on the traumatic ordeal:

> I could not sleep that night—it was too terrible. Within the very touch of my hand there were three young girls dying because no woman would help them. I spent much of the night in anguish and prayer. I did not want to spend my life in India. My friends were begging me to return to the joyous opportunities of a young girl in America. I went to bed in the early morning after praying much for guidance. I think that was the first time I ever met God face to face, and all that time it seemed that He was calling me into this work. Early in the morning I heard the "tom-tom" beating in the village and it struck terror in my heart, for it was a death message. I sent out my servant, and he came back saying that all of them had died during the night. I

shut myself in my room and thought very seriously about the condition of the Indian women and after much thought and prayer, I went to my father and mother and told them that I must go home and study medicine, and come back to India to help such women.[22]

Ida Scudder, missionary doctor to India.

Ida returned to America in 1895, where she earned her medical degree at Cornell Medical College before rejoining her family in India. She had publicized her anticipated ministry while in the States, and as a result she brought with her a check for ten thousand dollars to begin a program of medical work for women. This was the beginning of what became the Vellore medical complex, which included a hospital, clinics, and a medical school. Offering Indian women the medical services they so desperately needed was the incentive for building the complex, but medicine was never seen in isolation from evangelism. Annie Hancock, an evangelist, worked closely with Ida, following up on patients and leading many to faith in Christ.[23]

Medical work required large sums of money, and little could be accomplished without generous supporters back home. Indian nationals who were inclined to donate funds for humanitarian causes were not inclined to give to Christian endeavors. Ida was an able fund raiser, but the discipline was not without hassles and controversy. When it was necessary to transform Vellore into a co-educational institution to meet accreditation standards, some of the women contributors and board members cried foul. The plan was carried out, but it was a difficult time for Ida, who was abandoned by some of her staunchest supporters. Lucy Peabody accused her of disloyalty to the women's cause, and Hilda Olsen, a governing-board member, who later resigned, was incensed by the decision: "Vellore is as you say, God's work, but I would like to add God's work *for women*. Every dollar would have to be given back to the givers."[24]

Ida was still active in the work in 1950, when she helped plan the golden-jubilee celebration at Vellore. She had retired four years earlier and turned the work over to Dr. Hilda Lazarus, one of her students, but she remained actively involved for many more years. She was physically active as well. Indeed, at the age of eighty-three, she was still said to be "serving a wicked tennis ball." She had become a celebrity of sorts among supporters back home and through-out India. That fact was demon-strated when a letter addressed "Dr. Ida, India" was delivered to her—one woman in a nation of some three hundred million.[25]

### Lilian Hammer

Often the missionary doctors re-ceive the greatest recognition in the field of missionary medicine, but it is sometimes the nurses who perform the most heroic service. This was true of Lilian Hammer, who served as a nurse among the opium addicts of the Lisu tribe in Western China.

Lilian was a mill worker from Lan-cashire, England, who was forced to leave home by her enraged father when she announced, at the age of twenty-one, that she had decided to take a nurses' training course at a local hospital in order to prepare for missionary service. Her decision to pursue nursing was prompted by her fear that she would not otherwise be accepted as a candidate by the China Inland Mission. In 1943, after her nurses' training and study at a mis-sionary training school, she began her formal application process with the CIM. It was a more complicated ordeal than she had anticipated, and some of the expectations the Ladies Council had of her did not seem to her to be essential for China mission-ary service. "Can you play the pi-ano?" What relevance has piano play-ing, she thought to herself, for a pioneer missionary who might never encounter a piano in a lifetime of foreign service? "But she knew she must answer, and felt it would go against her if she did so in the negative. 'Yes,' she said firmly. Then,

after a momentary pause, she added, 'With one finger.' "[26]

There is no evidence that her in-ability to play the piano seriously influenced the outcome of her inter-view, but after all factors were consid-ered, she was informed that she would not be accepted as a candi-date for the CIM. It was a devastating outcome for Lilian. Her family ties had been severed and all her hopes had been focused on China. Now her future looked bleak. She accepted the decision as divine providence, how-ever, determined that she would not let the disappointment interfere with her priority to serve God. If China was closed to her, she would minis-ter at home. But within months after the CIM denied her service in China, the Red Cross gratefully accepted her services. Indeed, she had prepared herself so well for medical service that she was placed in charge of a unit, with two medical doctors an-swering to her.[27]

While fulfilling her contract with the Red Cross in China, Lilian be-came acquainted with CIM mission-aries who recognized her abilities and encouraged her to reapply to the mission. She did, and after her con-tract with the Red Cross was fulfilled, she was welcomed as a member of the CIM. Her years in China, however, were limited. In 1951, after the com-munist take-over, she was forced to leave. The following year she re-turned to the Far East, this time to work with John and Isobel Kuhn in their pioneer work among the tribes-people of Thailand.[28]

As a nurse, Lilian had an appeal that many other missionaries did not have, and her reputation for healing was carried from one village to another. "She would trudge over the muddy rice fields, up the slippery trail to the village on the Ridge ... dispensing simple medical remedies, binding up wounds and ulcers, showing Bible pictures and trying to explain them with the few Yao words she had learned." But it was her help in curing a self-inflicted malady that established her reputation the most. "It was mainly the plight of these drug addicts, and the desire of some of them for deliverance from the craving, that prompted the Yao to build a little hut for Lilian on the Ridge, and urge her to come and live among them."[29]

Other villages and tribes pleaded for her services as well, and with good reason, as Isobel Kuhn has related:

Lilian had been one of the nurses in our Tali hospital in China, and she had helped Dr. Powell when that skilled medico treated opium addicts until they were cured. Lilian had learned the technique and put it to use now, so that her opium patients suffered as little as possible. Her fame spread for this as also for her midwifery skill, and we could fill pages with her errands of mercy up and down mountains to other tribes as well as Yao.

One of her opium patients ... was so impressed with Lilian's skill that, unknown to her, he persuaded the Lisu village where he lived to build her a little shanty and invited her up among them.... Others too were interested, so down the mountain trotted a delegation to invite Nurse Lilian up to preach to them! Not suspecting their hopes, Lilian consented and went.... "This is yours!" they told her with delight. "It was built just and only for you, and we want you to come and live

with us. Many are wanting to break off their opium and become Christians."[30]

Lilian was well aware that a medical cure for opium addiction was not enough. "She knew that there was little hope of a lasting deliverance from the opium craving unless the medical cure was accompanied by spiritual healing." The fear of demon power over them drove many tribespeople to opium, and that fear had to be replaced by faith in a loving God. "When demon shelves remained in the home and unbelief in the heart, the lure of the short-lived false peace of the pipe usually proved too strong." She had sought to make the opium treatment easier by restricting her care to Christians, but that rule led to many false professions and many disappointments for her when "converts" later renounced their faith and went back to their addiction.[31]

During most of her years in the mountains of Thailand, Lilian worked alone. She lived in utterly primitive conditions with little privacy. Although she enjoyed reading classics, loneliness at times became overwhelming. "How I would love to escape from it all," she wrote. "I find it very hard to endure.... I am hoping to have a fellow worker some day. For twelve months I have been alone, since there has been no one to send for my help. However, whether alone or with a companion, the Lord is able to work." Her CIM regional supervisor had sought to find a partner for her, but without success. A young woman joined her for a short time, but left due to illness, and Lilian was alone again. Some missionaries thought that was best:

"Lilian is a loner," her fellow missionaries agreed between themselves sometimes, as they saw her taking, quite unconsciously, an individual line, or sticking determinedly to her own ideas about how things ought to be done. . . . She had ploughed a lonely furrow for so long that mealtimes and prearranged schedules were airily ignored if they interfered with what she was doing. The very qualities that made her such a successful pioneer among the tribes were those that made her a fellow worker rather difficult to live with.[32]

Lilian's reputation had preceeded her when she returned home for furlough in 1955. People thronged around her wanting to hear of her pioneer medical work among the primitive tribesmen. "With her lively descriptions of her life among the Lisu her experiences were recounted before spellbound audiences," and before she returned to the Far East, she toured South Africa, telling harrowing stories of witch doctors, demonism, and opium addicts, and how she as a nurse had been able to reach out through the love of Christ.[33]

Lilian's lonely existence was an anomaly in the region where she worked. The people "cannot conceive how I can climb the mountains alone, live alone, work alone," she wrote. "In the East people go everywhere in twos or in larger groups. It seems strange to them for anyone, especially a woman, to be any length of time alone." Yet, at the age of forty-three, she had little hope that her situation would change. She had committed herself to missionary work, and despite the dangers of a solitary existence in the remote mountain region where marauders sometimes plundered innocent travelers and troublesome enemies. But Lilian had vowed to continue, though she wrote, "I must confess that I am sometimes tempted to turn back instead of going on."[34]

Whether she fully realized the potential for danger among the mountain tribes is unclear, but it was ever lurking in the shadows. In 1959, while journeying through the jungle trails alone, she was attacked and killed. A sawed-off shotgun was the weapon. The assailant was not found, though some years later it was discovered that the murder was committed by an opium addict. "He had accepted a bribe from a witch doctor and a Chinese quack who saw they were losing their power over the people because of Lilian's medical and spiritual work." In the years that followed her death, the work continued among the Lisu, and later a Lisu church was built near the site of her slaying.[35]

## Chapter 16

# God's Word in Every Tongue: Bible Translation and Linguistics

Bible translation has historically been regarded as a male profession. Indeed, in the nineteenth century and the early decades of the twentieth century it was no more appropriate for a woman to be a Bible translator than to be an ordained minister or a seminary professor. That restriction began to weaken, however, by the 1930s. Wycliffe Bible Translators, founded by William Cameron Townsend, helped women as well as men catch the vision for translating the Bible for people in remote tribes. Still, there was strong opposition. Not only was it thought to be inappropriate for women to be translating (and interpreting) the Word of God, but their carrying out this work in dangerous remote tribal regions was even more controversial. Before they were accepted on a par with men, women had to prove themselves worthy of the task.

Townsend more quickly accepted women than did most of the other officials of Wycliffe Bible Translators. It took years to convince some that in the work of Bible translation women were fully equal to men—and in some cases far superior. The fears of women being killed by "savage" tribesmen were generally unfounded. Indeed, they were typically exposed to less danger than men. An example is the case of Loretta Anderson and Doris Cox, who went to Peru to work among the headhunting Shapras in 1950. There translation work was successful, and within a few years many of the people had become Christians. Years later, Tariri, the tribal chief confided to Townsend: "If you had sent men, we would have killed them on sight. Or if a couple, I'd have killed the man and taken the woman for myself. But what could a great chief do with two harmless girls who insisted on calling him brother?"[1]

## Eunice Pike

When Eunice Pike and Florence Hansen enrolled in the Summer Institute of Linguistics (an arm of Wycliffe Bible Translators) in 1936 to prepare for a ministry of Bible translation with the Mazatec Indians in Mexico, they were given a less than enthusiastic welcome. They "did not impress Legters [the co-founder of the mission] as appropriate pioneer material. This he felt was a job for rugged men. He had not encouraged women to join the crusade—but these two had turned up."[2]

There were other grim warnings these young women had to contend with, as Pike later related. "Some people had reminded Mr. Townsend that Latin American women never traveled alone, never lived alone, and were always well chaperoned. With genuine concern for Florrie and me, they had said that any attempt on our part to live in an Indian village would be misunderstood by the people and could only end in disaster."[3]

Despite the objections they were assigned to do linguistic and translation work among the sixty-five thousand Mazatec Indians, ninety percent of whom spoke no Spanish. They lived in Chalco, a remote town with a population of two thousand, a ten-hour horse-back ride across the mountains from the nearest link with civilization. Many may have viewed it as inappropriate for women to be involved in such activity, but without Eunice and Florence the Mazatec language might have gone untranslated for many more years. "When we first arrived in Mexico almost nothing was known about the Mazatec language. Three and a half years later we were talking it—with lots of errors— had figured out something of the grammar, and had our opinions about the alphabet with which it should be written."[4]

Women had certain advantages over men in tribal translation work. For reasons of propriety, a language informant had to be chosen very carefully. Men and women alone together were presumed to be involved sexually. Women informants were difficult to find among the Indians because so few knew Spanish, yet those that were available often proved to be the most reliable. Securing a competent informant who could endure the hours of tedious conversation was not an easy task. Tribal men were particularly vulnerable to boredom, because language work often took them away from more exciting activities. Women, on the other hand, would sew or do other sedentary work while doing their job as an informant. Marta was one such woman, and Eunice depended heavily on her. She "seldom tired of repeating, and she especially enjoyed helping us to translate Bible stories. Eloisa, her sister, liked them too, and she listened while sewing or cooking nearby, and added her suggestions whenever Marta hesitated."[5]

Sometimes it was difficult to translate the Bible precisely in the Mazatec language. Eunice tried for days to get a correct translation of the word "adultery" from Marta, who only offered imprecise phrases. Finally Eunice asked a visiting anthropologist to get the correct word from one of the men in the tribe. He eagerly honored her request, but when Eunice tried the word out on Marta, she got a surprising reaction: "For a second or two Marta looked at her in blank amazement. Then she hid her face in her hands and shrieked with laughter. Between her fingers we could see tears running down her

Eunice Pike, Wycliffe Bible translator to Mexico.

red face." When Marta was able to get control of her emotions, she angrily demanded to know who had divulged the word, and when Eunice refused to tell, she ran out in the yard and demanded an explanation from her sister. Her sister denied having mentioned the word, insisting that she only taught Eunice and Florrie "good words." The incident had taught them a valuable lesson—that the most correct word is not always the best word to use. If a word in a Bible translation could create such a stir, it was better not to use it.[6]

In 1941, after less than five years among the Mazatec Indians, Eunice and Florrie completed the first draft of the New Testament. It was a great accomplishment, but just a first step. "We did not celebrate the finish of that first draft, perhaps because we knew that this was only the beginning—many revisions lay ahead of us." During the years that followed, Eunice and Florrie continued to live among the Mazatec, but their work was often interrupted by other assignments—assignments that sharpened their skills and aided their revisions. Eunice returned to the States to teach for a time at the Summer Institute of Linguistics, and in 1946 she was given the task of helping two young women translators begin their work among the Mixtec Indian tribe in Mexico. All the while she and Florrie (who had since gotten married) continued to work on the revision, and by 1949 the Book of Acts and 1 John were ready for the printers and then distribution among the people.[7]

In the years that followed Eunice

worked with other partners and spent much of her time in village work, using her nurse's training to the advantage of the gospel and selling Scripture portions and Christian books that had been translated into the Mazatec tongue. She demonstrated through her years of ministry that single women could effectively carry out the work of Bible translation in remote tribal areas, and the example she set encouraged hundreds of women to follow in her footsteps.

## Marianna Slocum

Many single women missionaries indulge in the fantasy that one day the man of their dreams—a handsome single male missionary—will appear on the scene and romance will follow. And for women translators, isolated in remote regions, the yearning can be all-consuming. For most of them, however, the fantasy is no more than an idle dream. The number of single male missionaries to be encountered on the jungle trails is severely limited. For Marianna Slocum, though, that dream became a reality. After completing college and training at Camp Wycliffe in the summer of 1940, she and her female partner began their translation work among the Chol tribe in Southern Mexico. Stationed nearby, working with the Tzeltal tribe, was Bill Bentley, and in the months after her arrival they fell in love and became engaged. They returned home in the summer of 1941 to prepare for a late August wedding, but it never took place. Six days before their wedding, while Bill was staying in her home, he did not come down to breakfast.

Marianna's father found him lifeless in his bed—he had died in the night of congenital heart failure.[8]

Marianna's dreams were shattered, but in the midst of her sorrow she vowed that she would return to Mexico and finish the work Bill had started. Following his funeral in Topeka, Kansas, she went to Camp Wycliffe and then on to Mexico, alone, but soon to be joined by another single woman. Her days were spent in long tedious hours of language study. It was a hard life, which only the heartiest of women could endure. Several women came to work with her but they did not stay—until Florence Gerdel, a nurse, came in 1947 to help out "temporarily." They began a partnership that would last for decades.[9]

The work among the Tzeltals was slow. It took seven long years with them before she began to see real changes, but then things happened quickly. Her very first convert left the village, scorned by his family and friends, and went to another village where he soon had a congregation of eighty believers. In the years that followed, while she translated the Bible and Florence nursed the sick, "congregations of Christians came into being everywhere." With every step forward, though, there were setbacks. "Enemies of the Gospel set several chapels on fire; some of the Indians were jailed; one was shot and killed for his faith in Christ."[10]

In 1956, fifteen years after she had come to work among the Tzeltels, the first edition of her just-completed New Testament was ready to be distributed. It was a big day when the shipment arrived aboard a small aircraft, and the Indians eagerly stood in line to buy copies with their hard-earned pesos. It was a day that also marked a turning point in the ministry of Marianna and Florence. Their work was done. They not only had given the tribe the New Testament, but they had also established churches and had taught people how to read and write and handle their own medical needs. Yet, the two women felt a keen obligation to these people who had opened their hearts to them, and they did not wish to leave without their blessing. So it was that they were commissioned by the Tzeltel Indians to reach out to another needy tribe, the unreached Bachajon people who also lived in the Mexican state of Chiapas.[11]

Marianna Slocum, missionary translator to Mexico and South America.

The work among the Bachajon people was similar to their work with the Tzeltels, and in 1965, after eight years of toilsome labor, a New Testament was again ready for distribution. On the day that this precious cargo arrived, people from many miles around and from more than forty congregations came to celebrate and to buy their own personal copies. "How much does it cost?" was the oft-repeated question as the Indians stood in line. Seventeen and a half pesos was, of course, the answer to the question they had in mind, but the actual answer could never be given in pesos. Loneliness, illness, unfriendliness, primitive living conditions, and the sacrifice of marriage and family all made up the cost of the Bachajon New Testament. It was a heavy price, but one Marianna gladly paid. And when her work with the Bachajon people was over, she and Florence started all over again in the mountains of Colombia.[12]

### Marilyn Laslo

The work of Wycliffe Bible Translators that began initially in Latin America quickly spread worldwide, reaching into some of the planet's most remote and primitive regions. Papua New Guinea, with its seven hundred different languages, was one such region. Here were people who had never heard the gospel and for whom the Bible had never been translated—tribal peoples like the Sepik Iwams who had a history of headhunting and sorcery and a deep hostility toward outsiders. It was this group of people who lived in the village of Hauna along the Sepik River that Marilyn Laslo and her partner set out to reach in a dugout canoe in 1969.

Marilyn's initial arrival in Hauna

was greeted with amusement and utter dismay. The villagers had never seen white women before, and they could not imagine what would bring them to their village. When Marilyn finally was able to communicate to one of the young men (through Pidgin) that they wished to live in the village and learn about the people, there was immediate resistance. The chief was suspicious. Stories had circulated through the region about white men who came and sometimes killed the villagers. But at the same time the chief found himself in a predicament, and he realized there was only one solution. "We are strong men, of a strong tribe. What harm could they do? Our enemies would laugh at us if we showed ourselves afraid of two women!"[13]

Marilyn had grown up in Valparaiso, Indiana, and first felt the call to missions one day at the age of nine when she was driving the tractor on her family farm. During her high school years, however, the call became less clear as she involved herself in sports and social life, and after high school she drifted from job to job with no clear focus in her life. It was not until her pastor challenged her to go on to school to prepare for missions that she decided to enroll at Bryan College. Once again, though, her vision for missions was blurred. She became active in the athletic program and reigned as homecoming queen in her junior year, and after her graduation she enrolled at Indiana University where she earned her masters degree in 1961.[14]

After four years of teaching, Marilyn once again felt the call of God on her life for foreign missionary service. She still had financial debts, however,

and so she made a bargain with God that she would follow that call if He would give her time to pay off her debts. She meant business. She quickly found a new teaching position and in addition worked from five o'clock until midnight as a waitress and short-order cook. When the school year was completed she had paid off her debts and had money in the bank.[15]

When Marilyn enrolled in the Summer Institute of Linguistics at the University of Oklahoma she was uncertain about her future geographical location and even about her ability to withstand the rigors of missionary life. But as she became acquainted with other Wycliffe members, her dream became more focused.

And there were other unplanned influences. Among them, the lives of such missionary greats as William Carey, George Grenfell, Adoniram Judson, David Livingstone. In the SIL library, Marilyn immersed herself in biographies of such missionary greats, reveling in their dedication and courage, measuring her own willingness to sacrifice by theirs.

Of all these towering figures, however, she found herself attracted most to James Chalmers, of the London Missionary Society, whose book, *Pioneering in New Guinea*, was everywhere regarded as a missionary classic. . . . In Chalmers' audacious courage, Marilyn felt a zesty challenge, and wept openly whenever she read and reread of that Easter morning in 1901 when, going up New Guinea's wild Fly River, Chalmers and a companion were attacked and beheaded, their flesh cut into pieces, cooked with sago and eaten on the same day.[16]

Reading such an account of cannibalism would have quickly checked the enthusiasm of many would-be missionaries, but to Marilyn it was pure inspiration—inspiration she desperately needed once she arrived in New Guinea to live on the banks of the Sepik. "On their first night in the borrowed shack, they were assaulted by swarms of vicious mosquitoes, flying ants and other insects" that came right through their mosquito nets. "Meanwhile, king-sized cockroaches scampered across the floor and the tops of their nets. And over it all were the jungle night noises— cries of wild birds, grunts of crocodiles, sounds of night animals, insects and bats."[17]

Morning brought relief from the night terrors, and Marilyn quickly realized that this tiny town of four hundred was a bustling little community. "The village throbbed with round-the-clock activity, its women pounding sago into paste, weaving baskets, keeping the children out of the way of the men spearing fish, felling trees for new homes, bringing in the sago palm, making dugout canoes, carving intricately designed shields." Even the children were assigned their chores and kept busy throughout the day. Marilyn and her partner adjusted to the routine, ever curious about the habits and customs of their neighbors, who were ever curious about them. "Each day brings what seems like a million bright and unblinking eyes to follow every move we make," wrote Marilyn. "It's like living in a glass house. But we are beginning to adjust to it all, and we thank the Lord for giving us so many wonderful little friends."[18]

The most frustrating aspect of life in Hauna was the difficulty in communicating. Marilyn had expected her work to be difficult, but never could she have imagined how arduous the task would be of breaking down such a difficult language. The difficulty and variety of languages in this region had caused James Chalmers a century earlier to lament that "this country must be the authentic site of the Tower of Babel," and Marilyn echoed his frustration. She spent long days walking through the village pointing to objects that a villager would identify and copying down the phonetic sound of the words. Nouns were easy. Verbs were in a different category altogether.

> Take, for instance, the verb *to cut.* Cutting down a tree to build his house, the Sepik Iwam will use one word; if he's cutting it down for firewood, he will use another and very different one. The vocabulary goes on endlessly. Cutting bananas off the stalk, or whiskers off his face, or sago palm leaves for his roof—whatever the action or its reason, he uses words that sound like no other, no matter how close their context.[19]

Marilyn quickly discovered that learning a language involved far more than simply learning words. As she began to communicate with the people, she realized that "the center of life and seat of emotions was the *throat.* Thus, in the tribal tongue one would never say, 'I've asked Jesus to come into my heart.' Instead he would say, 'I've asked Jesus to come into my throat.'" The more words she wrote down on her notebook— or banana leaf, as the villagers called it—the more ignorant she realized she was. She was often discouraged, and sometimes she needed to be reminded why she was there. One day an old man asked her why she was carving with a thorn on a banana leaf (translated: writing in her notebook). She explained to him that she was learning the language so she could write God's word on a banana leaf.

Marilyn Laslo, missionary translator to New Guinea.

Incredulous, the old man put out his hand, gently touched the paper, and said, "You mean to say, Mama Marilyn, that God's talk and our talk can be carved on the banana leaf for us to see and understand?" Assured that this was so, he turned away, hesitated a moment to shake his head, then said softly, "Marilyn, oh, Marilyn, why did it take you so long to come?"[20]

This old man was not alone in his desire to better understand who God is. The villagers were very superstitious. Health problems were immediately determined to be caused by evil spirits. In Hauna alone there were more than fifty witch doctors who had individualized remedies for every ailment known among them—some remedies more effective than others. Demonism was a fact of life, according to Marilyn: "In America demon possession may be discounted by some, but out here it's a reality one can't deny."[21]

In her struggle against some of the most disturbing practices of the witch doctors, Marilyn began practicing a simplistic form of medicine herself—dispensing medicines, lancing boils, and pulling teeth. It was not easy for her. "The last thing I ever wanted to be was a nurse," she wrote. "I can never go into a hospital to visit the sick without feeling sick myself. If anyone even suggests he or she is about to vomit, I beat them to it." What Marilyn found most effective and gratifying was preventative health measures. "Convinced that many of the illnesses came from the polluted river water, she launched one of her most ambitious projects: the installation of four 2,000-gallon tanks to catch the rain water and pipe it to locations convenient to all villagers."[22]

Like all members of Wycliffe Bible Translators, Marilyn was expected to observe tribal customs and write an anthropology paper to submit to headquarters to be made available to other missionaries or researchers. This was a challenging aspect of the work but was also at times very distressing. It would have been easier on many occasions for Marilyn to turn her back and escape the reality of life in Hauna. One such occasion was when her friend Neemau was buried. Marilyn had known Neemau was sick, but was perplexed when she received the news that she had been buried. She hurried to the grave site only to discover that Neemau was still alive. "That's my good friend Neemau!" she cried. "She's not dead. Can't you see she is still breathing. You can't bury her! Let me take her to my house and revive her!" But the people ignored her pleas. Neemau was not talking. Her throat had died. Therefore she was dead.[23]

Once Marilyn had an adequate command of the language, she began teaching the villagers to read and write. So eager were they to learn that in 1974, only five years after she entered the village, she inspired the construction of a school, ninety feet long and twenty-four feet wide, with ten separate class rooms. The men of the village also built a clinic, a church, a shop, and a house that was designated for translation work. For her translation project, she selected ten of her best students and divided them into five teams of two each to translate each of the four Gospels and the Book of Acts. "Marilyn herself moved from team to team, helping to clarify a passage." Periodically she took some of these helpers with her to the mission base down river to go over material with experienced translators.[24]

In 1977, three years after the translation work had begun, Marilyn and her co-workers had completed the rough draft of the first five books of the New Testament. It was a monumental accomplishment, but in reality only a beginning. There would be many more revisions of what had already been done and much more raw translation work to do. In the process, however, many had become Christians, and the Hauna villagers could genuinely worship in the church they had built.

# PART III

# MINISTRY CHALLENGES

Twentieth-century overseas missionary work has presented many challenges to women—challenges that have often involved agonizing decisions and confrontations with the establishment. By the early decades of the twentieth century, the place of women alongside men on the front lines of the missionary advance was well established, but that did not make it any less difficult for them when they were charting new territory and entering ministries that until then had been the exclusive domain of men.

For Mabel Francis, the challenge involved her own national loyalty. After World War II broke out she was faced with a difficult decision. Should she defy the orders of her mission board, endanger her life, and remain at her post with the people she was ministering to in Japan? Or should she abide by the ruling of her superiors, demonstrate her patriotism to her homeland, and return to the security that it offered? Betty Olsen faced a similar challenge. Without the security of marriage that she so longed for, she left the comforts and friendships of home and entered the war-torn jungles of Vietnam, only to be captured and killed by the enemy.

The challenge for Constance Padwick did not pose the physical dangers that Mabel Francis and Betty Olsen faced, but it did involve courage—courage to think about issues and strategies for mission. Missiology, the science of missions, had been regarded as a sphere for men, and women were simply not expected to trouble their minds with issues of mission strategy and concepts. In her effort to reach out to Muslims, however, Padwick realized that she had to challenge some of the time-worn methodology, and in doing so she became a respected missiologist whose publications were numerous. Other women entered the arena—sometimes developing new strategies without realizing how significant their work was. Joy Ridderhof and

B. V. Subbamma are examples of women who made contributions that have had a significant impact on modern mission strategy.

Women have also taken up the challenge of presenting missionary work on a popular level through the pen. Frequently this challenge was met after a time of tragedy when writing became a catharsis and a means of offering to the public an explanation or insight into the meaning of what otherwise might have appeared to be a tragic waste of human life. Elisabeth Elliot began her writing career in this way and went on to write some of the greatest missionary classics ever written. Among the other women also took up this challenge is Isobel Kuhn, who wrote of her struggles in missionary service in the Orient.

Since the beginning of the modern missionary era, women have faced challenges in team ministry with their husbands, but these challenges have involved new issues in the twentieth century. With the innovations of modern medicine and the expansion of mission hospitals and clinics, the life span of missionary wives vastly increased. The loss of life in childbirth no longer took its heavy toll, and wives became full-fledged missionaries in their own right. With that change came new challenges in ministry. What place did the wife have in making crucial decisions about the type and location of the assignment, about furlough, and about the children's education? Balancing team ministry with marriage and motherhood was a struggle for women like Ruth Shaffer, who with her husband worked among the Maasai in Kenya, and Pat Dale, who worked with her husband among the stone-age tribes of Irian Jaya.

A challenge closely related to that of team ministry was the rearing of children on the mission field. Determining where little ones should be educated was a difficult issue that faced many women, including Evelyn Brand, who served with her husband in India, and Dorie Van Stone, the author of *The Girl Nobody Loved*. But if marriage and motherhood posed a challenge, so did ministry as a single woman. Since the late nineteenth century, single women had been going overseas as missionaries, but it was not until decades later that they faced some of their greatest challenges in dealing with the male missionary establishment. In an era of women's liberation, it became a challenge for women to view their singleness as an asset—to realize that in many ways their ministry could be enhanced by their unencumbered life style. Maude Cary discovered this during her many long years in Morocco, as did Helen Roseveare, a missionary doctor in the Congo.

Another challenge missionary women have come to grips with in recent years is the challenge of power encounter and charismatic gifts. Mildred Larsen struggled for many years with the concept of demon possession before she began to understand its reality through her close contact with native Christians, and Evelyn Quema, a native of the Philippines, enhanced her own ministry through her dependence on charismatic gifts. One of the greatest challenges of missions in recent years has been the challenge that faces the non-Western church, and women as well as men have been eager to meet this summons. Rosario Rivera, through her breakfast program in the ghettos of Lima, Peru, and Young Sawa Kim, through her crosscultural work in Japan, have demonstrated their commitment to world evangelism. The greatest challenge of all, however, that has come out of the non-Western church has been that of Mother Theresa and the Missionaries of Charity, who have spread out from India to circle the globe.

## Chapter 17

# Onward Christian Soldiers: Preaching the Gospel in Enemy Territory

By the very nature of their work, missionaries are often required to fill dangerous assignments or are caught in a situation that is life-threatening. In such circumstances, women are generally more safe than their male counterparts because they pose less of a threat. It is for that reason that women have been able to serve faithfully when men have been evacuated or prevented from entering a hostile area. During World War II women stayed to head up the work of the Gospel Missionary Union, and it was women who entered Auca territory after five men had been killed. The argument that women should be permitted to accept assignments that are too dangerous for men is not one that is readily accepted by most mission leaders. This was true when Mabel Francis requested to remain in Japan during World War II.

## Mabel Francis

Mabel Francis grew up in New Hampshire in the late nineteenth century, and began teaching school at the age of fifteen at the invitation of a young man who himself was a school teacher, but who was too ill to continue full-time. She "developed a deep attachment to him," but his death dashed her hopes of marriage. It was a depressing time for her. She continued teaching, but reminders of him were everywhere—even just outside the rural schoolhouse, where through the window she could see his grave, which she faithfully decorated every day.[1]

As she taught school in this little New England community, Mabel's conscience was pricked about her failure to share the gospel. She heard the voice of God saying, "Why do you weep over this young man who has gone on to heaven? You must tell the people of Tamworth that you know my love and that they should also know it." From then on she began holding Sunday afternoon church services in the schoolhouse, and soon there was a revival. Even "the hard-handed old farmers with their smell of tobacco" were "being moved for God." The revival spread to the village after the local pastor heard of her ministry and invited her to speak at his church. After that she became a well-known figure in the region. "One village after another called for me in those teen years to testify and speak about the Christian gospel. We really had a big revival in South Tamworth, and many lives of people in the town were transformed. We had similar meetings and revivals in Sanburnton, Meredith and other New Hampshire communities."[2]

When she was nineteen, Mabel felt the call of God to missionary service in Japan. She decided that she needed formal education if she were to become a missionary and enrolled in Gordon Bible School, founded by the great missionary statesman and supporter of women in ministry, A. J. Gordon. Her financial situation was precarious during this time, and sometimes her food money came from small stipends she was given for preaching. In 1900 she rented a store front in Brockton, Massachusetts, and began a city mission work, which she left in the hands of others two years later when she decided to continue her education at Nyack Missionary College.[3]

Mabel began her ministry in Japan in 1909, at the age of twenty-nine and served there for fifty-six years. That in itself was an accomplishment equalled by no other missionary. Unlike her colleagues, she refused to return to the States when all missionaries were recalled in the early 1930s due to the economic crisis in the mission brought on by the Great Depression. It was an agonizing decision for her, because she had no desire either to

defy the mission or to be deprived of her financial support. But the needs of the Japanese church were too great in her mind to simply abandon the work.[4]

Life was not easy in Japan for missionaries. Funds were scarce, and housing was generally poor. Travel by bicycle was the most economical, and Mabel often thought "how nice it would be to have money to ride the bus." The hilly terrain and the rough unpaved paths, often brought a sigh of dejection: "O Lord, where are the men who ought to be riding these bicycles up and down these trails?" The need for men was felt not only in a general sense, but also in a very personal way—at least during her early years of ministry. "When I was so discouraged, and the job seemed so terribly big," she wrote, "I thought, 'Well, now, if I was married, I could follow on with my husband.'" But God did not agree: "The Lord said, 'You are on the wrong track. I have a plan for your life and it is not for you to be married. . . . Your only work in life is to spread the gospel among the Japanese, and if anyone should come and ask you to marry, he would be out of My will.'" It was a difficult proposition for Mabel to accept, but she later revealed that "the whole thing passed out of my life like a cloud passing away, and that was many years ago. The thought of marriage has meant nothing to me since that time—nothing!"[5]

Mabel spent most of her years in Japan ministering in and around Hiroshima. Her brother joined her in Japan in 1913, and together they established twenty Alliance churches. In 1922 she teamed up with her widowed sister, Anne, and they spent

Mabel Francis, missionary to Japan.

much of the next forty years together, with Mabel ministering as an evangelist and Anne as a teacher.[6]

Mabel conducted a very successful evangelistic and discipling ministry in Japan. Her first convert was a young banker who quickly became a leader in the local church and later organized a number of churches in new areas. Her second convert was a well-to-do young woman who lived with Mabel and worked as her assistant for several years. There were other converts, including Mr. Ogata,

the postmaster of Fukuyama, who later became a faithful pastor, and Mitsuko Ninomiyo, who later became a missionary to the Japanese in Brazil. As a young girl, Mitsuko was intrigued by Mabel because she was the bicycling American who was always smiling. Later she was invited by a friend to attend church, and "much to her surprise," wrote Mabel, "she found out I was the preacher when she got into the church."[7]

During the 1930s as Japan became more and more militaristic, it became increasingly difficult for missionaries—especially the men—to continue their regular ministries without being hampered by authorities. This was true of Mabel's brother Tom. He made arrangements for furlough "because he was so frustrated with the questions and suspicions wherever he went." Mabel fared better. Even after the bombing of Pearl Harbor she was allowed to remain in her home. She was technically under house arrest, but she was allowed to have visitors and travel as long as she kept a record for the police. Later Mabel was taken to Tokyo, where she was interned in a Catholic monastery. But even there Mabel was able to share her faith, and as a result of her testimony the man in charge of the internees later became a Christian and served as a deacon in a church in Tokyo.[8]

Unlike other missionaries, who might have appeared to have come into Japan as victors after the war, Mabel and her sister had suffered through the devastation with the Japanese people. She was sixty-five at the close of the war, and she was deeply respected by Japanese Christians and non-Christians alike. But she and her sister were only two in the midst of such a vast population with such overwhelming needs. Mabel was particularly concerned about the women, whose status had been raised through the influence of General MacArthur.

They were wonderful women, but there were so many more soldiers than there were missionaries—and they led them in another direction. The American officials wanted them to have recreation, and then wanted them to

drink and things like that, and they got them to do it.

If only we could have had enough missionaries to lead them out. Those women had high standards, and they would have become wonderful Christian mothers and Christian women, but there were not enough of us to reach them.

That's where America failed in Japan. Our churches didn't grasp the opportunity—they didn't send a thousand missionaries!

During the first ten years after the war, the Japanese people were really very open and seeking.... Now ... it is much harder to reach them.[9]

After the war Japanese officials honored her and her sister and invited them to speak at official functions, and in 1962 the emperor honored her with Japan's highest civilian honor, membership in the exclusive Fifth Order of the Sacred Treasure. This was one of many ways appreciation was bestowed on Mabel for her sacrifice for "the welfare of the Japanese people in their distress and confusion at the time of their defeat" and for "the long years spent in leading hundreds of Japanese to the knowledge of God, to Peace of heart and mind."[10]

## A. B. Simpson

Mabel Francis often related her fond memories of A. B. Simpson, who founded the Christian and Missionary Alliance (then known simply as the Christian Alliance) in New York City in 1887, and then traveled throughout the country promoting the missionary cause. His "attitude toward women," according to Leslie Andrews,

must be viewed against the backdrop of his consuming passion to evangelize a lost world before the return of the King. He did not seek to placate those whose ecclesiastical agendas were, in his opinion, secondary to the task of world evangelization. If women furthered the primary mission of the Church to reach lost souls for Christ, then he enthusiastically endorsed their ministry to achieve that objective.[11]

Simpson was criticized for his open policy toward women in ministry, but he was quick to defend his position. After a series of meetings in Atlanta he responded to attacks by saying the matter was an issue "which God has already settled, not only in His Word, but in His providence, by the seal which He is placing in this very day, in every part of the world, upon the public work of consecrated Christian women." He concluded by chiding the pastor who led the attack: "Dear brother, let the Lord manage the women. He can do it better than you, and you turn your batteries against the common enemy."[12]

Simpson's theology also reflected his attitude toward the female sex. A chapter title in one of his books was "The Motherhood of God." Here he rejected the common belief that God was of the male gender and confessed his appreciation for the feminine qualities of God.

The heart of Christ is not only the heart of man, but has in it all the tenderness and gentleness of woman. . . . He combined in Himself the nature both of man and woman even as the first man Adam had the woman within his own being before she was separately formed

from his very body.[13] In reference to the Holy Spirit, Simpson wrote: "As our heavenly Mother, the Comforter assumes our nurture, training, teaching, and the whole direction of our life."[14]

## Gladys Aylward

The heroic ministry of Mabel Francis was matched by another woman who also served in a war-torn Asian country—in China, the enemy of Japan. She was Gladys Aylward, whose life was portrayed in the film "The Inn of the Sixth Happiness," starring Ingrid Bergman, and in the book *The Small Woman* by Alan Burgess. She was a celebrity and yet she was among the most humble of human beings. She was committed to what she perceived to be the call of God, and she refused to let the danger of enemy artillery deter her from her mission.

Gladys had no preparation for the type of work and atmosphere she was to find when she arrived in China in 1933. She had been employed as a parlor maid, a genteel term for domestic servant. She had no academic or language preparation and no candidate orientation for the work. She simply came to China on her own to share the gospel with the people she encountered. Few missionaries have gone abroad with less apparent potential for success. Yet, her determination made up for what she lacked in recognizable qualifications, and her work was accompanied by success.

For Gladys, a missionary career was a ticket out of the hum-drum daily existence that most lower-class single women faced as they looked into their futures. While working as a maid she had experienced a life-changing spiritual encounter with God, and she immediately caught the vision for foreign missions. She was in her late twenties—a factor that would not be in her favor—but she reasoned that the China Inland Mission would attach more importance to her enthusiasm and commitment than to her age, as it had done with so many prior candidates. It was with bitter disappointment, then, that she learned she had been rejected. This was clearly not a matter of sex discrimination. The CIM had an illustrious history of promoting the ministry of women. Gladys, in the eyes of the mission leaders, was simply not missionary material.[15]

The problem was her low scores in classroom testing—which may have been caused by a learning disability. Although she was not noticeably dense conversationally, academic studies were unbearably difficult for her. She tried but, according to her biographer, "when it came to imbibing knowledge by normally accepted methods, Gladys's powers of mental digestion seemed automatically to go into neutral, and occasionally reverse."[16]

So convinced was Gladys that she was called by God to be a missionary to China that she did not let the rejection obscure her plans. She began making arrangements independently of any mission-board oversight, which included depositing money each week for her overland train fare with the local ticket agent and making contact with a resident missionary in China who would oversee her initial ministry. When she departed from the Liverpool station in the fall of 1932, she could have

been mistaken for a gypsy rather than a missionary. She was wearing an orange frock over her coat and carried a bedroll and suitcases with pots and pans and a small stove attached with a rope.[17]

It was a harrowing journey across Europe and on into Russia and Siberia. Much of the time she was traveling with Russian military troops who were on their way to participate in a border war with China. She could not understand or speak any of the foreign languages she encountered, which resulted in confusion and delays. One incident occurred in Siberia when she was ordered to get off the train in a small town. She refused, insisting she go to the very end of the line. The train went some miles further and then stopped. The soldiers all exited, and she was left alone. She had no choice but to collect her belongings and trudge back to the town. Alan Burgess vividly captures the scene:

> The Siberian wind blew the powdered snow around her heels, and she carried a suitcase in each hand, one still decorated ludicrously with kettle and saucepan. Around her shoulders she wore a fur rug. And so she trudged off into the night, a slight lonely figure, dwarfed by the tall, somber trees, the towering mountains, and the black sky, diamond bright with stars. There were wolves near by, but this she did not know. Occasionally in the forest a handful of snow would slither to the ground with a sudden noise, or a branch would crack under the weight of snow, and she would pause and peer uncertainly in that direction. But nothing moved. There was no light, no warmth, nothing but endless loneliness.[18]

Amazingly, Gladys eventually reached her destination hundreds of miles into the remote interior of China in relatively good health and spirits. The widowed resident missionary, with whom she had arranged to work, was serving alone— and probably with good reason. Jennie Lawson was an abrupt and abrasive woman, who was not impressed with the details of the overland trauma that Gladys had just endured. She immediately assigned Gladys to carry out the laborious task of cleaning the rooms and stables at the muleteer inn that Jennie operated. Her ministry was that of witnessing to the muleteers who stopped for a night's lodging, and she was relieved to have a dedicated helper. For Gladys, missionary work suddenly seemed less romantic than she had envisioned it, and her parlor-maid experience must have seemed like a truly genteel profession.[19]

The difficulty Gladys endured in getting along with Jennie increased as time went by, and finally Jennie ordered her to leave. For a time Gladys worked with some CIM missionaries, and later she acquired a position as a "foot inspector." Chinese law forbade foot binding, but it was a decree that was difficult to enforce. Chinese women who served as inspectors sometimes sympathized with the tradition and failed to adequately report infractions, and it would have been an indiscreet job for a man. So a foreign woman was the ideal choice. It was a job that suited Gladys well. It gave her opportunity to visit many homes, and as she traveled from village to village she was able to present the gospel to those she encountered. Her language

skills were feeble, but there was a body language of love that overcame her verbal deficiencies. "She had very few years of formal schooling," writes Alan Burgess, "but she had an intuitive gift for observation and evaluation."[20]

Gladys Aylward, missionary to China.

During these years of serving as an inspector and as an itinerant evangelist Gladys was little concerned about what went on beyond the mountain ranges. But significant changes were taking place in China that would have a major impact on her and on her work. Mao Tse Tung was beginning to build his revolutionary army, and Japan was amassing tens of thousands of troops on China's Manchurian border. War was looming on the horizon, and Gladys would soon be embroiled in the conflict.[21]

It was during the summer of 1937 that the once peaceful mountain villages of Shansi where Gladys lived suddenly became a war zone. Bombing raids were common, and whole villages were wiped out by the hated Japanese enemy. With the ever-present dangers, it would have been natural for a lone missionary to leave the war zone. Gladys had recently adopted Chinese citizenship, however, and she was determined to stay with her people who, faced with the casualties and other problems associated with combat, needed her more than ever.

In the spring of 1938 her own village of Yangcheng was bombed. "Nothing in her life before had prepared her for the sight which confronted her. The walls and gate were untouched, but the center of the town appeared completely pulverized. Dead and dying, wounded and bombshocked, lay everywhere." In the midst of the terror and confusion, Gladys took charge. She organized teams to attend the injured and children and to search for bodies under the rubble, and then she laid out plans for an escape route to safety. Her plan was effective. When the Japanese troops arrived a few days later they found the village deserted.[22]

As traumatic as the enemy invasion had been for Gladys, it was a time for her to demonstrate her strength of character. She realized that she was more capable of leadership activities than she had previously dreamed possible. Yet, at the same time, she realized how vulnerable she truly was. She was forced into leadership roles when she would have rather relinquished the decision-making and the responsibility to someone else. More than ever she longed for words of assurance and the strong arms of a husband to bolster her timid spirit. It was in light of this emotional backdrop that Linnan, a Chinese military officer, entered her life.[23]

Initially their relationship revolved around their mutual concern to resist the Japanese. Gladys eagerly cooperated with the Chinese military and enthusiastically agreed to Linnan's request that she function as a spy behind enemy lines. What began as simply a collaboration in a common cause, however, turned into a romance. It happened before she had time to fully think it through, and when she did, she struggled with the propriety of her emotions. "She was a missionary dedicated to God," writes Burgess, "but God had also made her a woman full of the natural tides and forces which stir womankind. If she was falling in love, she reasoned, then it was God who allowed it to happen."[24]

Marriage was something Gladys had always dreamed of. She had fantasized that her prince charming would one day walk through the gates of Yangcheng, and she would be ready for him. But he never came. And when Linnan entered her life, he was somehow not the image she had of her prince charming, but he was a man who could share some of the physical and emotional burdens of her war-ravaged life. Together they talked of marriage, and Gladys wrote home of her plans. "But the marriage never took place. In the devastated war-torn countryside nothing short of death seemed certain, and plans were made to be broken."[25]

For Gladys, involvement in the war effort was not a matter of choice. Her conscience would not have allowed her to turn her back on her people when they needed her most. And she was involved in far more than humanitarian endeavors. Her work as a spy was so significant that for a time there was a reward of one hundred dollars (a large sum in the 1930s in China) by the Japanese Army for her capture. She was described simply as "The Small Woman, known as Ai-weh-deh."[26]

The most terrifying wartime experience Gladys endured was her escape over the war-torn mountains with some one hundred children. Without families to care for them the children were being housed at a compound near the enemy lines. Their lives were in critical danger and, knowing that, Gladys reluctantly agreed to guide them and some other children to safety over the mountains and across the Yellow River to Sian, the capitol of the Shansi. Her greatest fear was that she might escalate the danger to the children because of the reward that was being offered for her. But in other respects she was ideal for the task. She was familiar with the terrain, and children responded well to her. "Her mind was in a turmoil nevertheless, and she could not bring herself to leave until an urgent message from God Himself, as she firmly believed, convinced her that she must go."[27]

"It was one thing to journey through the mountains alone," writes Alan Burgess,

quite another to take a hundred children. . . The first day had been troublesome enough, yet all the children were fresh, and she was crossing country she knew intimately. . . . Seven nights out . . . found them camped in the heart of a mountainous region unknown to her. . . . Everyone was filthy with dust and dirt. They had no food. Keeping a hundred children out of sight and earshot of enemy soldiers who were often in the region was the most strenuous aspect of the long journey, but incredibly, they arrived at their destination safely—except for Gladys, who was exhausted to the point of delirium.[28]

In 1943, three years after her harrowing trek and after the Japanese had retreated, Gladys was once again sharing the gospel in her simple way with the Chinese people. For her, it was hardly a cross-cultural ministry. She had become Chinese by citizenship and by identification. Indeed, so Chinese was she that when she reestablished herself in Chengtu after the war, she became employed by the local church as a Bible woman—a lowly position that had heretofore been filled only by nationals. For most missionaries accepting such a position might have been humiliating. It was fitting, however, that Gladys serve in this capacity. She was a humble woman, and she was not fully comfortable with the fame that was soon to befall her. Her greatest service had been rendered through clandestine wartime activities, and international exposure somehow seemed inappropriate.[29]

## Betty Olsen

Like Mabel Francis, Betty Olsen was a missionary with the Christian and Missionary Alliance who served faithfully in enemy territory. Her missionary career ended in the jungles of Vietnam, after having served only a short time. She was a registered nurse and a graduate of Nyack Missionary College, determined to make her life count for God in the war-torn countryside where her expertise was so desperately needed.

The sacrifice involved in missionary work carried no surprises for Betty. She had grown up in Africa with her missionary parents, and had known the pain of separation and the difficulty of adjusting to boarding school. She was rebellious and insecure as a teenager, and the death of her mother while she was in high school only multiplied her problems. Her difficulties continued throughout her years in college and nurses' training. Her dream was to marry and return to the mission field, but bitterness and self-pity plagued her. Knowing she would be turned down as a missionary candidate, she returned to Africa without mission support and worked with her father and stepmother until she created so many problems that she was asked to leave.[30]

It was while she was living in Chicago that Betty was able to turn her life around. She began to go for counseling with a church youth director who helped her develop principles to live by. That counselor was Bill Gothard, and many of the principles he developed with Betty he later incorporated in his seminar known as the Institute in Basic Youth Conflicts. After that, Betty was accepted by the Christian and Missionary Alliance and was appointed to serve as a nurse at the mission station at Banmethuot. It was there on January 30, 1968, that the Tet offensive began. The Viet Cong forces overran the mission station, killing five missionaries and a young child. Less fortunate than the dead were Betty and another missionary, Hank Blood. They were taken captive with Mike Benge, an American AID worker, and for months they endured indescribable torture on the steamy, insect-infested jungle trails.[31]

After five months of sheer agony Hank Blood died. Betty and Mike lingered between life and death. By the end of eight months they were almost walking corpses. "Their hair turned gray. They lost their body hair, their nails stopped growing. Their teeth were loose with bleeding gums"—all signs of malnutrition. Betty's legs were so swollen that she could hardly walk. She begged her captors to leave her behind, but the torture continued. Finally, she "became so weak that she couldn't get out of her hammock" and "she had to lie in her own defecation." She spent her thirty-third birthday writhing in pain in her filthy hammock, and two days later she was dead.[32]

Soon after her death, Mike was imprisoned in a POW camp in North Vietnam, where he remained until his release in 1973. It was only after his release that the story of Hank and Betty's grueling death march through the jungle was told to the outside world. In Betty, the once rebellious and bitter young woman, Mike had found "the most unselfish person he had ever known." His own life had been changed through the testimony of her Christ-like love. "She never showed any bitterness or resentment. To the end she loved the ones who mistreated her."[33]

## Chapter 18

# Developing New Ideas: Missiology and Mission Strategy

The image of the female missionary as a rugged pioneer in a remote jungle village or as a persevering individualist working among famine victims and refugees is a familiar one. Women have been on the front lines of missionary advance for more than a century, and their sacrificial achievements have been many. Ann Judson, Lottie Moon, Mary Slessor, Amy Carmichael, and Ida Scudder are only a few of the women who have won recognition and acclaim for their courageous missionary service. They and thousands of other women missionaries plunged into the demanding and often daring work of cross-cultural evangelism, eager for challenging opportunities that could not be found at home. Many of these women no doubt surprised themselves in their ability to supervise mission endeavors when men were not available. Maude Cary and three other single women missionaries were the only representatives of the Gospel Missionary Union left in Morocco during World War II. They kept the work going and conducted orientation when new missionaries arrived after the war. Indeed, missionary service has been one of the only vocations in which women have been more prominent in adverse situations than men. "The more difficult and dangerous the work," writes J. Herbert Kane, "the higher the ratio of women to men."[1]

Despite their noble contributions in field service, women have had very few opportunities to hold leadership positions or to develop mission strategy. Except in extraordinary situations they were not welcome in the male-dominated missiological think tanks. This was true even though they had proven their worth in the areas of mission leadership and strategy during the heyday of the Women's Missionary Movement in the late nineteenth and early twentieth centuries, when more than forty "female agencies" were founded. It was a time when women were more involved on the organizational and strategy level of foreign missions than they have ever been before or since. The Central Committee operated extensive educational and publishing programs that brought millions of women in touch with the world scene.[2]

This involvement in missiological thought and education was viewed as an essential part of the task of world evangelism, and developing effective field strategy was seen as equally paramount. Indeed, women were involved in this arena by necessity. They had no choice but to assume the customary responsibilities of mission-board secretaries and field directors. This trend, however, was short-lived. With the demise of the Women's Missionary Movement, prompted by numerous mergers of female mission societies with general mission boards, women quickly lost their positions of responsibility. As a result, women during most of the twentieth century have had very little input in the field of missiology—in setting goals, planning strategy, and developing new concepts for more effective world evangelism.

Although women in general have not been in leadership positions that encourage their efforts in developing mission strategy, many women have individually formulated new ideas that have contributed significantly to the missionary enterprise. The area of specialization that women have traditionally been excluded from is missionary aviation. Yet, it was largely through the innovative ideas of a woman pilot that this specialization developed. During World War II, after having served in the Air Force, Elizabeth Greene wrote an article for a Christian magazine presenting the need for missionary aviation. The article was spotted by a Navy pilot who contacted her, asking that she join an effort already underway to form a missionary aviation support service. That mission later became known as Mission Aviation Fellowship, and she served as one of the mission pilots in Mexico, Africa, and Irian Jaya.[3]

Although she had broken ground herself in the area of women's involvement in missionary aviation, she took a strong stand against the idea of other women entering the field. When asked if she would "encourage a girl to go into this sort of work," she replied, "MAF definitely frowns upon it, and so do I." Her reasons were that few women were mechanics, that heavy lifting was often required, and that women were less safe in remote areas than men. Her own greatest contribution, then, was not that she paved the way for women to follow her into this difficult field of mission specialization, but that she had offered new ideas and principles to this developing support ministry that would become an indispensible part of missionary work overseas.[4]

Missionary life style and effectiveness is an area on which Elizabeth Brewster and her husband, E. Thomas, have concentrated in recent years. They developed the LAMP (Language Acquisition Made Practical) program which has been viewed as highly creative by some and impractical by others. Their emphasis on bonding has been a particularly controversial issue, and here, though they write together, Elizabeth's perspective comes through loud and clear as she compares a missionary's bonding to nationals with a mother's bonding to an infant.

"We have a new little boy who was born into our home just a few months ago. In preparing for his natural childbirth at home we were introduced to the concept of bonding."[5]

This is not the way most missiological articles are introduced, but it is indicative of the creative concepts that emerge when women are permitted to participate in developing mission strategy. Bonding, from the Brewsters' perspective, involves adopting the native lifestyle by eating their food, sharing their housing, using their transportation, and otherwise making themselves as much a part of the culture as possible. It is certainly not a new concept, and many of the Brewsters' ideas are controversial, but it is a concept that has been enlarged through the ideas of a woman.

Most women who have contributed new concepts and ideas to mission strategy have not been professional missiologists. They simply developed their efforts on their own or with the help of others and went about the business of doing missionary work. There have been some significant exceptions, however, and Constance E. Padwick is an outstanding example.

### Constance Padwick

Constance Padwick was a first-rate missiologist who ministered in the Arab world for forty years, beginning in Egypt in 1916, and later serving in Palestine, Sudan, and Turkey. She was born in Sussex, England in 1886. As a young woman in the Anglican Church she was deeply interested in spiritual concerns, as is seen in her active involvement in the Student Christian Movement and her study of New Testament Greek. In 1910, the year of the great Edinburgh Missionary Conference, she traveled to Palestine—a journey that marked the beginning of her life-long concern for the Muslim world. During the following five years she worked in the home office of the Church Missionary Society, editing a children's magazine. Although her ambition was to serve abroad, the mission denied her request for health reasons. So determined was she, however, to be in the front lines of service that she left on her own for a short-term mission to Egypt with the Nile Mission Press. Her tenure with that mission ended, however, when the CMS agreed to sponsor her missionary career which extended over most of the following four decades.[6]

Padwick's specialized field of ministry was writing. She was a gifted writer and cross-cultural communicator. As a proficient Arabic linguist and a keen observer of Islamic society and religion she effectively ministered to Muslims through literature in a way that few other missionaries had been able to do. For many years she edited *Orient and Occident* a Christian magazine published in Cairo, and she "inspired and became the energetic mainspring of the Central Literature Committee for Muslims," which sought to coordinate the scattered mission efforts to provide Christian literature for Muslims.[7] This work was followed with deep interest by the great ecumenical missionary statesman William Paton, who viewed Padwick as one of the innovative leaders in mission literature.[8]

In Egypt, Padwick's involvement in literature work won the recognition of H. D. Hooper, the Africa secretary of the CMS, who wrote in 1938 of the "remarkable ventures in the field of literature which owe so much to the genius of Temple Gairdner and Constance Padwick." She held "the conviction that Christian literature . . . should be something more than a dispensable handmaid of the church and mission" and should be "integral to any Christian advance." She and her colleagues were critical of much of the existing literature to Muslims—literature that was often "filled with the spirit of disputation rather than of worship and love, and apt to hammer rather than to woo and win."[9]

Besides writing for Muslims, Padwick was heavily involved in presenting the mission to Muslims to the Western church, which she believed had too long ignored the Islamic world. She served as a consultant to Hendrik Kraemer in the writing of his widely acclaimed book *The Christian Message in a Non-Christian World*. He was an internationally-known Dutch theologian and missiologist, whose influence on twentieth-century missions was enormous, and her collaborative work was an important factor in his ministry.[10]

She was a prolific writer in her own right as well. Over the course of her lifetime she authored several full-length books as well as many scholarly journal articles, the last one published shortly before her death when she was eighty-one years old. The all-pervasive theme that runs through her writing is her belief that it is the solemn obligation of the Christian Church to share the message of salvation with the Muslim world. Her focus on Islam, however, was questioned by some, and she posed the same question herself: "Can it really be right, when in mass movement areas souls are pressing into the Kingdom, for whom we cannot find shepherds, can it be right in these circumstances to send men and women to an Islam that consistently rejects their message?"[11]

But her response was unequivocal:

The church through long centuries . . . showed not only the negative of neglect but the positive of hostility and retaliation. Therefore are we bounden (as members of that Church of Christ whose communion and solidarity is not limited to those contemporary with us on earth) to go, not in superiority but in penitent love to the Muslim, to make what loving reparation is allowed us to the heart of our forgiving Lord and to the unforgiving Muslim world. And this duty lies upon us, inescapable, whatever are the opportunities of joyful service elsewhere.[12]

Her recognition of the difficulty of Muslim evangelism more than anything else compelled Padwick to devote her efforts to developing sound mission strategy—though she was certainly not the first missiologist to focus on Islam. Centuries before her, Raymond Lull had developed an apologetic approach that he believed to be the most effective way to persuade Muslims of the merits of Christianity. Samuel Zwemer, the "Apostle to Islam," who went as a student volunteer to Arabia in 1890, also used an apologetic approach, while at the same time seeking to understand the Muslim mind.

At the urging of Zwemer and others, general conferences on missions to Muslims were initiated for the purpose of developing a more effective mission strategy. The second such conference, held in Lucknow in 1911, was attended by missionary delegates from around the world, including many women who actively participated in the sessions. One of the most impassioned addresses at that conference was delivered by Agnes De Selincourt, who challenged her female colleagues to strive for closer identification with the upper-class Muslim women:

> We need to give a larger place in our missionary plans to what has been well termed the Ministry of Friendship. It means infinite expenditure of time and sympathy and love to place ourselves alongside of these women, to enter into their lives, to share their aspirations in so far as these are rightful; it means willingness also to lay ourselves open to not a few snubs and repulses. In many ways it is harder than contact with the poorer classes, who often quickly and gratefully respond, and do not so speedily pull us up by their hot resentment the instant we show the cloven hoof of our fancied superiority and behave as if we had come to India to "work among them," rather than to love them and seek their friendship."[13]

So, Padwick was not unique in her approach to Islam. Like Zwemer and De Selincourt, she stressed the importance of love and understanding as underlying prerequisites to any kind of meaningful mission work to Muslims. Indeed, her strong conviction that the Church was "bounden . . . in penitent love to the Muslims" was at the very core of her philosophy and strategy of missionary work in the Islamic world. The missionary must reach out in love to his Islamic brothers and sisters, and this love is best demonstrated through an intimate understanding and even an appreciation for the Muslim faith.

Some of Padwick's missiological thought was radical for her day and would, indeed, be considered so in many circles today. But the revolutionary impact of her writing was softened significantly by the form in which it was presented. Much of her writing was in the form of biography, a form that gave her the freedom to select her subjects and the particular focus she wanted to take regarding the subject. In this way she was able to present new concepts for mission strategy that were more readily accepted than they might have been had they been presented in an article—particularly in an article written by a female missionary.

Her first major biography that related significantly to Muslim missions was *Henry Martyn: Confessor of the Faith*, first published in 1922. Her deep admiration of Martyn was understandable in the light of what might be termed a "feminine" missiology. She emphasized the importance of building bridges with Muslims through love. As was to be expected, there was strong opposition to his presence and to the work he was doing. At one point some of the most orthodox Muslims became so hostile that they demanded he defend his faith before their own noted scholars. Of this experience he wrote, "I am in the midst of enemies who argue against the truth with uncommon subtlety." Padwick was quick to point out, however, that it was not his apologetics that made the greatest impression on his Muslim associates. When the New Testament was completed and Martyn was preparing to return to England in 1812, "they could hardly let him go. They took him out to a garden and seated him on a bed of roses, and made him read them the Bible history for hours at a time. 'Their love seemed to increase,' he said, as the time of his departure drew near."[14]

Padwick's most widely recognized biographical work was *Temple Gairdner of Cairo*, published in 1929. Again, Padwick presented effective mission strategy through biography. Like Martyn, Gairdner identified closely with the Muslims. He was a skilled linguist and a gifted musician, and he combined those talents to reach out to Muslims as no other missionary had done before, among other things by studying Arab music and introducing classical music to his Muslim friends.

The last full-length biography Padwick wrote was *Call to Istanbul*, published in 1958, which featured the life and ministry of Lyman MacCallum, who began his ministry in Turkey with the American Bible Society in 1925. Like Gairdner, she knew Mac-Callum personally and had observed a mission strategy that she herself could soundly endorse. He was (as were the other subjects of her biographies) committed to breaking down barriers between Christians and Muslims, and it was that message more than any other that Padwick sought to convey to her readers. In the introduction she wrote, "The significance of Lyman MacCallum's life, and the reason why it should be recorded, lies in his behaviour. . . . He differed radically from most of the missionaries . . . in that he did not feel, and indeed was essentially *not*, a foreigner among the Turks." This

difference was obvious to Muslim Turks, as one of his friends testified: "I came to know one Christian who did away with the chasm which separated us from all Christians. He filled it in completely and made the path absolutely level. I have tested him for years. I came to believe that if there could be one such real Christian, there must be many more. I loved him and in his person I loved all Christians."[15]

Padwick's many other books and articles also emphasize the necessity of building bridges through love and understanding. The work that stands out above all others in demonstrating that philosophy behind her own mission strategy was *Muslim Devotions*. In this volume she presented a compilation of Islamic devotional writings that she hoped would help Western Christians more fully comprehend the deep personal faith of the Muslims they sought to win to Christ.

## B. V. Subbamma

One of the greatest cultural barriers to the gospel in modern history has been the caste system—a powerful institution in India that has frustrated the work of missionaries for centuries. Although significant legislative reform has reduced the influence of caste and abolished discriminatory laws against untouchables, much of India is still deeply enmeshed in the caste system. How to approach the caste system, therefore, continues to be a knotty issue. One of the most significant missiological studies to appear on the subject in recent years has come from the pen of B. V. Subbamma, a caste-Hindu whose own pilgrimage to Christianity was hindered by caste.

Subbamma was introduced to Christianity as a child while attending a Lutheran mission school. She initially resisted biblical teachings, believing Christianity to be a religion of the Harijans (outcasts). Eventually, however, after reading the Bible for herself, her life was transformed: "The name of Jesus became so precious to me that I could hardly believe it. . . . I was supremely happy, having the assurance that Jesus Christ had suffered for my sin and had forgiven me and blessed me with salvation." There was a major obstacle, however, that loomed before her: "The question of baptism disturbed me. I was definitely not prepared to leave my own Kamma people and join some other community. At the same time I longed to be baptized since I understood one had to be baptized if he wished to be a disciple of the Lord."[16]

After enduring considerable personal turmoil and opposition from her family, Subbamma was baptized and, according to missiologist Donald McGavran, "paid the tremendous price of complete identification with the existing Church made up of Harijan Christians."[17] In the years that followed she conducted women's work in India, and it was during that time that she began to explore alternative concepts of caste evangelism—particularly in Christian ashrams and house churches. Though she deplored the caste system, she realized that it was a cultural institution that could not be ignored in the propagation of the gospel. Her own experiences and interest in reaching caste Hindus prompted further study at the School of World Mission at Fuller Theological Seminary, and the capstone of her research there was *New Patterns for Discipling Hindus*, a thought-provoking book that cautions Christian missionaries against disrupting caste exclusiveness. Although her work certainly has not ended the debate on evangelistic strategy in reaching Hindus, it is a significant contribution to the field of missiology that has application far beyond a ministry to people in one particular religion.

In her work she not only deals with the caste system but with other aspects of cross-cultural evangelism as well. She speaks at length of the significance of women's work. Indeed, she defends the concentration on women's work in South India. According to her, "sociological study . . . indicates that religious change can best be brought about . . . through women. In South India society the mother-son relationship is the most crucial of all family relationships." How is this women's work being conducted?

> The Bible Women's work is vital to the mission of the Church. Two hundred and fifteen Bible women in the church comprise the main force of evangelistic workers. All doors are open to the women, but not to men workers. The strength of the Bible woman lies in the personal friendships she forms with Hindu women.[18]

### Joy Ridderhof

Women have not only been in the missiology "think-tanks," but they have also been involved in developing field strategy—especially in the area of mission specializations. One of those has been Joy Ridderhof who founded Gospel Recordings in 1941. As a single missionary to Honduras, she had seen success in her work but had left the field due to poor health. In her attic apartment in California, while recuperating from her illness, she conceived the idea of sending taped messages back to Honduras on inexpensive records to be played on gramophones. With the help of another missionary who was on furlough from Central America and of some local musicians, she was ready to produce her first record in Spanish that would appeal to the people she knew back in Honduras. When the production was completed, she sent her first shipment (less than two dozen records) off and waited.

The letters she received exceeded her highest hopes in their enthusiasm. She was almost sick with excitement. The record was wonderful! People had listened to it wide-eyed, wanted to hear it again and again, and not only the believers, either. Some who had been utterly indifferent or even strongly opposed were strangely moved by it.[19]

As successful as this first attempt was, the effort was flawed—at least in the eyes of Joy. The report from the field had concluded with the comment that the people listened to the records so much that they "could repeat them just as they had heard them—American accent and all." From that point on she determined that only those who were speaking in their native language should do the actual speaking or singing on the records. It was a momentous decision that would eventually lead her around the world to capture voices.[20]

So successful were her first efforts

that missionaries from other areas began requesting her services. Her first assignment involved a record for the Navajo Indians. It was after this that Ann Sherwood, an old friend, offered to assist her in the work. Little did they know that this partnership would last for many years and take them all over the globe. Their first trip outside the United States was to Mexico, where they recorded the language of the Mazahua Indians. They traveled there together in a station wagon that had been donated for the work—the first of many large donations that would carry the work of this mission through its infancy. While in Mexico, they recorded thirty-three languages, which they brought back to Los Angeles and made into records. Before returning, though, Joy fulfilled a promise to visit Honduras, where she was able to see the fruit of her labors. When they arrived back in Los Angeles they dedicated the new headquarters of Gospel Recordings—a building that had been refurbished by volunteers and was much more suited for this growing operation than Joy's attic bedroom had been.[21]

The next extended recording trip Joy and Ann made was to Alaska, where they visited Eskimo tribes and painstakingly made recordings of gospel messages and songs by using interpreters to correctly record the languages that had not yet been learned by missionaries. Here their journey took them by station wagon as far as they could go and then by train or steamer, and on to remote areas by light planes or fishing boats—recording once in a Russian cemetery and at other times in wigwams. It was while in Alaska that a missionary suggested the great need for such a ministry in the Philippines, where there were hundreds of languages and dialects in which the Bible had not yet been translated. It was that comment that prompted Joy to begin planning a trip to the Philippines.[22]

Joy Ridderhof, founder of Gospel Recordings.

Initially, Joy worked alone with Ann in her travels, but eventually other staff assistants joined the team. Her method was to locate bilingual tribespeople in remote areas where the gospel had never been preached, and to rehearse with that individual a short evangelistic message that could be put into the tribal tongue. This method was used over and over again as she and Joy trekked through the remote islands of the Philippines. One language they recorded was Palanan Negrito, which required the assistance of three individuals—a Filipino woman who knew English and the Ibanog language, an Ibanog man who understood, but could not speak, Palanan Negrito, and a Negrito man who understood the Ibanog language.

It took hours to get the whole message recorded. Each sentence was not only played back to the negrito himself, but everything he said was translated back to Joy and Ann, to ensure that he had understood correctly what he had been told. Later on, when Ann edited the recording, preparing the negrito's own language for a finished record, she had to make one hundred and fifty splices in it! But although she did not understand the negrito language, she knew what that record contained. It told of the Son of the Chief of Sky, who came to earth to die on a tree tied crosswise, to bear the punishment of the sins of all people on earth, to save them from the wicked village down below, place of fire. It told that whoever believed in Yesu, Son of Chief of Sky, would himself become a child of Chief of Sky, and when death came would enter immediately into the good village above, everything pretty and happy there. It told of the Holy Spirit (spirit shadow good belong Chief of Sky), Who would come to dwell in the heart of the one who believed in Yesu.[23]

In the eyes of many critics, Joy's efforts were superficial at best. They questioned the value of entering a tribe with no resident missionary and giving only a sketchy summary of the gospel. But in spite of the critics, the mail brought Joy testimonies of conversion in remote tribes all over the world and convinced her that the ministry was a valid one. Though she would not be viewed as a missiologist, Joy made a significant and lasting contribution to the missionary enterprise through a creative idea and through the dedication of her life to its development.

Chapter 19

# The Power of the Pen: Missionary Writing

One area of missions in which women have not taken a back seat is missionary writing. Many of the most insightful and honest books about the realities of missionary work have been written by women. Amy Carmichael is one of the best known. She captured the hearts of men and women for more than a generation with her books about life in India and Indian nationals. Mildred Cable and Francesca French opened the vast country of China to their readers. Helen Roseveare wrote of terror and triumph in Africa, and Eunice Pike of the struggles of translation work in Latin America.

Without the woman's perspective, missionary literature would be sorely deficient. The trials of family life and the inner spiritual struggles are often dealt with in greater depth by women, and women are often more open in admitting their own personal conflicts than men are. This is true in the writing of Elisabeth Elliot and Isobel Kuhn. Elisabeth confesses to weaknesses and temptations that are rarely dealt with in missionary literature, as does Isobel, who shares her struggle with doubts and pride and tells how she was initially denied full candidacy with the China Inland Mission. Though Elisabeth speaks to problems and concerns that relate particularly to single women and Isobel does the same for married women, their writings speak to everyone who has a heart for missions and posses a timeless quality that guarantees a place for them among the great Christian classics.

## Elisabeth Elliot

The most widely-publicized drama of modern missionary history might be virtually forgotten today were it not for the facile pen of one of the surviving widows. Operation Auca, which claimed the lives of five American missionaries, was related in detail in three publications authored or edited by Elisabeth Elliot, including the classic *Through Gates of Splendor*. Through this ministry of writing

*195*

she inspired and challenged tens of thousands of Christians to deepen their commitment and to carry on in their involvement in overseas missions, be it home support or on-site efforts. In addition to her ability to string words together in a very creative and masterful style, Elisabeth had a strong message to convey—a message that did not always depict a pretty picture of missions. This was true especially of her novel *No Graven Image* and her autobiographical account of her early years as a single missionary, *These Strange Ashes.*

*These Strange Ashes* is far more than a mere autobiography. It is a handbook for missionaries—single women in particular—who are considering ministry in remote tribal regions. The excitement and adventure of such work quickly dissipates in the pages of this volume, and the tangibility of loneliness and deprivation become a stark reality. The missionaries in the book, including Elisabeth herself, are real people who are struggling with the irritations of everyday life as well as the inner conflicts that arise when anything that would qualify as human success seems so elusive.

The main missionary characters in the book are Elisabeth and her partners, Dorothy, Doreen, and Barbara—all single women, who, except for Barbara, "badly wished to be married." They were dedicated in their commitment to reaching the Colorado Indians for Christ, but they were struggling with the pain of loneliness and their desire for marriage and family. Even Barbara, who had been engaged before she felt called to missionary service, was afraid she still loved her ex-fiance

and did "not dare to return to England" for fear she would be deterred from her first priority. For Doreen, the desire for marriage involved a relationship with an Ecuadorian. "She had gone through agonies of decision for several years but nothing was resolved. 'Mixed' marriages— racially or religiously mixed—were generally frowned upon by the missionary community." For Dorothy, the situation was even more controversial. She "never tried to hide her eagerness to get married. She, too, had had her interests in the past, and now an Ecuadorian divorcé appeared on the scene, professing conversion to Protestantism and asking her to marry him."[1]

Elisabeth's situation was somewhat different. She had known Jim Elliot from her college days at Wheaton, and they had corresponded since they had both come to South America as missionaries. "Each time a letter came I opened it with trembling hands. Might he by now have decided that life alone in the jungle was not what he wanted after all? Certainly it was not what I wanted."[2]

There were other problems and issues that plagued these women separated by miles of rugged jungle roads from the nearest reminders of modern civilization. Little things they had taken for granted suddenly became the very things they missed the most. "One of my recurring dreams was of going into a dimestore," wrote Elisabeth. "That became to me almost a dream of paradise—to be able to wander freely among the displays of vegetable parers and shining posts, dishclothes, notebooks, Scotch tape, nail files, the little ordinary things that made the difference between a civilized life and the life around us."[3]

There were other reminders of their distance from civilization. Drinking water and even milk had to be boiled before it could be consumed. Indeed, "the book said to dip everything, lettuce included, in boiling water for a few seconds. This could be counted on usually to kill amoeba and always to kill one's zest for salad." Meal preparation was a long ordeal that distracted from language study. But Elisabeth found herself looking for distractions. Breaking down an unwritten language was tedious work and self-discipline was a constant battle:

> None of us felt sorry for ourselves with having to cope with inconveniences. Inconveniences belonged to missionary life. The proportion of time, however, which was consumed with these temporal matters bothered me. When I was fiddling with the stove, I felt that I ought to be working on the language, the real work I had come for. But what perversity of my nature was it that made me put off the language work even when the dishes were being done by Edelina, the clothes were hung on the line, and the bread had been baked? I would hie myself over to the study and sharpen pencils. I would find that the desk was littered with scorched bugs from the lamp the night before and would have to set about a major cleaning operation. I would rearrange file cards and dash off a few letters. . . . The awful truth was that I really preferred housekeeping. I loved order and neatness and organization but did not like to concentrate. After an hour or two of sheer effort of will power to stick at the job, I was relieved when I had to go back to the house and check Edelina's progress with the lunch.[4]

She wrote to Jim that "the days drag by" and that she was "fed up with life" in the jungle. "I find that because nothing actually presses me to activity, I dawdle in quiet time, let my mind wander in prayer, and daydream when trying to study."[5]

The struggle with self-discipline often created doubts in her mind as to what the will of God actually was for her. But even darker doubts clouded her consciousness—especially when tragedies occurred that were beyond her control. When she and Barbara had sought so desperately to save Maruja (a Colorado Indian) and failed, she was distraught. "If God had spared Maruja's life," she reasoned, "The whole Quinones tribe might have been delivered from spiritual death. In my heart I could not escape the thought that it was God who had failed. Surely He knew how much was at stake. . . . To my inner cries and questionings no answer came. . . . There was nothing but darkness and silence."[6]

Later similar doubts resurfaced when Macario, her language informant, was murdered. She began to question her call to missions, and reflected on a previous experience when she had knelt down "asking for assurance that the call was God's voice and not a figment of my own mind." She struggled with her lack of accomplishment and the obstacles that confronted her and asked, "Had I come here, leaving so much behind, on a fool's errand?"[7]

Life was difficult for Elisabeth and her colleagues, physically and emotionally. And marriage, as it so often is, was seen as a solution to their problems. By the end of the book, "Dorothy was engaged, Doreen, too, had made up her mind to marry Abdon," and Elisabeth was preparing to leave to live nearer to Jim, whom she would soon marry. Barbara was hanging on, "making progress in the Colorado language."[8]

Although *No Graven Image* is a novel, it speaks with stark honesty about missionary life. The story is about Margaret Sparhawk, a missionary among the Quichua Indians in the mountains of Ecuador, who struggles with cross-cultural adjustments and experiences both success and failure in the process. The story might have been about just another single woman missionary risking her life to save lost souls, but it turned out to be more than that. It was a story that raised issues and sparked controversies. Indeed, some mission board leaders sought to keep the book out of book stores after its publication in 1966 and objected to their candidates reading it.

The book is engaging and offers the humorous side of missions as well as the tragic side. Her description of language learning is one that ought to be read by all missionaries who struggle to learn a language from scratch:

> *"Imatai?"* I said, pointing to the sheepskins. She mumbled the answer so that I did not hear. The children repeated it for me. Rosa was not enthralled by the game and was finding it difficult to entertain a visitor whose vocabulary was limited to a single interrogative. I tried a new tactic. I stood up and sat down, using the Spanish word for "I sit down." It was clear, from Rosa's expression, that she questioned my sanity. I laughed and tried it again. The children watched mystified and delighted, but offered no information. Rosa was at a loss. She said something to me which I did not understand. Several possibilities came to mind: "Are you crazy?" "What is the matter?" or "When are you leaving?" I thought it most likely that she was trying to tell me she did not understand. Well, enough of this, I decided, and resorted to drawing pictures in the ashes on the ground for the children. Still Rosa did not sit down but busied herself here and there doing nothing. Then she spoke sharply to one of the children and the child went outside, perhaps to get the cow, I thought, or fetch water. Their life must go on, and my intrusion was inhibiting the process. Rosa had done all she knew to make me welcome. Beyond that she was at a loss, and my presence confused her. I could not explain my mission and it would be a very long time before I would be able to. But this was a beginning. A visit to an Indian home, a bare beginning on the language—six or eight nouns and a question form plus the word for "yes." Well, some other day.[9]

Elisabeth's description of the missions scene was telling, but not necessarily the picture that missionaries wanted their supporters back home to see. After settling into her work, Margaret (who relates the story in first person) has some sober thoughts about the Quichuas: "Well, they aren't headhunters, I reflected with a slight trace of disappointment, for it was beginning to dawn on me that my position among these Indians was not really a very dramatic one. Where the need is not obvious, as it is . . . among wild aborigines, sacrifice to meet the need loses some of its nobility." This is an interesting observation in light of her own husband's death at the hands of the Aucas.[10]

Elliot's cynicism about the missionary community is not what could be described as subtle. She describes a mission council meeting that most missionaries could easily identify. "I noticed in the coffee hour something that has escaped me when I watched the men coming into the church before the meeting. There was a hail-fellow-well-met spirit among them here, but they seemed to see only one another; they acknowledged the presence of women, but without looking any of them straight in the eye." And, what of the women? "The women on their part—young, pregnant wives, single women with hope in their eyes, overweight older ones, attractive and unattractive—looked as though they had sacrificed much for the cause of Christ, and, stabbed with shame, I thought, Who am I to be their judge. God looks on the heart."[11]

The most controversial aspect of the book related to Margaret's effort to give medical help to Rosa's husband, who had injured his leg. Though she was not a nurse, she nevertheless gave basic medical treatment—in this case an injection of penicillin. Without her aid, Pedro would no doubt have recovered; with her aid, he died—perhaps from a reaction to the injection. "Was it the medicine? Would streptomycin have worked? No, no. You have to go back much farther than that. . . . A dozen accusations confronted me." In her despair she blamed God. "O ineffable, sardonic God who toys with our sacrifices and smashes to earth the humble, hopeful altars we have built for a place to put Your name! Do you mock me? Why did You let him die? Why did You let me kill him? O God! I came to bring him life—*Your* life—and I destroyed him in Your name."[12]

It is in that tone that the book ends. It is a book that speaks to reality—indeed, the very reality Elisabeth herself experienced when her husband was killed—but it was not the message missionaries or missionary leaders wanted to hear.

Elisabeth Elliott, wife of Auca martyr Jim Elliot and best-selling author.

The books that relate to Elisabeth's married life with Jim Elliot were actually written before her books that focus on women missionaries. In some ways they are not as analytical and critical of missions—perhaps because they were written earlier and in the aftermath of a tragedy that took the life of her husband. Indeed, some might suggest that *Through*

*Gates of Splendor* and *Shadow of the Almighty* were written in part to dispel the criticism that had surrounded the questionable methodology of Operation Auca and the tragedy that resulted. Although Jim Elliot is presented as a man who endured struggles in his spiritual life, he almost takes on the image of a super saint who is larger than life. In her later writings about herself and other women, no such picture is presented.

Elisabeth's personal response to the Auca tragedy stands out as truly heroic. She alone of the five widows made it her mission to return to Ecuador in an effort to reach the Aucas. With Valerie, her little daughter, and Rachel Saint, who had studied the Auca language and was the sister of Nate Saint who had piloted the plane for Operation Auca, she entered Auca territory after two Auca women came out and requested their presence. This led to the opening of the work, which took place without the secret plans that had accompanied Operation Auca a few years earlier. "There were no newsmen or photographers to record the breakthrough, for there was nothing to record except that two women were once again venturing into the jungle to preach the gospel—routine missionary work."[13]

In recent years, as Elisabeth herself has reflected back on Operation Auca and the aftermath, she has offered a more realistic appraisal. "For those who saw it as a great Christian martyr story," she wrote, "the outcome was beautifully predictable. All puzzles would be solved. God would vindicate Himself. Aucas would be converted, and we could all 'feel good' about our faith." But that is not what happened. "The truth is that not by any means did all subsequent events work out as hoped. There were negative effects of the missionaries' entrance into Auca territory. There were arguments and misunderstandings and a few really terrible things, along with the answers to prayer."[14]

## Isobel Kuhn

Another female missionary writer whose books have been widely circulated is Isobel Kuhn, who served for many years in Asia with the China Inland Mission. As with Elisabeth Elliot, much of her writing was prompted by misfortune. In 1954 she underwent surgery in Thailand for breast cancer, a disease she fought for more than two years before it took her life in the spring of 1957 at the age of fifty-five. Those years of fighting, however, were productive years. In 1956 alone, she completed three books and began writing another. Her writing of missionary books had begun years earlier, when she served in China, and continued when she was isolated in a shanty high in the mountains of northern Thailand while her husband, a mission superintendent, was away sometimes months at a time overseeing his regional work.[15]

In her book *By Searching* Isobel tells of the struggles of faith she encountered as a young woman and the obstacles she faced when she began focusing on a missionary vocation. Although she was reared in a Christian home and had a strong Christian heritage—her grandfather was an ordained Presbyterian minister and her father "an ardent lay preacher"—she grappled with doubts when she left home and enrolled in the University of British Columbia. When she confessed in her English class to believing the Bible, her professor had sneered, "Oh, you just believe that because your papa and your mamma told you so." As painful as his remark was, she soon realized that he was right. "I would not call myself an atheist," she wrote. "But I called myself an agnostic—I frankly did not know if there was a God or not."[16]

Although Isobel had been honest in admitting that her childhood faith was based on her parents' belief, not her own, she became acutely aware of the fact that even that faith— superficial though it was—was not so easily abandoned. She found no peace in her doubting; yet, outwardly she appeared to have a happy life. She was a socialite, so much so that her 1922 yearbook pictured her with the caption "And oh the tilt of her heels when she dances!" And she had made a name for herself as an actress in the University Players Club, but she was devoid of inner happiness and peace. Finally, during a time of stress following a breakup with her fiance, she realized her need for God. The onset of this turn-around came, paradoxically, through the very subject that had led her astray. Her English professor, a disciple of Matthew Arnold, had challenged her faith in God while at the same time introducing her to his hero, and it was while reading Matthew Arnold's essay on *The Study of Poetry* that she came across a quote from Dante: "In His will is our peace."

Now that sentence wrote itself across the dark of my bedroom. Dante believed in God. What if there were a God, after all? If so, I certainly had not been in His will. Maybe that was why I had no peace? An idea struck me. No one was watching to see if I were a fool or not. Sitting there on my bed's edge, I raised both hands heavenward. "God, if there be a God," I whispered, for I was not going to believe in what did not exist just to get a mental opiate, "if You will prove to me that You are, and if You will give me peace, I will give You my whole life. I'll do anything You ask me to do, go where You send me, obey You all my days." Then I climbed into bed and pulled the blankets over me.[17]

The end result of Isobel's bartering with God led to a recommitment of faith—a faith that was rooted in Bible study and prayer. Along with this faith came a concern for reaching out to others and a certainty that "His will" for her was foreign missions. Her pilgrimage through Moody Bible Institute was strewn with obstacles and answers to prayer, especially those that are so gratefully elucidated by impoverished Bible school students—answers involving money. As her schooling drew to an end she initiated the application process with the China Inland Mission. She was a good student and had not thought that her candidacy would come into question. Indeed, it was a shocking and humiliating ordeal, as she later confessed in *By Searching*, when she was told that one of the individuals who wrote a reference for her would not recommend her for missionary service: "The reason given was that you are proud, disobedient, and likely to be a trouble-maker."[18] Isobel was not unaware of her dominating personality and her condescending attitude toward those who were not as capable as she herself was, but she had prided herself in her good reputation among teachers and administrators and found the censure devastating.

On the basis of this negative reference, she was told that she would have a probationary period before final acceptance: "The Council decided to accept you conditionally.... The Vancouver Council will be watching to see if any of these characteristics show themselves. If you prove that you have conquered them, you will then meet with the Western council and be accepted fully." Although she had been asked "not to spread it around," she shared her disappointment with some of her closer friends. One of these friends responded less sympathetically than the others. "What surprised me most of all was your attitude in this matter," he wrote. "You sound bitter and resentful. Why, if anyone had said to me, 'Roy B., you are proud, disobedient, and a trouble-maker,' I would answer: 'Amen, brother!' And even then you haven't said the half of it! What good thing is there in any of us, anyway?"[19]

Isobel was finally accepted by the China Inland Mission and she sailed for China in 1928. In many ways she was a very different young woman than she had been two years earlier when she had been humiliated as a prospective candidate. In the interim she had served with a Christian organization, the Corner Club, and she had begun to realize her own limitations and inadequacies. Again, as with her doubt and humiliation, she candidly wrote of these experiences for the benefit of her readers:

I worried about my own failure at the Corner Club. I did not have the gift of evangelism. Young lives were constantly being cleansed, rededicated and built up in Him, but I did not see that. I looked just for souls to take the initial step of salvation. Pentecostal girls were urging me to seek the baptism of the Spirit. One of them was a gifted evangelist, a golden-haired, angel-faced girl, and I fell into the snare of comparing myself with others. Peggy had something I didn't. Was it really the speaking in tongues? Inwardly I fretted. But the Lord was carefully holding me.... I had never spoken in tongues, but I seemed to have had everything else they claimed to have experienced.... I always felt there was a peril in seeking just an *experience* from the Lord...[20]

After her first year of language study in China, Isobel married John Kuhn, whom she had known from Moody Bible Institute. Although they were both deeply committed Christians and had dedicated their lives to missionary work in China, they encountered attitude problems and personality clashes—routine marital adjustments. But if such marital strife is routine for missionaries, it is rarely attested to in autobiographical accounts. Isobel, however, was not one to cover the realities of missionary life with a veneer of super-sainthood, and she refused to pretend that her marriage with John was without discord. In a seventeen-chapter autobiographical sketch, *Vistas*, she openly confessed to many struggles in her marriage.[21]

She was four years his senior—he was in his early twenties when they became engaged—and she was perceptive enough to foresee potential conflict. Before she responded in the affirmative to his hand-written marriage proposal, she weighed her doubts: "There was no question in my mind as to what my answer was, yet as I spread that precious letter out before the Lord there was still a problem. John and I are of very opposite dispositions, and each likewise is rather strong minded." How these two strong-willed natures could coexist harmoniously was a mystery, and she humorously confessed her apprehensions: "Now Science has never discovered what happens when the Irresistible Force collides with the Immovable Object."[22]

One of the first collisions that occurred between Isobel and John revolved around their household help. John had brought into the marriage Yin-chang, a Chinese cook, who himself got married—making a foursome of two sets of newlyweds in one household. Though she had vowed she would be a good mistress, Isobel immediately clashed with them. In her eyes Yin-chang was lazy. His loyalty was to her husband, and and both he and his wife were moody in her presence and borrowed her things without asking permission. Finally the situation exploded when Isobel criticized Yin-chang's work to John in front of him. To her surprise, she later wrote in her *Vistas*, "John turned on me, siding with Yin-chang." That was too much for Isobel.

Hot with temper, I said nothing but put on my hat and coat and walked out of the house, down through the town and out onto the plain, angry resentment boiling within. I wasn't going to live in a house where a lazy servant was condoned and given preference over the wife! And so on. For hours I walked, blind as to direction, not caring what

happened to me, but just determined to get away from it all.[23]

When Isobel returned the situation was tense, but John conceded and told her that she could dismiss Yin-chang and his wife, which she promptly did the following day. The matter was not so easily settled, and when the Chinese pastor and church leaders came in a delegation to speak in Yin-chang's behalf, John initially left Isobel on her own to defend her actions. In the end, her decision stood—a decision she questioned when all the domestic duties suddenly fell on her shoulders before she was able to secure suitable help.[24] There were other incidents that prompted Isobel to walk out on John, but she always came back. There was no place to go in the remote mountain regions of China and Thailand.

Another area that created conflict in their marriage was the writing of prayer letters. For Isobel, a letter to supporters back home was a creative work of art, and her friends enjoyed forthright honesty and humor. In the early years of their marriage they wrote the letters together and signed them jointly, but eventually Isobel took over. But that did not solve their differences. "Letter-writing day with its small arguments, became to her what she called 'an exasperating trial.'" When she related a story, John questioned the accuracy of the details, and when she tried to quote a conversation, he argued with her recollections and scoffed that she should "say that this is your interpretation of the conversation." Isobel later expressed her gratitude for John's criticism of her writing because it had an impact on her ministry as an author. "God was preparing to use my pen in relating stories of His work in human hearts. I couldn't afford to let that pen grow careless as to facts. The blue pencil showed me that a Christian writer can't be too particular that every point be according to reality." John, too, had a change of heart. According to her biographer, "he gave her entire freedom as to what she wrote and how she wrote it."[25]

Why did Isobel write so openly about marriage conflict in her *Vistas?* She was convinced that the problems of her marriage were not unique, but that the solutions were. "Certainly without God's help," writes her biographer, "most marriages never would have endured the shattering experiences she and John shared." As to their marital conflicts, Isobel was philosophical. She was grateful that tensions over minor differences could be resolved "with a spirit of patience, forgiveness, and mutual recognition of each other's gifts." Near the end of her life she reflected on the state of marriage in society, even among Christians:

> I feel many modern marriages are wrecked on just such sharp shoals as this. A human weakness is pointed out. The correction is resented. Argument grows bitter. Young people . . . are not prepared to bear and forbear. They are not ready to forgive, not willing to endure. Divorce is too quickly seized upon as the way out. It is the worst way out! To pray God to awaken the other person, to be patient until He does so—this is God's way out. And it molds the two opposite natures into one invincible whole.[26]

For Isobel, writing was gratifying. "If I have something to say, writing is just fun; it is housework that makes the ass long-faced and weary!" Although she spent most of her adult life in remote villages, she was always in the company of books and spent much of her leisure time reading.[27]

While living among the Lisu people, Isobel was actively involved in mission work. Her writing was only a secondary involvement. Meeting the needs of the people came first, and one of those needs was biblical education. On her own initiative she established the Rainy Season Bible School—an institution that was geared to the lifestyle of the tribespeople and considered by some to be her "greatest contribution as a missionary for twenty years in China." She felt at home in this work. "I love to teach the Bible," she confessed. "Evangelism was never my gift, but the opening of the Scriptures feeds and blesses the teacher even more than it does the student."[28]

By 1950, violent guerrilla warfare among the communist and nationalist Chinese had erupted in the region to the point where Isobel realized she must leave her home. Saying goodbye to John was difficult, but it was a relief to escape safely with her young son and to return to America to be with her college-age daughter, Kathryn. It was while she was living in a comfortable little apartment in Wheaton, Illinois, that she received a letter from John, telling her that he had been assigned to make a tribal survey of North Thailand. He spoke of the great need for evangelism among the tribes there, and then he confessed his personal desire to meet that need: "We can use the Chinese language. . . . I always found someone who understood me. . . . The field is before us. The door is still open. The government is friendly. The tribes are approachable. The time may be short."[29] Isobel was numb. "Of course my heart fainted," she wrote. "But once I stopped contemplating the disagreeable things that might happen and turned single-eyed to the Lord, He counseled me. . . ."[30]

She accepted the Lord's counsel as directing her to cheerfully take up the challenge of ministry among the tribe peoples in Thailand. But it was a difficult course to follow. "At fifty years of age, must she go pioneering again, climb up rough trails, learn another tongue? Already she had worked on the Chinese and Lisu languages. Now must she study Thai, too?"[31]

The story of pioneering mission work in Thailand is told in Isobel's book *Assent to the Tribes.* Here she told not only of her own ministry with her husband but also inspiring stories of colleagues who braved the primitive conditions to labor among the aboriginal tribes. She also related fascinating accounts of the tribal people, describing them in a way that gave the reader a true reflection of their character. Unlike many missionary writers who sought to convey the primitiveness of the tribal people, she emphasized qualities that showed some of the positive aspects of the culture. This is seen in her description of the old man who was her first convert among the Lisu, where she had been working with a single woman while John was involved in overseeing the entire region:

He spoke five languages fluently—Lisu, Lahu, Akha, Thai, and Chinese. He was a good talker and chatted the Gospel to all who came to the house. As soon as he learned a point of doctrine, he would turn and teach it to the man nearest him. He also became very fond of us, greeting us with a wistful, "I was love-longing for you to come back." We have found the Lisu Christian to be a person of deep affections, although he does not show it on the surface. . . . He had a gruff manner, and when his pains hurt him and discouraged him with thoughts that he would never be well again, he could be really grumpy. Yet on visit after visit he would let loose occasionally some of those sweet little tender remarks which a Lisu uses only when his emotions have been deeply touched.[32]

It was not easy for this man to live a Christian life in Lisu society. He stood alone in his commitment to Christianity. Four other families had initially shown interest, but when the tribal leaders threatened them they turned their backs on him, and even his wife did not share his convictions. So, he "found himself on a lonely pathway." Because of this and his continuing health problems, there were reversals in his walk of faith. "He was tested severely. . . . When the rainy season returned and his joints ached again and gnarled up, he saw clearly that he had not been granted a permanent cure, and he started to smoke an occasional pipe of opium to numb the ache, and perhaps, to cheer himself up." At times his faith wavered, especially when he reflected on what he had given up to become a Christian. "A fellow gives up smoking and drinking and the heathen festivals," he lamented to Isobel, "and—well, there isn't any fun in being a Christian, is there?" When he died, his neighbors refused to bury him, and his frustrated survivors had to search for outsiders to carry out the task.[33]

Isobel's writing also included accounts of converts who turned completely against the faith they had once professed. This is a problem that missionaries frequently are forced to contend with, but it is not subject matter for a glowing prayer letter that only includes success stories. "Part of the heartache of all missionary work," wrote Isobel, "is the bright promising convert who turns out to be a mere puffball, crumbling like a macaroon under the least pressure."[34]

Isobel and John's work in Thailand was barely two years old when Isobel was diagnosed as having breast cancer. Surgery was performed on the field, but soon after that she was sent home for further treatment. The months that followed were some of the most difficult in her life. The treatment took a toll on her physically, and the departure of her daughter Kathryn to serve in the Orient with the CIM took its toll emotionally. The painful memories of sending her away to boarding school as a child resurfaced as she realized that "one thing was practically certain; this parting would be final." Isobel lived alone with her eleven-year-old son Danny, while Kathryn sailed to Singapore, where she would be greeted by her father, who had remained behind to continue the work.[35]

Alone while Danny was in school, Isobel realized her days of writing were numbered, and writing would be the one legacy she could leave behind that would reach the hearts of people long after she was gone. Yet, the last two years of her life were a constant struggle. Her health improved enough for her to accept speaking engagements, but the cloud of death always loomed in front of her. When she was informed that she would have to undergo more surgery—not to cure her, but only to prolong her life—she initially declined. She was distressed by the medical costs she was incurring for the Mission, and she did not want to hinder the pioneer work of her husband who had returned home to be with her. It was her writing ministry, however, that prompted her to change her mind. "The disease is growing rapidly," she wrote to a friend, "and I knew if I were to go on writing *after* Christmas something must be done to retard it. So I consented to the surgery."[36]

It was her writing more than anything else that buoyed her spirits during the last year of her life. She was confined to her bedroom, but she was nevertheless able to write, "I thoroughly enjoy each day." She wanted to complete all the writing she possibly could in those final months, but she was ready to die— except for one factor: "Danny would be my biggest reason for wanting to stay." Yet even here she was philosophical: "But having a mother in Heaven may help him spiritually."[37] Her death in 1957 was a painful ordeal for her husband and two children, but they were comforted by the fact that she would ever remain alive in her eight books and many articles.

## Chapter 20

# Double Duty: Marriage and Team Ministry

Effective husband-wife team ministry in overseas mission has been conducted by Protestants from the very beginning of their missionary endeavors. Roman Catholics had no such teams. They had single men and single women, but no married couples with children to model family life for new converts. Protestants, on the other hand, emphasized the importance of the family in the expansion of the gospel message around the globe, and mission leaders gave high praise to the missionary wife and her crucial role in the work.

The loneliness that is often associated with single women missionaries was also a problem for women working in a team ministry with their husbands—especially those who were involved in isolated pioneer situations. A picture of this seclusion was graphically painted by Walter Lowrie who in the 1850s visited a missionary couple who were working among the Chippewa Indians:

On reaching this station I was much impressed with the spirit of self-denial needed to sustain the missionaries in these solitary and distant stations. On the border of a scattered Indian village, in the midst of a dense forest, mostly of beech and sugar trees, is a plain frame house, a school house, and a small enclosure for a garden. The whole opening, less than two acres, seems to be cut out of the solid wood, so dense is the forest. This is the residence of a missionary and his wife. Their nearest white neighbors are at the station of Little Traverse on the south, eighteen miles distant, and Mackinac on the north, forty-five miles distant. In the winter there is scarcely any communication, even with the nearest points. Surely the people of God ought not to forget in their prayers, these laborers in the wilderness, nor consider it a burden to sustain them in their work of love.[1]

One of the most enduring husband-wife teams of the early generations of modern missions was that of Robert and Mary Moffat, who served together in Southern Africa for a half century. Their team ministry stood in stark contrast to the ministry of their son-in-law, David Livingstone, who left his wife, Mary, and their daughter behind while he conducted his missionary endeavors.

Effective team ministry required that the husband and wife share the mission work in a true partnership. This did not mean that they were always working side by side. Indeed, sometimes the strength of their partnership was demonstrated in their times of separation, when the husband fulfilled one aspect of the ministry and the wife another. In many instances, what promised to be an effective partnership broke down because of lack of confidence on the husband's part or inability to cope with the situation on the part of the wife. Nevertheless, it has been through husband-wife team ministry that much of the work of foreign missions has been achieved.

### Ruth and Roy Shaffer

A noteworthy husband-wife team ministry to Africa in the twentieth century was that of Ruth and Roy Shaffer, who gave their lives to work with one of the most unreceptive tribes in East Africa—the Maasai. They began their ministry with the Africa Inland Mission in 1923, after graduating from Moody Bible Institute, and for thirty-five years they made their home at Siyabei, a gruelling three-day walk across the Rift Valley from the mission base at Kijabe. The work at Siyabei had begun five years earlier, and Roy and Ruth were to replace the resident missionary couple when they left for their furlough. Language study—seven hours a day—began immediately after they arrived, but it was at Maasai prayer meetings that Ruth picked up words and phrases most readily. After six months they took the required language exam. "It wasn't quite as hard as I had expected," wrote Ruth. "My grade was 92. Roy's was 86. Yet I still feel as though I knew nothing."[2]

Six months later, Ruth and Roy were on their own at Siyabei with their two small children, and they were quickly initiated into Maasai life. One of the Maasai church leaders was accused of adultery—an all-to-common problem in the Siyabei church. It was a Maasai custom for a widow or an abandoned wife to go to another man in the tribe and ask him to give her a child. "To them, adultery meant little or nothing. Far worse was the stigma of barrenness." So distraught were these women that they would often take a "long safari on foot from kraal to kraal, singing and dancing and begging food, cents, a goat, meat, or anything to give to the medicine man or witch doctor who claimed to be able to cause them to conceive." Dealing with these problems as well as other problems, such as female circumcision, became a joint effort for Ruth and Roy. They faced questions of their own, however, when Annie Grover, a single nurse, came to live with them. Although she was fifty and Ruth and Roy were still in their twenties, many Maasai "couldn't understand a man's having only one wife and were sure that, according to their custom, the oldest one . . . was Roy's first wife" and Ruth "was his second."[3]

Within a year after ministry with the Maasai had begun, Ruth and Roy

Ruth and Roy Shaffer and children, on safari with the Maasai. (Courtesy of Ruth T. Shaffer.)

began doing itinerant evangelism among the outlying villages. It would have been much simpler if Roy had gone by himself, but the Shaffers were a team, and it was important that they go together to reach both men and women and to struggle through language barriers together. Their mode of operation was to leave early in the morning, on foot, and to arrive by evening in time to pitch their tent near the kraal and then to introduce themselves and begin their ministry right away. "We held the meeting right inside the kraal, in the midst of the cattle and sheep by the light of our Coleman lamp," wrote Ruth of their first such endeavor. "We even took the portable Baby Estey Organ to stimulate the singing. . . . About half of the eighty people living in the kraal left their huts and came

out to look and to listen attentively to the Words of God." A roaring lion kept them awake much of the night, but early in the morning they were back in the kraal for another service and a medical clinic that Annie Grover conducted. Their trip was a success, and they were invited back.[4]

Ruth's ministry was specifically focussed on the Maasai women, but without a team ministry with her husband it would have been very difficult to penetrate the barrier of the Maasai culture. They quickly learned that "among the Maasai a woman was rated below a cow in real value to her husband. She seemed never to live in any state other than utter subjection to men, always seen but never heard." The condition of the young girls was even worse than that of the women. From the age of six until puberty they were sent to live in a *manyatta*, "a free love kraal" set aside for the young warriors.[5]

One such girl was eight-year-old Dora, who was brought to Ruth's girls' school by her widowed mother in hopes that she could escape the abuse and degradation of the *manyatta*, but when the young warriors discovered her missing from the kraal they came after her. "Dora was trembling from head to foot," wrote Ruth, "for she knew they had come to take her away to their *manyatta*. . . .
The warriors lied and said her mother had sent them to bring her home. I grasped her right arm and a warrior grasped her left. . . ." It was Roy's intervention that saved Dora. Most girls were not that fortunate. "For many more years to come, it would be only the lucky few mission school girls who would escape spending their childhood in a warrior *manyatta*."[6]

If life was deplorable for young girls prior to puberty, it was hardly any better during their initiation rites and afterward. Indeed, the utter subjection of women by the Maasai tribesmen was graphically illustrated by the appalling rituals young girls were forced to endure. "When the girl reaches puberty, she is taken back home to her parents, who arrange for her to join a group of four or more girls who are to be circumcised, in many cases against their will." Ruth vividly recalled the ceremonies she observed in the 1920s at Siyabei. Early in the morning, "the girls were led down the hill to the icy cold river, in which they sat all morning until they were numb. They were then rushed back to the hut where screaming women carried on a frenzied ritual to

build up the girls' courage, but actually it was very frightening." What followed was literally torture.

The clinical term for female circumcision is "clitoridectomy." The excision of the clitoris was done by an old *Engoiboni* (female *Oloiboni*) in a dark hut. Fresh, green cow manure was used to curb bleeding. . . . Others used fat and ashes. . . . Maasai female circumcision involves not only clitoridectomy but in addition, parts of the labia minora are cut off, which has a profoundly damaging effect on fertility. It leaves a gaping vulva into which germs pass much more readily to produce inflammatory pelvic diseases. . . .

During many days of healing, the newly circumcised girls were kept in a separate group, bedecked with beads all over their faces, necks and arms. Vivid designs were painted on their faces with white lava dirt, black soot or with red ochre which was evidence that they had completed this traditional rite. It is proof that they have been able to withstand extreme pain honorably, and have earned the status of women. They were herded like sheep, kept in motion all day long, crawling about on hands and knees. They were not allowed to sit down and they just couldn't stand up yet.[7]

After the scarring had healed to the point where the girl could resume normal activities, she was sold in marriage to a man (often much older than she) and sent to live in his kraal. She was then expected to tend cattle and have babies—the latter being a sign of her worth, though her ability to reproduce had been severely curtailed by her circumcision which "causes so much scar tissue that few Maasai babies can survive birth alive and mothers often die in childbirth as well."[8]

The team effort that Ruth and Roy brought to their ministry helped in dealing with issues like female circumcision. Unless the men could be persuaded that these traditions were harmful and ought to cease, there was little chance the practice would stop. Through their efforts and those of other missionaries, the tradition gradually began to diminish.

There were other customs of the Maasai that were less harmful, but that were no less difficult for Ruth to adjust to. Indeed, she was grateful that Roy had a stronger stomach than she did so that at least he could show proper appreciation for their hospitality. "Roy always did the right thing in accepting all gifts of milk offered to him. I was a coward and would say, 'No, thanks, I'm not hungry'; very poor taste, indeed, but I just couldn't overlook the Maasai method of washing gourds." That method invoked catching calves' urine in the gourd and thoroughly rinsing it before scrubbing it with a cow tail brush. Then fresh milk was stored in the gourd until it soured and was ready to drink—or on special occasions mixed with blood.[9]

Despite these customs, Ruth and Roy developed a powerful bond of love with the Maasai. They felt at home with them and came to appreciate many of their customs and traditions. Apart from bringing them the gospel, perhaps their most enduring contribution to them was their modeling of Christian marriage and family life. One of their first and most faithful converts was Sitoya, who "never wavered in front of the medicine men" and who "refused all the liquors offered him." He married Noolmusheni, one of the mission school girls, who was beaten almost to the point of death before she submitted to circumcision. Despite her condition she bore ten children, which they regarded as a sign of God's blessing on their marriage. She "was a staunch leader of the women at church," and he "was an excellent speaker each time he gave the message at church on Sunday." So appreciated was his testimony and service that he was officially ordained at the age of eighty.[10] When the Shaffers finally retired they left behind Maasai Christians—husband and wife teams to carry on the ministry. Other missionaries would continue to come, but in many respects their work was complete.

### Lillian and Jim Dickson

Some of the most effective team ministries involved couples who worked so closely together that they could take each other's place on a moment's notice. This was true of Lillian and Jim Dickson, who were pioneer missionaries among the tribal people of Taiwan. They came to Formosa in 1927, soon after they were married. Lillian herself was not a missionary—at least not in the eyes of the Board of Foreign Missions of the Canadian Presbyterian Church, which did not commission wives for missionary service. They were expected to support their husbands' work and work with women, but they were not acknowledged as actual missionaries themselves. Lillian did not allow that stipulation to restrict her ministry, however, nor did her husband. He recognized Lillian's capabilities when he married her, and he knew that their ministry would be impeded unless she served as a full partner.

It was through the ministry of a native woman that the work among the tribal peoples was initiated. "One day," wrote Lillian, "my husband came back from the far East Coast and about twenty feet behind him trailed a barbaric-looking woman. She had heavy tattooing across her whole face—a wide band from ear to ear which gave her a fierce expression." She was the first believer in the head-hunting Tyal tribe, and when Jim informed Lillian that he had brought her to be enrolled in the Bible School, she scoffed at the idea, insisting the woman was too old. "But he was right and I was wrong," Lillian confessed, "for this was Chi-oang, who later was to start an underground movement of Christianity among the people of the hills and lead a thousand souls to Christ."[11]

Chi-oang's ministry had an amazing effect that was later referred to as "The Pentecost of the Hills." Lillian described the impact this had on their lives and ministry:

Up the wild mountain regions where "foreigners" had not been allowed to go during the time Japan ruled Formosa, now the missionary went, filled with overwhelming gratitude and wonder at what God had wrought. He found whole villages converted, all the people Christians and often a little church built in the middle of the village as their place to worship God. He found more than a dozen such churches in the mountains. Always he would ask the people there, "Who brought you the news of the Gospel?"

Often they would say, "Chi-oang came bringing us the story of the one true God and the Saviour whom He sent." . . .

In 1946, right after the end of the war, there were four thousand believers among the Tyals. They came down the mountains by hundreds, knocking at the doors of the little Formosan Chinese churches scattered along the foot of the mountains, asking to be prepared for baptism.[12]

Although Lillian and Jim had not come to Taiwan to work with the tribal people, they could not refuse the pleas of the people to come and teach them the Word of God. It was very difficult work that required stamina and physical endurance. They had to cross raging mountain torrents on precarious rickety bridges that could give way at any moment, and there was danger from unconverted tribesmen who resented their intrusion. But there were also times of humor. On one occasion, after days of arduous travel, Lillian was offered a bath. Water was heated and then, to her amusement, she was led to a pigpen, where she bathed in an iron kettle used for butchering. It was the only place where the family could insure her privacy.[13]

Because of heavy responsibilities as the principal of the Theological Seminary of the Formosan Chinese Church, Jim was unable to adequately supervise and disciple the tribal churches. That obligation, therefore, fell largely on Lillian. On one occasion, at her husband's request, she was away for four months, during which time she visited seventy churches, accompanied by a Formosan pastor. Such excursions among the mountain tribal people became the norm for Lillian as Jim worked with the Chinese on the plains.[14]

Lillian Dickson (on left), missionary to Taiwan, with family.

In addition to her work of overseeing the churches and Bible teaching, Lillian became deeply involved in humanitarian services among the impoverished mountain people. Because she was not considered a missionary—only a missionary wife—by the Canadian Presbyterians, she was unable to raise funds through that mission, so she formed her own relief organization, Mustard Seed, Inc. Through this channel, with the help of World Vision and con-

cerned individuals, she distributed food and clothing and established a large medical clinic that housed more than eighty beds for in-patients and served some seven thousand out-patients each month.[15]

Despite her selfless service, though, there was criticism—especially from those who felt she should have limited her ministry to evangelistic work.

I knew people at home thought that we tried to do too much. But if you were there how would you stop, and where would you stop? If you walked into a mountain village with Christ and found more than eighty per cent of the people sick with tuberculosis, the bright-eyed children playing around all in danger, would you walk out again saying "too bad?"[16]

Although Jim's ministry was largely with the Chinese, he became involved in Lillian's relief work. At times he took the responsibility of distributing needed supplies to outlying churches, and on one occasion, while traveling to a small island, he was feared lost at sea. Finally, after days stretched into weeks, Lillian received word through the weather bureau that he was alive and would be returning home the following week. It was a difficult time for her, but an inevitable part of their team ministry. "While I admired him for going on, not sparing himself in the service of the Lord," she wrote, "the human part of me longed for him to be safe at home, his mission accomplished."[17]

For Lillian and Jim, team ministry usually meant separate activities. To double their effectiveness, they conducted their meetings and directed their supervisory work individually

213

with the help of nationals. Lillian's schedule was busy. On Sundays when she was not traveling in the mountains she left early on her "round of Sunday services, the Church of the Lepers, the Boys' Home, the Children's Homes, the Church of the Blind and an orphanage."[18]

Through her self-sacrificing service Lillian's humanitarian and teaching ministry grew, and reports of her work rapidly circulated among missions enthusiasts back home. Yet, she was surprised when she received a phone message inviting her to fly to the States and appear on a television program honoring Bob Pierce, the president of World Vision. It meant leaving Jim and stepping aside from her busy weekly schedule, but Jim was convinced that such publicity would be to the benefit of the tribal people, and he urged her to go. It was a crucial time in their ministry. They were overseeing some two hundred and fifty churches in which poverty and health problems were on the increase. Because of government policy and a massive influx of mainland Chinese the standard of living for the tribes people had severely declined, and Lillian accepted the opportunity of presenting their needs as an answer to prayer.[19]

Through television and later through writing opportunities Lillian told the story of her team ministry with her husband, but the focus of her message was on the aboriginal tribes people. The title of her book captured her emphasis—These My People.

## Pat and Stan Dale

An effective husband-wife team is generally characterized by two people who respect each other's gifts and abilities and who yield to each others needs. Domineering, demanding individuals do not make good team members, and yet many missionary women have found themselves isolated in a remote corner of the world in a ministry partnership with a man with whom it was difficult to co-exist, let alone work effectively. For some missionary families that problem—whether its cause lay with the husband or the wife—has resulted in returning to the homeland and resigning from the mission. For others it simply meant learning to live with the problem and going on in team ministry despite the handicap. This was the situation with Pat Dale, who served with her husband in a remote tribe in Irian Jaya.

When Pat McCormack married Stanley Dale in 1949, she had just completed nurses' training and he had just been dismissed from active service as a missionary with Unevangelized Fields Mission. The reasons given for his termination included "marked individuality, bombastic attitude toward leadership and toward nationals." His personality problems were well known, but he was several years her senior and she looked up to him and admired his strong will. Less than a year after they were married, right after the death of their one-month-old son, Stan left for New Guinea to begin work with another mission organization, Christian Missions to Many Lands (CMML), while Pat remained in Australia with his mother. In less than two months he sent for her, and together they worked with the Wapi tribe. They served there together for four years, until Stan was again dismissed. The reason given was that his colleagues objected to his manner of "disciplining the natives," but others put it more bluntly that he "simply never learned to control his temper."[20]

Despite his record as a missionary, Stan applied again for foreign service and was accepted by the Regions Beyond Missionary Union (RBMU), and fourteen months later, in 1960, was once again stationed in a remote tribe with Pat and their four young children. A year later, Stan was given permission to work in an entirely unevangelized area.[21]

During their first six months of work in this new region, Bruno, a single male missionary, worked with Stan, and Pat remained at the mission base with the children. As was true in his previous association with other missionaries, Stan did not get along with Bruno, and he suggested that Bruno seek another assignment. For Pat, there was no such option. She was married to him, and she was relegated to a life alone in the tropical jungles with this most difficult and erratic man. After the annual field conference she and the children joined Stan in his remote mission outpost in Irian Jaya. She shuddered when she emerged from the aircraft that was surrounded by "naked Yali men, cold and sinister in their black cosmetic," and "her heart sank further upon seeing the 'house,' a grass-roofed, dirt-floored hut, far too tiny for a family."[22]

It was obvious that six people could not live in the tiny hut, so Stan and Bruno, who once again joined the work, began building a perma-

nent residence. Yet, as Don Richardson relates, it was a difficult time for Pat:

Many times during those harrowing two months in the little hut she wept silently in the darkness when everyone else was asleep. She wept with loneliness for family and friends in Tasmania, with concern for her children and their education in this savage, heathen environment; with the dreadful feeling that many Yali did not want them there and might eventually turn against them; and with dismay over the many inconveniences, the problems in cooking, washing and bathing.[23]

Unlike many women who would have buckled under the strain of such difficult circumstances with such a difficult man, Pat accepted her role and became a full partner in the ministry. Among the Yali, women had no role in religious rituals. It was a man's world, and the women simply accepted their fate. Challenging this custom was a top priority with Stan, though it was one more factor that separated him from the very men he sought to reach with the gospel. Reaching the women was high on his agenda, and it quickly became Pat's special concern. It was not an easy assignment. The Yali women, unlike typical tribal women, did not acknowledge Pat when she arrived, and they maintained their distance for many months.[24]

In 1963, more than a year after her husband had first settled among the Yali, Pat welcomed her first female visitor. After that first visit more came, and a month later she conducted a meeting for women, at which time forty of them came—"the first ever women's meeting in the Heluk Valley." It was a radical development, considering the sex-role customs of the Valley, but the women were excited about the change. They honored Pat with the title *nisinga* (our mother), and admired her free lifestyle—the fact that she could smile and be happy, that she lived in the same house with her husband, that she educated her own children, even her sons, and that she could talk about sacred matters without being punished—all of which were unknown to Yali women. Pat's meetings with the women led to further innovations. "Yali women and girls began attending the preaching services held almost daily by Stan. They sat apart from the male listeners with their eyes to the ground, but listening all the same."[25]

Pat's work might have progressed well had it not been for her husband's impatience in dealing with the tribespeople. He was intolerant and had on more than one occasion been involved in physical scuffles with them. By 1964, she was desperately in need of a furlough, and Stan reluctantly agreed to return to Australia with her. He may have feared that it would be difficult to persuade her to return. It was. "She sensed with foreboding that martyrdom awaited at least her husband if he returned to the Yali people. And her five growing children desperately needed the educational benefits available in Australia."[26]

Stan's wishes prevailed, and the family returned the following year to be greeted by the missionary couple who had lived in their vacant home and who had graciously finished the interior and "beautifully landscaped" the exterior "with rock retaining walls and profuse flower beds." It was their way of showing their love for Pat. Stan, however, was not pleased. It was a show of luxury that missionaries had no right to enjoy. "He dismantled the walls and used the hundreds of rocks they contained to improve the airstrip still further." For Pat, it was only a small sacrifice in comparison to what she had already given up, but it was a gift rudely taken from her that might have brought her an element of joy in that otherwise hostile environment.[27]

Almost immediately upon their return Stan made the decision that all professing Christians should burn their fetishes in order to make a complete break with their pagan practices. He was well aware that this action would probably lead to a violent attack by the non-Christians of the tribe, but he was determined to carry out his plan. The violence that ensued almost ended Stan's ministry entirely. In June of 1966, he was critically wounded and two of the Yali Christians were killed. He was flown to a mission hospital where he miraculously recovered, and by late August he and the family were back at the mission post preparing believers for baptism. Many were baptized, but Stan was determined to defy those Yali who had wounded him, and he made plans with another missionary to travel in an area that he was warned would be unsafe. It was indeed unsafe, and the two missionaries were killed.[28]

Amid her grief, Pat turned to the other widow and said, "I hope you won't blame me for Phil's death." She was Stan's wife. She had married him in spite of his serious character flaws. She had stood beside him in ministry when she would have rather returned home. And she felt responsible for his actions even now that he was dead. With his death her missionary service ended. The partnership in team ministry had been dissolved.

*Chapter 21*

# Heartbreaking Separations: Juggling Motherhood and Ministry

Like their nineteenth-century predecessors, missionary women of the twentieth century struggled with the difficulties of rearing children in foreign lands. Frequent deaths were no longer dreaded as an inevitable aspect of going abroad, but long separations from school-age youngsters brought anguish to the mother's heart and doubts about her call to overseas missions. The children struggled as well. Ida Scudder had to be torn out of her mother's arms when she was left in Chicago with relatives, and Paul Freed, who later became founder of Trans World Radio, recalled how he became so homesick as a youngster that he ran away from the missionary children's school and took a train home to be with his parents. It was the mothers, though, who usually suffered the most pain when children were sent away to school.

Statistics indicate that the children generally adjusted well to missionary children's boarding schools. But the mothers often agonized over the prolonged separations, and in many cases their ministry was hampered or redirected as a result. This was certainly true in the case of Isobel Kuhn. Her daughter Kathryn followed in her parents' footsteps and joined the China Inland Mission, despite the extended separations from her parents which she endured as a child. But for Isobel the gnawing pain was sometimes almost unbearable. She was fully aware of the issues involved: "How can the child of missionaries, especially pioneer missionaries working on a far and primitive field, get an education?" she questioned. "This is the most ticklish of all missionary problems, and feelings run deep and warm on the subject." Her own feelings were mixed. She did not want to send her daughter away, but neither did she want to keep her at home. "To keep a child alone among adults, especially one of Kathy's gregarious disposition, was a positive cruelty. The way she would simply tremble with delight at the idea of playmates used to stab my heart."[1]

When the time came to actually carry out the decision to send her six-year-old child to boarding school, the real test of commitment had to be faced. "I went down to our cabin to get Kathy ready," she later wrote.

She was asleep in the top bunk, her pretty curly lashes dark against the soft pink cheeks. As I stood and gazed at her the thought came, "You will never again have the joy of caring for her, watching her grow and develop." I was pierced to the depths. . . . I was in torture. Never can I forget the agony of those hours. . . .[2]

The pain Isobel felt is not uniquely a female emotion, but mothers generally have acknowledged the anguish more than have fathers. Isobel's husband sympathized with her grief, but he apparently did not feel it to the same extent that she did. "John's kindness and patience," she wrote, "is a memory for which I can never cease to bless God. For the twenty-four hours after Kathryn left and before our own ship was due to leave, he walked the streets with me. . . . He just stayed with me until I was so physically exhausted I could lie down and drop into oblivion." The agony of separation was further compounded when the Kuhns received word that their daughter and the other children in the boarding school had been taken captive by the Japanese. They were separated for six years—sometimes going for months without even contact through correspondence.[3]

Some fathers showed little sympathy for the anguish their wives and children endured at times of separation. This was apparently true of Alexander Duff, a nineteenth-century missionary to India. His son later reflected on the ordeal with a less than favorable review of this father's conduct:

I . . . well remember how my mother's and my own heart were wellnigh breaking, and how at the London Bridge my father possessed himself of the morning Times, and left us to cry our eyes out in mutual sorrow. . . . And so we parted . . . a sadder parting as between mother and son there never was. The father buried in his Times . . . parted from the son without any regret on the latter's part.[4]

For those mothers who did seek to educate their own children, the burden of domestic cares sometimes became almost overwhelming. In 1890 Jennie Campbell, a missionary to China, wrote of this problem: "My time is so much taken up in my home cares and in teaching children's lessons, that I do a very small amount of real missionary work. I find more and more what a poor sinful Christian I am. I do long to grow more like the Savior, and have him in my life." Some months later she confessed that her "spiritual life seems just as dead as possible and yet be called life."[5]

## Evelyn Brand

The anguish of being separated from little ones was not a factor Evelyn Brand considered when she sailed for India in 1911, already past the age of thirty and still single. Yet there may have been more than an idle hope that she would marry and have children. She had sensed the missionary call to India while listening to a powerful missionary challenge by a handsome young man who was on his way back to India with the hopes of pioneering a ministry among the hill people of the South. Evelyn was too shy to make his acquaintance at that time, but after she arrived in India, she gratefully accepted any invitations that brought them together. She was devastated, however, on hearing that he was engaged to a young woman in England to whom he had sent a silk wedding dress. She "fled to her room. . . Oh, again she had played the fool! . . . She had let herself fall hopelessly in love with Jesse Brand, and he belonged to another."[6]

Evelyn's hopes for romance with Jesse were revived when they were separated and he began writing to her. Rumor that the young woman back in England was too frail for missionary work also came as good news. Their friendship deepened, and in 1913 they were married and Evelyn joined him in the house that he had prepared for her among the impoverished hill people. Less than a year later their first child was born. Almost immediately Baby Paul "accomplished what months of words and deeds had failed to do. At last the hill women accepted her as one of themselves. She had delivered a man-child, a mark of divine favour. Their common motherhood surmounted differences of dress, culture, colour."[7]

Two years later Connie was born. The family was now complete, except for the four native children, unwanted by their parents, who would be taken into the home and the many other children who would be cared for in boarding schools. But Paul and Connie were her own flesh and blood, and from the time of Connie's

birth, Evelyn began to dread the day that she would have to relinquish her children to relatives back home. "She counted each day, each week, each month as if they were priceless pearls slipping through her fingers. Three years . . . then furlough, when they must leave their precious ones in England. It was the price one must pay for the high privilege of service."[8]

Although Evelyn was eager to return home to see her family after her years in India, she dreaded the thought of leaving her children so much that she convinced Jesse to postpone their furlough for a year. Finally in 1923, after serving for ten years among the hill people, they were on their way home. "The children were old enough, Paul nearly nine, Connie six, to be left to attend school in England." Yet, the thought of leaving them was an ever present heartache:

> The year was blessing . . . and it was torture. Everywhere the message was well received. . . . But as the sands of the year ran low the constant dread of parting turned into agony. To leave her children . . . for five or six whole years! Why Paul would be almost a man, and Connie, her precious golden-haired treasure, now scarcely out of babyhood. . .

> "I can't do it," she blurted suddenly to Jesse about a month before they were due to sail. "Paul, yes. He's old enough to stand the separation, and he must have his schooling now. But Connie, my little darling . . . Jess, I must take her."

> Jesse's face reflected the pain in her own, but he shook his head. "I know. But, my dear, it would be cruel to separate them." Then, looking into her ravaged eyes, he relented. "Very well.

Why not take Connie apart and ask her if she would rather go back with us?"

Evie thankfully grasped at the thread of hope. Connie regarded her gravely. "Can Paul come too, Mummy?"

"No, darling. Paul must stay here and go to school."

The child shook her head. "Oh, not without Paul, Mummy. Not without my Paul."[9]

The day finally arrived when Evelyn had to leave her children behind. The night before the children reviewed the Tamil scripture verses they would be reciting weekly during the years of separation, and Evelyn gave them each hand-painted decorated plaques to hang by their beds. For Connie: "As one whom a mother comforteth, so will I comfort you." For Paul: "I will be a father unto you." The next morning the children left for school, knowing that when they returned home that afternoon their parents would be on the way to India not to return for several years. "Evie stood by the gate looking after them, eyes so blurred with tears she could scarcely see the waving of their hands before they ran around the corner." It was a moment of utter anguish: "As I stood watching them, something just died in me."[10]

The years of separation were more difficult for Evelyn than they were for Jesse. When their furlough in 1929 was delayed for a year because "another missionary family seemed to need it more than they did," he "cheerfully" accepted the decision while she agonized over it. To her an additional year of waiting seemed "interminable," but she agreed—a decision that must have haunted her

the rest of her days. The pain of not seeing her children proved to be slight in comparison to the affliction the additional year in India would bring. Jesse became ill with blackwater fever, and a few weeks later he was dead. Evelyn blamed herself for not taking him to a medical center, and in the months that followed "she plunged into feverish activity," seeking "to drown her own despair" and to make up for his loss to the ministry.[11]

It was six years after she had left them that Evelyn was reunited with her Paul and Connie. Paul was fifteen and she hardly recognized him. She had changed, too, in the eyes of her son. She was not the mother he remembered. What he saw was "a little, incredibly little, shrunken old Lady! This is Mother, he had had to tell himself over and over, trying to make himself believe it. This is my beautiful, tall, graceful, sparkling Mother!" It was a furlough year that Evelyn cherished, and one that she despaired of leaving behind, but the work among the hill people could not be abandoned. "She sailed in the autumn of 1930, weak, fearful, intolerably lonely. . . ." The next five years were filled with activity as she sought to do the work of two people. She traveled on horseback from village to village, preaching and teaching as Jesse had done.[12]

When Evelyn returned on her next furlough in 1936, her children were adults—or so they seemed to her. As has been so true of vast numbers of missionary children through the generations, both Paul and Connie were making plans to follow in their parents' footsteps and become missionaries. In fact, both applied for missionary service but were turned down because of their youth. So, once again Evelyn returned to India alone. Because of World War II it would be almost ten years before she was to return to her now-married children and to a grandchild. In the years that followed her son Paul would become a missionary medical doctor, known internationally for his breakthroughs in leprosy, and Connie would serve with her family in Africa. And Evelyn, known by nearly everyone as "Granny" would continue actively to minister among the hill people until past the age of ninety-four. She had retired from the mission board more than two decades earlier, but she could not leave her hill people—and the only real home she had ever known.[13]

### Dorie Van Stone

Children can be one of the greatest liabilities in a husband-and-wife team ministry in overseas missions, but they can be a tremendous asset as well. Children are often the first to learn the language and their presence helps to build bridges crossculturally. Mothers have a lot in common with each other no matter how different their cultural baggage is, and the interaction between missionary women and nationals about child care and domestic matters have often helped to break down barriers more quickly. Yet it has been the children who have often been the cause of their parents' leaving the mission field. Education is the primary factor, but physical and psychological health concerns also enter the picture. It was the latter that

became a living nightmare for Dorie and Lloyd Van Stone.

The Van Stones sailed for New Guinea in 1952 with their two small children, Burney and Darlene. Soon after they arrived they were assigned to open up the Baliem Valley—the land of the "stone-age" Dani tribe. It was an exciting opportunity, but the excitement was dampened when Dorie became ill and was advised to return to the United States with the children. "I preferred to stay and die in New Guinea," she wrote, "But Lloyd reminded me, 'Honey, we must take responsibility for the children.'" It was a difficult parting, as Dorie later recalled: "As the plane circled I saw Lloyd sobbing openly, unashamedly. I would have bailed out of that plane had I not been confident that we were obeying our Lord." A year later, she and the children returned to live with Lloyd among the Danis.[14]

Their ministry was fruitful, and they soon felt at home. "We developed confidence in the Danis. Our children played with the Dani children and picked up the language rapidly." Yet they were never fully secure. The Danis were made up of warring factions, and there was always the possibility that the Van Stones could be caught in the crossfire. And there were misunderstandings that sometimes led to tense stand-offs. At one point the tensions became so high that the Dutch government ordered an evacuation of all women and children from the valley. Dorie and the children left, and when the tension moderated they returned—until Dorie became ill and had to leave again.[15]

Pioneering mission work in the

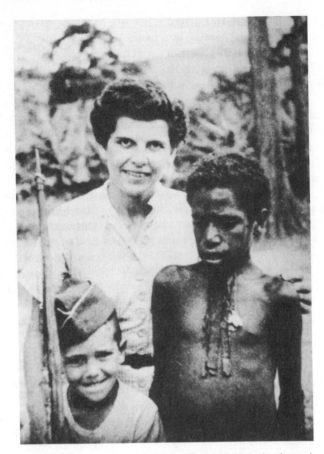

Dorie Van Stone. (From *Dorie: The Girl Noboby Loved*, by Dorie Van Stone with Erwin W. Lutzer. Copyright 1979, Moody Bible Institute of Chicago. Moody Press. Used by permission.)

Baliem Valley had been very difficult for the Van Stones, but when they arrived back after their furlough for their second term in 1957, they were optimistic about the future of their evangelistic ministry with the Danis. In the next two years, other missionaries joined them, and great progress was being made in language study. "As far as we knew," wrote Dorie, "we would be there for years." But life for them as they knew it as a family unit had changed. Educational priorities required that Burney and Darlene attend boarding school. "During our first term in the valley I had taught both the children," wrote Dorie. "But when we returned after our first furlough, Burney, nine, and Darlene, eight, attended the missionary children's school at Sentani." For Burney, the decision was like a prison sentence. "He vowed he would never leave us. When we *forced* him to stay at the school, he was terrified. His concern for our safety had turned into worry and fear, a terrible burden for a nine-year-old boy."[16]

The agonizing conflict Dorie and Lloyd faced in leaving their children—especially when the children resist—is an age-old problem that missionaries have confronted for generations. "As we saw it, we had no alternative," wrote Dorie. "In accepting the missionary call, we had realized we would have to sacrifice. We also believed we must be totally obedient to the mission society. That meant Burney and Darlene *had* to go to school . . . away from their home, or we would have to return to the United States."[17]

Then, in 1959, the Van Stones received a message from Santani that Burney had run away. He had been discovered missing that morning, and the school staff and children had searched in vain for him. "Something within us died," wrote Dorie. "Lloyd's knees buckled; he held onto the plane to steady himself. Frightful thoughts flooded our minds." Lloyd immediately flew to Sentani, and at noon radioed back to Dorie that Burney had been found hiding in an aircraft. "Childish imagination had his escape into the valley all planned: he would hide in the plane, and when the pilot made the next flight, Burney would soon be back in the valley with his father and mother!"[18]

Burney and Darlene were excused from school to return home to the valley with their father to spend a week at home. But at week's end, Burney refused to return. It was an anguishing struggle. "Burney still clung to me, and I had to pry him forcibly away," wrote Dorie. "That was like pulling away a part of my life. Lloyd and I knew that such a decision could not be justified—how could we be separated from our children when they needed us the most? . . . Yet paradoxically, we also knew that God had called us to the Baliem Valley." It was their certainty that God's call had been "unmistakable, direct, clear," that enabled them to send the children away again. "But Burney did not adjust. He would not eat, he did no schoolwork, and he even refused to speak. We decided that I should fly to Sentani to be with Burney for a few days. When I arrived he had been sobbing for two days. . . . The next day . . . sobbing turned into weak grunts."[19]

It was during that visit that Dorie, whose own health was deteriorating again, realized that she could not leave Burney again: "I wanted with all my heart to win Danis. But my first responsibility was to win Burney and Darlene. God had used us to be trailblazers in the Baliem. Someone else would reap the harvest." It was painful to turn back on what had so clearly been the call of God. "Reluctantly, we faced the fact that our days as missionaries in the Baliem might soon be over. Unresolved conflicts churned within us. God had called us, yet now we had to return." Back in the States, the conflict was kept alive by well-meaning supporters. "You've disappointed us," one woman commented. "Why didn't you trust God for healing out there? He'd have taken care of you and your children." Dorie responded, but not with a verbal reply: "I stood in the church lobby and wept." Her response could have been another question, one of the questions Darlene had often pondered: "Why does Jesus ask us to do such hard things?"[20]

*Chapter 22*

# Solitary Success:
# Capitalizing on Singleness

In the nineteenth century and even on into the twentieth century, the prospect of being a single woman missionary was not considered demeaning or something to be avoided. And once single women became established in their work they often wrote enthusiastically of their work and leisure time. Lucy Mead, who lived with several other single women, summed up her attitude in a letter home: "Someone occasionally mentions 'the serious melancholy, lonely, dull life of missionaries in China' which words bring peals of laughter. Not even in the most hilarious of college days have I had more fun than right here in this bunch of 'old maid missionaries.'" Single women often spoke of the freedom they enjoyed, sometimes confessing that "their strong personalities unsuited them for marriage's compromises." When Ida Lewis felt family pressures regarding marriage, she wrote, "then it will be for me to hunt a wife—I couldn't manage a husband."[1]

Despite such testimonials, it has often been regarded a handicap for women to be single, especially if they are missionaries. This view articulated in the nineteenth century by Daniel C. Eddy, in his book *Heroines of the Missionary Enterprise,* which reflected the morose feelings of sympathy people had for unmarried women missionaries:

Almost all the heroines who have gone forth from the churches of America, to dot heathen soil with their lowly graves, have been attended by some stronger arm than that of weak, defenceless [sic] woman. Many of them have had husbands on whom they relied for support and protection, and to whom they could turn with the assurance of sympathy, in hours of anguish and gloom.

But Miss Macomber went out attended by no such kind companion. She resolved on a missionary life, without the offer of marriage being connected with it. No husband helped her to decide the momentous question, and when she resolved, it was to go *alone.*[2]

Such pious prose is not suitable for describing single women missionaries today, but there are other subtle ways of characterizing them that places more emphasis on their single status than actuality would warrant. In the middle of a chapter on natural disasters that struck Taiwan, Lillian Dickson (a married women), without warning, inserted a statement about some of her female colleagues: "Our 'unclaimed treasures' (single lady missionaries) said they wandered through the house. . . ."[3] Why did she feel it necessary to describe them in such a patronizing manner? She might have simply said "single lady missionaries."

Some single women have sought to respond to such "put-downs" with humor and forthright discussion of the subject, and one who has succeeded is Jeannie Lockerbie, a missionary to Bangladesh and the author of mission books, including *By Ones and By Twos*. In that book she tells the story of a missionary friend who always responded to the question of whether or not she was married by saying, "No. My husband died at birth." Jeannie expressed her annoyance with the emphasis that mission societies placed on singleness.

I had never run into the term "single missionary" until I became one in the eyes of others. In the business and professional world a person is a secretary, a waitress, a nurse; not a *"single"* secretary, waitress or nurse. I don't know where or when the label "single" was affixed to an unmarried missionary woman. I was introduced to the term in missionary candidate school.

She argued that "separating the group by marital status seems to emphasize differences rather than promote unity and harmony."[4]

Other writers on the subject have pointed out the unique problems and opportunities for single missionaries—the majority of whom are female—and maintain that these issues should be specifically addressed while at the same time avoiding the typical stereotypes that are associated with single women missionaries.

It is true that the majority of single women missionaries have not chosen singleness as an ideal. Many of them, including Mary Slessor, Lottie Moon, Adele Fielde, Maude Cary, and Gladys Aylward were at one time engaged to be married, but for a variety of reasons remained single. But all might have wished that the ideal single male missionary would have entered their lives. Yet most of these women acknowledged the many benefits of singleness and most of them used it effectively to their advantage in ministry. Maude Cary, a tireless missionary evangelist to Morocco with the Gospel Missionary Union, was one such woman, and her life illustrates the lonely struggles as well as the laudable successes that were juxtaposed in the course of life for the single woman missionary.

### Maude Cary

Maude Cary was raised on a Kansas farm and sailed for Morocco in 1901 to begin her fifty years of ministry there. She was an independent and competitive young woman who created some consternation when she manifested these tendencies in language school. She was accused of pride and aggressiveness in her course work, while her male competitor, who scored fractionally higher than she did on the major exam, was presumed to be behaving normally for his sex. Single women were required to be self-reliant and courageous enough to forsake home and family for a life of privation abroad, but they were expected to know their place when relating to the male sex. Maude had over-stepped her bounds, but she realized her failing and, according to her biographer, "prayed daily for cleansing from the sin of pride."[5]

Despite her efforts, however, Maude did not adequately reform her ways in the eyes of the mission. She attended a field conference following her second year, and learned at that time the extent of the resentment that was harbored against her.

> From all that was said, her first two years on the field had been a total failure. The mission would have been better off without her. She was selfish and forgetful. She had written at least one unspiritual letter. She didn't always pray with the Muslims to whom she witnessed. Gaiety, friendliness, laughter—these had all been misconstrued. Added to her tendency to idle talk and her pride of dress, they became a mountain over which her co-workers had stumbled.[6]

Soon after this traumatic experience Maude was asked by the president of the Gospel Missionary Union, who was visiting Morocco, to make plans to terminate her ministry. It came as a devastating blow to Maude, who had dedicated her life to overseas missions. Not only would her career in ministry be over, but she would have to face the humiliation of going back home to her family and friends and admitting that she had been a failure. Her plea to remain, however, was granted, and she gratefully stayed on, vowing to serve ever more faithfully.[7]

Maude Cary, missionary to Morocco.

This would not be the end of the humiliation for Maude as a single woman missionary, however. The difficulty of finding a suitable partner has been a problem that has plagued single women for generations. Maude was no exception. She had made arrangements to live with two other women missionaries, but after a time they left and moved to another section of town. "Maude was stung by the conviction that they preferred to be without her."[8]

Another humiliating experience involved her relationship with the opposite sex. Like so many of her female counterparts, she longed to be married. That yearning was often the butt of jokes at the field conference. At one of these meetings, one of the mission leaders made light of the subject in front of the whole group. "Perhaps some of you young ladies would like to have homes of your own when you move inland. Cast your eyes about, and if you find anything you would like to have in your homes, feel free to speak of it!" It was an embarrassing moment for Maude, who "couldn't bear to lift her eyes toward any of the fine young men seated with them at the table."[9]

Despite the jest, it was the intense desire for marriage that prompted her to take a course of action she hoped might lead in the direction of marriage. She began studying the Berber language, in addition to Arabic, so she could have a ministry with that tribal group. It was a difficult language, and as she struggled with the grammar she had to weigh her motives. Was she really interested in the people themselves, or was she far more interested in a single male missionary, George Reed, who was working among them? She had corresponded with George, and she hoped that her new-found interest would kindle their relationship.[10]

Maude's groundwork paid off—at least that is the way it initially appeared. In January of 1908, George Reed proposed to her.

> The days of spring and summer were filled with the happiness known only to those in love. George was not well, and Maude was concerned about him. Meantime, Maude's weakened condition was a constant worry to George. He gently cared for her, even scrubbing the floors of the mission house when her turn came to do it.[11]

In the fall of 1908, George left Maude and went to work with the Berbers, and the following year, Maude followed, though she was not assigned to the same area. They kept in contact with each other, but no date was set for the wedding. George apparently had doubts about the decision he had made, and he encouraged Maude to return to America. She refused, and he went back to his mission post without her. Maude was frustrated by the indecision, but she refused to give up hope. Still single on her thirtieth birthday, she reflected on her past struggles and selected a motto for the remainder of her life: "Seek Meekness," prompted in part by the fact that "George Reed said he wanted a humble wife."[12]

Whether or not she became truly humble is uncertain, but that she was once again humiliated is beyond doubt. For six more years she lived in a state of uncertainty before George decided to leave Morocco and begin a work in Sudan. His actions clearly revealed what he could not communicate in words, and Maude finally knew with certainty that the engagement was off. It was a difficult time for her as she came to terms with the reality of her future—spending the rest of her life, as she predicted, as an "old maid missionary."[13]

Despite the humiliation Maude encountered as a single woman missionary, those very experiences helped prepare her for the difficult work of reaching Muslims with the gospel message. The work itself was demeaning, and it was necessary to be "thick-skinned" to deal with the animosity so often aimed at the Christian missionary. The longer Maude remained on the field, the more her senior status allowed her to be herself. What was earlier viewed as impudence and pride came to be accepted as an asset. Indeed, it was her strength of character that propelled her on through her many years of tireless service. Yet she had misgivings about her contribution to the work in Morocco. After twenty-three years she returned home for her first furlough and had time to reflect on her years of sacrifice. What was there to show for all she had done? Very little. She was grateful for the little band of converts she had helped nurture, but even they were shaky in their faith.[14]

Maude had changed considerably in the years she had been gone, as had the nation she returned to. In some ways, however, she was the same. Indeed, she arrived wearing the same style dress she had worn when she set sail in 1901—a contradiction for a woman who had years earlier been accused of "pride of dress." She seemed somehow entirely out of place in an America that was reveling in the reckless gaiety of the 1920s. But she was not there to join in the frivolity. Her aged parents needed her companionship, and she obligingly attended to their wellbeing. Both of them died during her furlough.[15]

Maude's remaining two and a half decades in Morocco were eventful. The work was slow, but there were always hopeful signs of progress. Yet many of the missionaries found the arduous toil in the barren soil of Islam, with its scant rewards, too difficult. For Maude, who was many times tempted to leave, there were no other real options in life. Thus it was that she found herself alone in Morocco in 1938, with one other single woman missionary to direct the entire outreach of the Gospel Missionary Union. They were joined by two more single women just before the outbreak of World War II, at which time the government barred additional missionaries from entering the country. During the war, the four women kept three stations open—with Maude and the other experienced missionary working alone.[16]

The prestige of having remained in Morocco as the senior missionary was clearly felt when new recruits began arriving after the war. Maude spent most of her time directing the orientation and language programs, but she continued to be involved in pioneering efforts as well. At the age of seventy-one she was designated to "open the city of El Hajeb to resident missionary work." In this assignment, she was assisted by a young woman who had not yet completed her language studies. Before they entered the city, a home had been secured for them by a fellow missionary—none other than George Reed—who had returned from the Sudan for a visit and had agreed to make the housing arrangements before the women arrived.[17]

After a furlough in 1952, Maude returned to Morocco for three years. She did not want to leave, but health problems forced the mission to retire their stubborn, but spunky, seventy-seven-year-old senior missionary. Twelve years later, in 1967, the Gospel Missionary Union was forced to terminate its seventy-five-year outreach in Morocco. It was a sad time for the missionaries and the tiny Christian church in that country. Back in the United States, another era had passed. An obituary appeared in a local newspaper, and "a small handful of people, seven of whom were ministers, attended the funeral. There were only two sprays of flowers, and hardly any tears."[18] Maude Cary's earthly struggles were over.

## Helen Roseveare

For Helen Roseveare, a medical doctor to the Congo, the problem of being a single woman became evident early in her missionary career. It was an issue that she had thought little about when she was in medical school, and the excitement of beginning her missionary service in Africa with the Worldwide Evangelization Crusade kept her mind on other things. As she began to develop her ministry, however, she was repeatedly confronted with situations that demonstrated that her sex and her singleness were distinct disadvantages.

She had no more than become settled in her hospital work when the mission informed her that she would have to move to a run-down leprosy camp at Nebobongo. She strongly opposed the decision, but she had no choice in the matter. In her new location she started with nothing and built a hospital with money she was able to raise from supporters. She cleared trees, dug ditches, fired bricks—working side by side with her African helpers. It was a tremendous accomplishment, and Helen was naturally proud of her work and defensive of her turf—perhaps too much so. Without her consent, the mission assigned John Harris, a young missionary doctor who had

just arrived on the field, to supervise the hospital. It was a devastating blow to her. "Now she had lost everything," writes her biographer. "She had always taken Bible class; Dr. Harris took it now. Dr. Harris organized the nurses, and Helen had always done that. Everything that had been hers was now his."[19]

After five years in Africa, Helen returned home to England for furlough. She was not well physically, she was under psychological stress, and she desperately needed rest. Indeed, there was a serious question in her mind as to whether she would continue her missionary career. She was burdened by the medical needs of the Congo, but she did not want to go back to Africa as a single missionary. With those concerns in mind, she set about to find a husband. She met "a Christian doctor whom she decided would be a perfect mate for her. She bought new clothes, got her hair permed, and even resigned from the mission in an effort to win him, but to no avail."[20]

It was a difficult period in Helen's life, but through it she was strengthened in her spiritual life and began to come to grips with the prospect of singleness:

The Lord spoke very clearly during my furlough that he was able to satisfy me. . . . I wasn't interested in a spiritualized husband. I wanted a husband with a couple of arms. Well, in the end I jolly near mucked up the whole furlough. . . . I couldn't find a husband in the mission, so I got out of the mission. God let me go a long way, and I made an awful mess. Then God graciously pulled me back and the mission graciously accepted me back.[21]

When Helen returned to the Congo in 1960, she found the political situation much more tense than when she had left two years earlier. Some missionaries were leaving, and she was cautioned about her plans to reenter. She was convinced that God wanted her back, and she eagerly returned to Nebobongo to relieve John Harris while he went on furlough. The three years that followed were fruitful ones for her, despite the tensions created by the growing Simba Rebel movement. "Reports came periodically of attacks against missionaries elsewhere, including reports of missionary women who had 'suffered' at the hands of rebels—an act so degrading and humiliating it could not even be named." Such reports seemed far away to Helen, who was so involved in her work that she had little time to think about her safety.[22]

By the summer of 1964, however, she could not ignore the Civil War that was raging as the rebels moved through the countryside, taking control of one village after another. Nebobongo was not spared. Rebel soldiers occupied the mission compound, and Helen was placed under house arrest. For more than two months she continued her work, living in relative security. Then one night in late October, a rebel soldier forced his way into her house and brutalized her. She had tried to escape, but to no avail. It was a night of sheer terror.

They found me, dragged me to my feet, struck me over head and shoulders, flung me on the ground, kicked me, dragged me to my feet only to strike me again—the sickening, searing pain of a broken tooth, a mouth full of sticky blood, my glasses gone. Beyond sense, numb with horror and unknown fear, driven dragged, pushed back to my own house—yelled at, insulted cursed.

Once she was back inside the house, the paralyzing ordeal was over in a matter of minutes. According to her biographer, the soldier "forced her backwards on the bed, falling on top her. . . . The will to resist and fight had been knocked out of her. But she screamed over and over again. . . . The brutal act of rape was accomplished with animal vigor and without mercy."[23]

"My God, My God, why have you forsaken me" were the only words that Helen could express in the terrifying hours of darkness that followed. At the time it would have seemed impossible that such a horrifying ordeal could have any positive value. Yet, after she was taken captive by the Simbas, she drew on that experience to minister to Roman Catholic nuns who had endured similar sexual brutality. One young nun, Sister Dominique, was particularly distressed. She had been paraded naked before the mocking soldiers before she was violently deprived of her virginity. She was convinced she had lost her purity before God and that there was no purpose in going on living. Helen, having suffered so deeply herself, reassured her of God's love and understanding. "If you know of Christ living in you, no one can touch your inner purity," she counseled. "No living man can touch or destroy or harm that real purity inside you. . . . You have not lost your purity. If anything, you have gained purity in the eyes of God."[24]

There would be many more horrors of rape before Helen was released, and she might have wished many times that she were a man and not forced to endure such suffering. But the joy of being free was quickly tempered when she heard the accounts of atrocities that had occurred among her missionary colleagues—men who had been tortured and killed. She had many emotional wounds that would take years to heal. "At that time we were not taught in missionary training school how to face up mentally to where rape fits into the picture," she later wrote. "It was a taboo subject. The strange thing is, of course, that the actual sexual experience of rape does stir you. You suddenly find yourself sexually awakened. And it was terrible because right in the suffering, in all the awfulness of prison life, beat-ups and everything, this other thing came too." By depending on God, however, Helen was able to work through this frustration. "God came to me in a very special way, and gave me such a warm experience of his loving presence that I understood in a new way Isaiah 54:5, 'Your Maker is your Husband.' "[25]

Back home in England, Helen initially had no thoughts of going back to the Congo. She had already sacrificed more than she could emotionally cope with, and she was satisfied with the prospect of remaining in England. That, however, was before she began receiving letters from her African friends begging her to return. In 1966, less than two years after she had left, she was back in Africa—once again training nurses and directing hospital work.[26]

Life was different after Helen returned. The spirit of independence had not subsided, and Africans were

Helen Roseveare, missionary doctor to the Congo.

less willing than they had been a decade earlier to accept the authority of white missionaries—especially women missionaries. Yet Helen had a rapport with Africans that few missionaries could equal. She credited some of this to her single status:

> When a married woman would go to visit the Africans, she had to guard against leprosy, lest she endanger her children. She would hesitate and glance around. Since I had no family, I walked right in.

> A married woman out visiting had to keep an eye on her watch to get the kids from school or prepare a meal. I had no such responsibilities. I could stay all night, if needed, and no one cared. The Africans sensed this difference immediately.

I wanted to be completely identified with the Africans. As a single woman, I could be much more closely identified than my married companions.

The Africans, particularly the pastors, had a tremendous love for us single women missionaries. They appreciated our giving up our homes to minister to them, and were so protective and gracious toward us.[27]

Helen's closer identification and easy manner with the African villagers was not duplicated with her nursing students. In the teaching context she was a hard driver and was not open to compromise when it meant unnecessarily jeopardizing health standards. Her students were obligated to take government exams, as were all such trainees, and she wanted them to do well and get good scores. Her tight discipline, however, was not universally appreciated by her students. Some of them rudely challenged her authority and made her teaching almost impossible. Yet she continued for seven more sacrificial years before she made plans to terminate her ministry. She had accomplished great things, but she left in 1973 disgraced and broken in spirit.

When I knew I was coming home from the field and a young medical couple were taking my place at the college and an African was taking over the directorship of the hospital, I organized a big day. It was to be a welcome to the two new doctors, a handover to my colleague, graduation day for the students in the college, and my farewell. A big choir had been practicing for five months. I got lots of cassettes to record everything and films to snap everything. Then at the last moment the whole thing fell to bits. The student body went on strike. I ended up having to resign the college where I'd been the director twenty years.[28]

In some ways that experience was as painful to Helen as had been the terrible months of the Simba Revolution. "It was a very, very lonely period," she wrote. "I was hurt so deep down inside I didn't know what to do with it."[29] Again, however, pain was turned into opportunity as Helen used the experience to help others. Any other missionary would have no doubt tried to cover up the failures and disgrace. Helen was different. She opened her soul to others who needed to hear of missionary failure as well as missionary success. And through her honest openness on the issue of singleness and other aspects of missionary service she has become an internationally recognized missionary speaker.

Chapter 23

# Signs and Wonders: Power Encounter and the Charismatic Gifts

The advent of the modern Pentecostal movement which began in the early years of the twentieth century did not open up a new era for overseas missions as the leaders of the movement had hoped. Indeed, when Agnes Ozman inaugurated the twentieth century by "speaking in the Chinese language" at a watchnight service on the last day of 1900, at Bethel Bible School in Topeka, Charles Fox Parham, the founder of the school "immediately began to teach that missionaries would no longer be compelled to study foreign languages to preach in the mission fields." According to his understanding of Scripture and of the "outpouring" that would occur in the "last days," one would "need only receive the baptism with the Holy Ghost and he could go to the farthest corners of the world and preach to the natives in languages unknown to the speaker."[1]

Pentecostal missions enthusiasts quickly discovered that their hopes were misguided. Although there have been claims of miraculous language gifts through the decades (and, indeed, centuries), Pentecostal missionaries have had to endure the rigors of language study, just like their non-Pentecostal counterparts. But if they did not receive a miraculous gift of tongues in the language of their choice, Pentecostals have had other advantages as they have reached out cross-culturally. In Latin America, Africa, and in parts of Asia, nationals eagerly gravitated toward the demonstrative faith of the Pentecostals and charismatics who did not stifle their emotions as many noncharismatic evangelicals did. And they were more eager to accept a faith that readily accepted the miraculous powers of God while at the same time recognizing the power of the demonic spirit world. This was true of Evelyn Quema's experience in the Philippines, and it was this aspect of Latin American culture that Mildred Larson came to grips with in her ministry with an Indian tribe living in the Amazon jungle.

## Evelyn Quema

The Philippines, like other areas of the Third World, has been deeply affected by charismatic religion. In some instances it was part of the native culture and in other instances it entered that area of the world through missionaries. Jim Montgomery's book *New Testament Fire in the Philippines* tells of this phenomenon and how it affected him as a missionary:

> It was like walking into a different world. As if a veil had been pulled aside. I had always believed, of course, that Christianity was a supernatural religion, but now I was encountering a dimension of the supernatural that I had before only read about, primarily in the pages of the New Testament.
>
> The difference was that this time I was talking with the participants in the remarkable events. Dramatic conversions. Churches spawning new churches almost faster than they could keep track. Miracles of healing commonplace. Speaking in tongues. Visions.[2]

Montgomery's book focusses on key individuals in the movement, one of whom is Evelyn Quema. Evelyn grew up in Manilla in the 1950s in a liberal Protestant family of ten children. Her turn toward a Pentecostal form of religion came in 1958, at the age of sixteen, when she attended a Foursquare Gospel church with her family. There she soon claimed the Baptism of the Holy Spirit which resulted in "a boldness in witnessing to others." Her parents and nine brothers and sisters were converted in the months that followed. Evelyn enrolled in a Bible school course, and it was during that time, while attending a religious meeting, that she received her "call" to ministry in true Pentecostal fashion:

> Among Pentecostals a common experience is to be "slain of the Lord." This is what happened to me that night. As I was praying I lost all consciousness of my surroundings and a vision appeared. It was of a high, high mountain. I kept climbing and climbing. Finally I reached the top and found a church there. I knew it was Baguio, the place of my birth, because of the pine trees.[3]

When she was twenty-two, Evelyn began a pioneer ministry in Baguio. She immediately rented a house and began holding meetings. Within a few months she had enough converts to form a self-supporting church, and in three years she had eleven "outstations, plus another dozen or more regular Bible teaching classes for children." Her work was not without opposition, however, and over a period of time several of her outstations were closed by Catholic priests. Yet the work continued to spread. As Evelyn's converts moved into other areas they often requested her to come and hold evangelistic meetings, and sometimes as many as thirty responded to the invitation at the end of her message.[4]

Opposition also came from Protestants. On one occasion five ministers came to visit her, "determined to put an end to this woman preacher business once and for all." She defended herself by pointing to the results of her ministry: "If I'm disobeying then there should be no fruit. If you want to believe that I am disobeying God's word, that is all right. Yet I will go on. It is not men of Foursquare that have called me, but God." At the same time, she insisted that preaching was not her primary gift. Rather, it was "the ministry of prayer"—a ministry that even women were permitted to have. It was through answered prayer—especially in regard to healings—that her ministry was enhanced. The healings were not as spectacular as some "divine healers" have claimed, but they were a natural part of her church planting ministry—a ministry that spawned four new churches and some two hundred converts in a matter of a few years.[5]

## Mildred Larson

In 1953 Mildred Larson began her work with the Aguaruna people, a widely-scattered Indian tribe of some twenty-five thousand, living in the tropical rain forest of Peru. When she arrived, she had only intended to work as a temporary assistant to Ray and Alice Wakelin, while she waited for her permanent assignment. She was a Wycliffe Bible Translator, and Cameron Townsend, the director of the mission, had requested that she delay her own translation work to help others.

I agreed. What a crucial decision that would prove to be! More than twenty years later I was still on my Aguaruna assignment. Before I could even help them, the Wakelins had to leave because of illness. I took up the study of the Aguaruna while I waited for their return. But once I began to study the language and to get involved with the people, there was no stopping. So much more needed to be done! When I found that the Wakelins could not

return, my choice was clear. I had my permanent assignment.[6]

Jeanne Grover, a nurse, joined Millie, and they moved into the thatched-roofed house that the Wakelins had left behind. They also inherited language notes and other materials that gave them a head start in their work. Immediately, they were introduced to the world of the spirits that was so much a part of the everyday life of the Aguarunas. Their house was built like the other homes in the village, except that it was more open, allowing for light and ventilation as well as opportunities to socialize. "We didn't have to worry about evil spirits coming in over the wall," as the Aguaruna did in their "totally closed" houses, wrote Millie.[7]

As they learned the language and continued to work among the tribespeople, Millie and Jeanne began to realize more and more how deeply the spirit world penetrated every area of the people's lives. They quickly realized that "sickness is more than germs"—that the real and imagined demonic power had virtual control over the health and well-being of the Aguarunas from birth to death. Looking back to 1956, two years after they had moved to the region, Millie later wrote, "We understood the language well enough by then that we could no longer live in blissful ignorance of the fears that plagued our neighbors."[8]

Despite these problems, Millie and Jeanne made progress as they continued their translation and medical work. Millie had two reliable male language helpers who confessed faith in Christ and eagerly taught the scriptures they learned in their translation work to their own people. The most helpful of the two abandoned his work for a time to return to his village. Millie had not been pleased with his decision to leave, but when he returned he reported to her: "I have good news! My mother and many others have come to know Jesus!"[9] Experiences like that made this most difficult life worthwhile.

Mildred Larson, Wycliffe Bible Translator to South America.

It was not until they had worked among the Aguaruna for nearly two decades that Millie and Jeanne began to comprehend the scope of demon oppression among the people. They were aware of the power of the shamans and of charms over the unconverted, but they did not realize the impact of demonic power on some of their staunchest converts. Nelson was one of those. Indeed, he came close to renouncing his faith because of the pull from the uncon-

verted tribal leaders and demonic oppression. Millie's own understanding of the problem was enlarged when Nelson's sister became ill.

It was a dreary, rainy evening when Nelson sent word to me of Elsa's sickness. As I entered the dimly lit thatched hut, I heard the eerie rhythm of the shaman's song. Elsa was chanting the song in a high, falsetto voice. Her husband and stepfather were holding her down as she lay on a sleeping platform.

Suddenly Elsa sat straight up, swinging her arms and shouting. Nelson and other men moved in closer to restrain her. After her violent outburst, she settled down again and continued to sing.

"I see you over there by the edge of the jungle," she chanted. "There are many of you. Don't come any closer."

"She has a demon, Millie," Nelson said to me. "Last time she was sick like this we all prayed and confessed our sins, and I wrote a song for casting out demons."[10]

While others in the hut held Elsa down, Nelson sang his song, and eventually she quieted down and fell asleep. Millie returned to her house and began reflecting on previous experiences, one of which involved a demon-possessed woman. The tribes people had recognized the seriousness of her condition: " 'She's been cursed; she's going to die; it's *tunchi*,' they all said." Yet, Millie felt powerless: "For the first time in my life, I knew that demons were real and powerful. Did I have the courage to cast them out, as Jesus gave his disciples power to do? If I tried and failed, would it do more harm than good? How did I know I could really exorcise a demon?"[11]

Two weeks after that Millie received word that the woman had died. In the meantime, she had endured an inner conflict that was the beginning of a turning point in her ministry. She had recognized that she had failed this poor woman because of her own unbelief. She had to confess that she had "always thought of demons as figments of the imagination of primitive peoples, as superstitions learned from their ancestors." She argued with herself: "I am translating Scripture into their language, but do I truly believe it myself?" Yes, she did, but she had been "brainwashed not to take too seriously the battle between Satan and God."

> During the years that Jeanne and I had worked among the Aguaruna, we had believed medicine to be the all-powerful force that would overcome superstition and sorcery. If we could prove that all sickness had a natural cause, people would be free from their terrifying fears of it, related to supernatural sources as they considered it to be. Whenever someone claimed to be sick because of *tunchi*, we would try to show how it wasn't actually sorcery. It must be parasites, or some germ—and usually it was.
>
> We had the all-powerful medicine as our weapon against sorcery. Since it is a figment of the imagination, we reasoned, surely more education and more medical training will lead to its downfall. If pills didn't work, the illness was surely just psychological. Tranquilizers ought to take care of a case like that.
>
> But in spite of our disbelief, shamans kept healing some people; others died

> of *tunchi*. People still talked about and acted out revenge against the curser. Even those who claimed to be believers and wanted to obey God went to the shaman as a last resort. He could tell them, as Jeanne and I could not, whether they needed medicine or his own ministrations because they had had a curse placed on them. . . .
>
> Many times . . . I had seen people that I knew must be possessed . . . but I felt no power to save these people from Satan's attack. . . .
>
> Now, with Elsa's attack, I had once again seen demons in action. But this time I had also seen Nelson, with much more faith than I, win the battle against them.[12]

Nelson would have further struggles with demonic power and with clinging to old tribal customs that glorified black magic, but he finally came to the point where he testified: "I renounced the evil spirits and asked God to deliver me from them. Then the other men prayed for me to be freed too. . . . I felt free! I felt clean! It was like coming out of the darkness of the jungle onto a wide road in the sunshine. I had peace; my depression and hatred were gone."[13]

Antun was another Aguaruna Christian who struggled with demons. Fifteen years after his profession of faith he was still struggling with night visions of an evil spirit who stood over him and terrorized him. Millie told this to a visiting pastor from the States, and with her he cast the demon out of Antun and prayed that the Holy Spirit would fill the vacant place in his life. From that time on he was a different man. It was this experience more than anything that helped Millie better understand how to reach the tribal people with whom she was working. The message they wanted to hear—more than the message that there was "a Savior who promised them life in the distant future"—was the message of "a Savior who had power to free them in this life from demons, to protect them from sorcery and to heal them of constant sickness."[14]

With her willingness to "openly acknowledge that spiritual warfare was real . . . and not a fiction or a superstition," Millie saw an increased interest in the gospel among the Aguaruna people. "Amazingly, when we at last understood how real Satan and his demons are, our Aguaruna friends opened up to us on a whole new level. 'When you didn't believe these things, sister,' they said, 'we were ashamed to tell you much. But now that you too believe, we are not ashamed to tell you, because we need God's power.' "[15]

## Chapter 24

# Picking up the Mantle: Outreach by Non-Western Women

From the onset of the modern missionary movement, native converts have been active in evangelistic outreach. This has been particularly true of women. It would be hard to imagine where the non-Western church would be today if it were not for the ministry of Bible women. They faithfully served the church—often in the face of heavy persecution and with only the smallest financial remuneration. "The Bible woman has become an institution," wrote Helen Barrett Montgomery in 1910. "Her work is indispensable; she multiplies the missionary's influence, goes before to prepare the way, and after to impress the truth. One of the humblest, she is at the same time one of the mightiest forces of the Cross in non-Christian lands."[1]

In most instances Bible women served the local churches and did evangelistic work in outlying villages. At times, however, they left their homes and families and traveled to distant regions to serve for lengthy terms. This sometimes meant leaving aged parents behind—a very difficult thing to do for Asian women who felt it to be their obligation to care for elderly family members.[2] Some Bible women served overseas as missionaries, as was true of Korean Bible women who went to Hawaii at the turn of the twentieth century. These "quasi-ministers" filled a variety of roles, including that of "evangelist, teacher, public health educator and social worker."[3]

Bible women who served abroad were generally single or widowed women, but non-Western women also served effectively as missionary wives. This was particularly true in the South Seas. According to Charles Forman, "The great period for indigenous missionary wives was the last quarter of the nineteenth and first quarter of the twentieth centuries." More than a thousand men and women from various South Sea Islands volunteered to carry the gospel to other islands. This meant learning a new language and adjusting to a new culture, despite their meager education their achievements were substantial. Although the women were not considered full-fledged missionaries in their own right, they "shared fully in the hard work involved. In places where women had little voice in society, missionary wives showed new possibilities."[4]

Non-Western women also supported foreign missions through lay ministries. In Burma, women's missionary societies flourished. Initially they were promoted by women missionaries from the West, but they soon became thoroughly indigenous, though patterned after Western models. By the mid-twentieth century, the Burmese Baptist Women's Society was supporting five full-time women evangelists, and the Karen Society (also of Burma) was also sending women to unevangelized regions.[5]

In some cases laywomen were themselves actively involved in evangelistic outreach. This has been true in Africa, where an organization known as Women of the Good News has proliferated in recent decades. It began in 1970, through the combined efforts of Virginia Jones, an American Missionary, and Rebeka Eliya, a Zairian pastor's wife. The organization has a broad appeal that spans a wide range of age groups and social classes and is very African in flavor. To join the "club" women must meet certain requirements, and after that their solidarity is promoted through uniforms, slogans, songs, and lively parades and rallies. Evangelism is a primary function of the organization, which itself has grown from a few hundred in 1970 to tens of thousands in various denominations.[6]

Despite these signs of optimism in various parts of the non-Western World, women who seek ministry often find many obstacles in their way. In India, for example, the church has failed to adequately train women and to encourage them to fill the leadership roles the missionaries once filled. As the church has become more indigenous, it has also become more male dominated. "Research suggests that women missionaries who were competent and financially independent were not replaced by Indian women because women's ministries were not held in high regard. . . . Indian women have been taught it is their fate to suffer in silence." This is the frank appraisal of Juliet Thomas, the secretary of women's ministries for the Evangelical Fellowship of India.[7]

Despite the restrictions in Christian ministry that women face in many areas of the Two Thirds World, individual women have in certain instances made great strides in obtaining leadership roles. Such recognition, however, does not come easily. This is seen in the story of Patricia Kim, known as the Korean "Wonder Woman." After studying at a Bible school and seminary, she was initiated into Christian service as a lowly Bible woman, planting churches on the unevangelized Chindo Island. She began her itinerant work living in a tent, as she went from village to village on a motor bike. She quickly discovered that "coastal Korean men traditionally look down on women, and the ancestor-worshiping peasants opposed her teaching." That began to change when "they saw her helping people cultivate their rice paddies, and keeping honey bees to support herself." It was while she was involved in this work that Kim caught the vision for unreached peoples in other areas of the world, and in 1985 she was accepted as a missionary candidate by the Sudan Interior Mission to serve in Peru.[8]

## Rosario Rivera

Rosario Rivera grew up in a poor family in the Andes mountains of Peru in the city of Huancayo. Her life was relatively routine until one night, as a teenager, she witnessed the police ruthlessly beating three union organizers, who were perceived as trouble-makers by the local establishment. Rosario was incensed by the injustice, and she left the scene, as she later recalled, "swearing to myself that one day I would see justice done. My political inclinations were born at that moment." From that time on she began reading revolutionary literature and she joined in a youth organization known as the Revolutionary Action group. At the age of eighteen she went to Cuba for guerrilla training and after that became closely associated with the notorious guerrilla leader 'Che' Guevara. In the years that followed, Rosario attended the university, had a baby, and planned a nationwide textile strike, all the while maintaining her strong sympathies with the leftist movement.[9]

It was during a time of disillusionment, when Rosario suspected that some of the textile strike leaders had been bribed by textile officials to abandon the planned walk-out, that she "clicked on the radio, and heard a Christian station advertise a meeting that night with evangelist Luis Palau." The location was a nearby theater and the topic was "Drugs, Sex, and Youth." She attended out of curiosity but was not impressed by what she heard and left in anger. That night, however, in her sleep she heard verses of Scripture being read. After getting up and searching in her Bible, she came across Matthew 4:4, and she began weeping. Her life was changed and she vowed she would turn her life around and serve God.[10]

Rosario was not readily accepted by other Christians, who were skeptical about her and uneasy about her effort to transform her leftist ideology into Christian social action. She became involved in civic projects, and "after five years' work, her community had water, sewage, and other services, plus better housing." So successful was she that she was offered a position as a community developer, but she turned it down, "feeling God had called her to full-time service and without a salary for Him." Her focus was on the poor—especially poor children. She took "missionary" trips throughout Peru and held evangelistic meetings for youngsters.[11]

Everywhere she went, Rosario was gripped by the needs of the children. Poverty deprived them of many of the necessities of life, and she desperately sought to remedy the problems—often taking on projects that were far beyond her financial means. She started the "I Am Jesus" Christian elementary school in her home, which soon had eighty students. Because of lack of funding, she could not obtain government approval, but she refused to give up. She insisted that her ministry would be operated entirely on faith, and when there

Rosario Rivera, ministering to children in Lima, Peru. (Courtesy of John Maust, Latin American Mission.)

were no funds there was only one course of action: "we just get on our knees."[12]

It was this style of ministry that, from the standpoint of many colleagues, made Rosario difficult to work with. She was not careful about financial details, and her work often suffered as a result. This was true of her breakfast program for young children that she started in 1984. She began with two hundred children, but soon "she announced her conviction that God wanted her to feed 1,000. Before long, she far exceeded that. By late 1986 more than 2,500 children were being reached." This included more than twenty breakfast centers and more than one hundred and thirty volunteer workers. It was a massive project that was a testimony throughout the whole city of Lima, but it was not without controversy and problems.[13]

Though Rosario considered her work a faith effort dependent on God alone, she did accept funds from the Siloam International Mission, and in the mid-1980s the Peruvian board of directors of that organization removed her as the chief administrator of the breakfast program. It was a difficult move to make considering her devotion to the work, but disorganization and "sloppy handling of funds" created problems with those who worked with her and those who supported the ministry, and it was determined that an individual with administrative gifts was needed for the position. Rosario, however, continued to head the Bible study aspect of the breakfast program and to develop other ideas for community activities.[14]

Rosario's work is one of many that has been developed by Third World women, and she, as a colleague has pointed out, is "only human" and "evangelicals should steer away from idolizing" her. Unfortunately there have been instances when this warning was needed. Some North American evangelicals have sought to "showcase" her, playing up "the fact that Rivera is an ex-communist . . . tearing Marxism down more than they are building Rivera up, and in so doing they manipulate her." She is simply a woman seeking to serve God, who like so many others who have gone before her often struggles with two opposing directives: God's and her earthly associates'.[15]

### Young Sawa Kim

In recent years Asian Christians have made great strides in establishing their own priorities for missionary endeavors, and Asians have become some of the world's leading missiologists. Although Asian women are generally behind Western women in procuring leadership positions in the church and in mission ventures, some have broken through the barriers. One prominent example is Young Sawa Kim, who has made contributions to the church in Asia as well as to the missionary enterprise. She is a native Korean and an ordained minister, serving as a pastor in Japan. Her concern for world mission has taken her to Mexico to observe and to serve, and to America, where she has engaged in research at the Overseas Ministries Studies Center.

Sawa was born in Pusan, the second-largest city in Korea, in 1948, the year that the part of Korea south of the thirty-eighth parallel officially became the Republic of Korea. The thirty-six-year annexation of Korea by Japan was over, and a new era was dawning for her people. When she

was seven her family moved to Seoul, and there she became part of the new generation in Korea—a generation of young people who were being educated in their own language and being educated to remember the past. Nationalism was almost a religion. "Hating the Japanese had the same meaning as loving Korea." Never again would the Koreans allow another nation to dominate them. During her youth, Sawa could not have imagined the turn her life would take in adulthood. "I had never dreamed that I would marry a Japanese and be a pastor in a Japanese church." For Sawa, serving in Japan became cross-cultural ministry in its truest form.[16]

Sawa grew up with a Christian heritage from both her mother's and her father's side of the family, although her father, a widely-read poet, himself was not a Christian. Sawa's maternal great-grandmother was the first in the family to become a Christian and was baptized on Easter Sunday of 1900. She was a successful business woman, and though she was unable to read, she memorized passages of Scripture and witnessed to her family and neighbors. Her daughter, Sawa's grandmother, married an educator who "was killed by the Japanese police when the famous nationwide independence movement occurred on March 1, 1919." After that, Sawa's grandmother educated her two children and then devoted the remainder of her life to serve as a Bible woman. Sawa's mother was a high-school teacher, but her first priority was that her children be brought up in the Christian faith. She attended church prayer meetings every day at

4:30 a.m. and saw to it that the children were also faithful in church. Each Sunday they were drilled in Scripture memorization.[17]

It was while she was studying theology at Yonsei University, the oldest Christian school in the country, that Sawa met a Japanese student who would later become her husband. Her initial reaction to his friendship was hostile: "I had hated the Japanese and did not want to marry a Japanese man. But I was moved by his enthusiastic proposal of marriage and his sincere concern for reconciliation between Japan and Korea under the cross of Christ." He had come to Korea for the very purpose of reconciliation, and she fit into those plans. For three years they lived in Japan, and then her husband was sent by the Japanese church back to her homeland to be a missionary.[18]

Since 1979, Sawa and her family have been back in Japan, where Sawa took further study at Tokyo Union Theological Seminary and was ordained to the ministry. Her decision to pursue the ministry in a foreign country was not an easy one. Friends and relatives warned her that as a woman and as a Korean she could never be successful in Japan. Her husband also discouraged her, as she relates: "Masahiko also tried to persuade me to give up my study. 'As a pastor, I need a wife who helps me, and our congregations also have expected you to take the role of a pastor's wife,' he said. But I could not abandon my dream of being a pastor. I promised my family I would carry out all my domestic duties as before."[19]

Convincing her family and friends

of her mission was only the first of the hurdles Sawa would have to overcome before she realized her calling. After her graduation, she requested that the seminary place her in a church as they did the other graduates. "But the faculty of the seminary was very surprised at my proposal," she relates, "and they told me very sincerely: 'In the Japanese church, in the case of the pastor's wife being ordained, she should work together with her husband.'" Sawa pointed out that her husband's church had only thirty members and that they certainly did not need two ordained pastors when many areas in Japan had no pastor at all. Under pressure, however, Sawa agreed to become the associate pastor in her husband's church.[20]

Although she did not have a church of her own, Sawa soon had more ministry opportunities than she could easily fill. Japanese were used to hearing messages from outsiders, mostly Western missionaries, but to have a Korean minister of the gospel in their midst was unusual—the hatred that Koreans felt toward the Japanese was generally too great. In her uniqueness, then, Sawa became somewhat of a celebrity, and she began receiving invitations to speak in various parts of the country. During her travels she was often asked about the rapid growth of Korean churches and what the Japanese church could do to foster similar growth.[21]

Sawa's active ministry in the church was not without opposition—the most frustrating of which was that from her own husband. "For more than 15 years, we had discussed things and sometimes we quarreled seriously," she wrote, "but I never gave up the hope of persuading him." Her hopes were realized after she published her autobiography in Japanese. It was only then that he began to understand some of the struggles she had confronted in her Christian pilgrimage. He not only understood her more fully, but he also gained a better understanding of himself. "I could get complete freedom, too," he confessed to her, "after I let you do anything freely."[22]

It is this freedom that has brought greater fulfillment to both Sawa and Masahiko as new doors of ministry opportunities open to them. Japan was only the first cross-cultural mission experience for Sawa. After that she was invited to minister in Mexico, and the future is before her.

## Mother Teresa

As the founder of the Missionaries of Charity, Mother Teresa has become one of the most celebrated missionaries of the modern era. By the mid 1980's, she was overseeing more than three hundred religious houses in some seventy countries around the world in an effort to minister to the "poorest of the poor." For this sacrificial service she was awarded the Nobel Peace Prize in 1979. Though born and raised in Eastern Europe, Mother Teresa is properly viewed as a representative of the non-Western world. She had become a citizen of India before she founded her Missionaries of Charity in 1950, and her base of operation and major source of recruits has been India.[23]

Mother Teresa was born Agnes Gonxha Bojaxhiu in 1910 into an Albanian peasant family. From her youth she was concerned about the poor in society and about overseas missions. "She was caught in the wave of enthusiasm for . . . spreading the gospel in the missions, an enthusiasm generated by the writings of Pope Pius XI." She prayed and meditated and investigated opportunities of service, one of which was with the Loreto nuns who served in Bengal. At eighteen she joined this religious order and the following year, in 1929, she found herself in Calcutta, where she soon became involved in teaching at the Loreto convent high school.[24]

From her earliest years in Calcutta, Sister Teresa was burdened by the needs of the poor who lived around her, but it would be some two decades before she would be able to leave the security of her convent and live among the teeming masses of impoverished humanity. "To leave Loreto was my greatest sacrifice, the most difficult thing I have ever done," she later reflected. "It was much more difficult than to leave my family and country to enter religious life. Loreto meant everything to me."[25]

But as difficult as the decision was, Sister Teresa knew she had no alternative. God had called as she was traveling by train to a Himalayan retreat in 1946. "It was on that train that I heard the call to give up all and follow Him into the slums—to serve Him in the poorest of the poor. . . . I was to leave the convent and work with the poor while living among them. It was an order. I knew where I belonged, but I did not know how to get there."[26]

Her call had not come independently of her own intense concern for oppressed masses right outside her window. "On the other side of a high concrete wall, guarding Loreto's green lawns and uniformed school-girls, is the Moti Jheel slum of mud lanes and wretched hovels. . . . She saw the dirt, the ragged children, the open sewers, the disease, the hunger in a city that was and is one giant quagmire of pestilence, poverty and famine." It took two years to obtain permission to leave her convent, but once that was accomplished she was ready to begin her work with a young female volunteer who joined her in 1949.[27]

Mother Teresa, receiving honorary degree from The Catholic University of America. (Courtesy of The Catholic University of America.)

From the beginning the Missionaries of Charity were different from all other religious orders. There were no "walls" of security. "Our Sisters must go out on the street," Mother Teresa insisted. "They must take the tram like our people, or walk to where they are going. That is why we must not start institutions and stay inside. We must not stay behind walls and have our people come to us." She recognized the need for hospitals and educational institutions, but she vowed that such would never become a part of her own work. Her nuns soon became known around Calcutta as "the running Sisters," as they hurried from place to place in their commitment to reach out to the neediest of society. In the early years they were confined to India, but during the 1960s nine foundations were established in other countries, and by 1975 there were more than a thousand sisters spread out all over the world.[28]

For the first twenty years the ministry went essentially unnoticed. The work was appreciated and well—received wherever it went, but it was not the kind of service that attracted attention. That quickly changed, however, after Mother Teresa was interviewed by Malcolm Muggeridge for the British Broadcasting Company in 1970. Although the interview was aired on late-night television, the response was enormous. A film and a book by Muggeridge that followed further spotlighted the ministry, and Mother Teresa was on her way to becoming an international celebrity. She was not comfortable with the role, as she later revealed. "This celebrity has been forced on me. I use it for the love of Jesus. The press makes people aware of the poor, and that is worth any sacrifice on my part." Speaking of her place in the limelight, she confessed, "For me it is more difficult than bathing a leper."[29]

In recent years the Missionaries of Charity have grown to over three thousand sisters and four hundred brothers. The order has expanded the ministry to meet the needs of segments of society that did not even exist when the order was founded. In Greenwich Village, Gift of Love was founded for AIDS victims to "provide a loving place for the afflicted to die, free of the fear and stigma that AIDS engenders."[30]

Mother Teresa's work is not entirely without criticism. Her stance on abortion has been a sore point for many who believe that poverty would be reduced if abortion was recommended for those women who cannot provide for their children. "Every child has been created for greater things, to love and be loved, in the image of God," she argues. "Once a child is conceived, there is life, God's life. That child has a right to live and be cared for. Abortion destroys two lives, the life of the child and the conscience of the mother. It's not only destroying. It's a killing."[31]

There have been others who have questioned Mother Teresa's ability to direct such a vast organization as the Missionaries of Charity, and, indeed, there have been suggestions of mismanagement. Her response is simple: "If you do it for Jesus, and if you do it with Jesus, everything is possible to him." She, likewise, is sometimes questioned about the underlying purpose of her mission—why she gives the people fish to eat when she might better teach them how to catch

fish for themselves. "But my people can't even stand," she responded. "They're sick, crippled, demented. When I have given them fish to eat and they can stand, I'll turn them over and you give them the rod to catch the fish."[32]

One of the most unique aspects of Mother Teresa's ministry is the spirit in which service is rendered—a spirit that pervades the entire religious order, as Malcolm Muggeridge has vividly written:

> Their life is tough and austere by worldly standards, certainly: yet I never met such delightful, happy women, or such an atmosphere of joy as they create. Mother Teresa, as she is fond of explaining, attaches the utmost importance to this joyousness. The poor, she says, deserve not just service and dedication, but also the joy that belongs to human love. . . . The Missionaries of Charity. . . are multiplying at a fantastic rate. Their Calcutta house is bursting at the seams, and as each new house is opened, there are volunteers clamoring to go there. As the whole story of Christendom shows, if everything is asked for, everything—and more—will be accorded; if little, then nothing.[33]

Mother Teresa is an enigma to many people. She could have wealth and ease and could enjoy the company of the world's most celebrated figures, but instead she chooses to remain as secluded as reporters allow her to be, serving in a lowly capacity with people who often do not even recognize who it is that is bending over them in mercy. When asked, while she was in Oslo, Norway, for the Nobel Peace Prize ceremonies, how she would identify herself, she offered a simple and unpretentious response: "By blood and origin, I am all Albanian. My citizenship is Indian. I am a Catholic nun. As to my calling, I belong to the whole world. As to my heart, I belong entirely to Jesus."[34]

Despite her humility and her lowly life, Mother Teresa has attained the highest position anyone could achieve. This is illustrated in a story told by Dee Jepson, who served as assistant to her husband who was a U.S. senator. She attended a Capitol Hill luncheon for Mother Teresa. "In came this tiny woman, even smaller than I had expected, wearing that familiar blue and white habit, over it a gray sweater that had seen many better days. . . . As that little woman walked into the room, her bare feet in worn sandals, I saw some of the most powerful leaders in this country stand to their feet with tears in their eyes. Just to be in her presence."[35]

Jepson later reflected on what Mother Teresa as a role model has to say to women in this era of women's liberation.

As I listened that afternoon, I thought, "Don't forget this, Dee. Here in this little woman, who doesn't want a thing, never asked for anything for herself, never demanded anything, or shook her fist in anger, here's *real* power." It was a paradox. She has reached down into the gutter and loved and given. She has loved those the world sees as unlovable—the desolate, the dying—because they are created in the image of the God she serves. Ironically, seeking nothing for herself, she has been raised to the pinnacle of world recognition, received the Nobel Peace Prize, and is a figure known to most people, at least in the Western world, and revered by many. She has nothing, yet in a strange way, she has everything. Is she so unlike what womanhood should be?[36]

Mother Teresa in many ways epitomizes the sacrificial service that has characterized women in missions for more than two centuries. She could not have imagined in 1950, when she launched her venture of faith, that within thirty years she would be honored and appreciated the world over. Like so many "guardians of the Great Commission" who went before her, she did not seek recognition, and yet through the recognition she was accorded countless others have been inspired to follow her example. Her life, like the lives of all the other guardians, serves as a motivating model for women of this and future generations.

# Conclusion

How has the face of missions changed for women in the past two centuries? In some respects very little has changed. Women still face many of the same struggles they encountered during the first generations of the modern missionary movement. They still sometimes find themselves serving abroad with no sense of call, except the call that tells them they should go with their husbands. And they still face forms of sex discrimination—even as Lottie Moon did a century ago. Dissention continues to cast its ugly shadows over the missionary community and women are not immune from such "sin in the camp." The problems are much the same as they were two centuries ago.

The challenges women face today are not so different than they were a generation or two ago, either. The trials and triumphs of husband-wife team ministry today are similar in many respects to those confronted by Ruth and Roy Shaffer as they worked with the Maasai earlier in this century, and the pain of leaving little ones still haunts missionary women—though the options for education have vastly increased during the past decades. Singleness still remains an important issue for women missionaries. Although the percentage of single male missionaries has increased (largely due to short-term programs), single women still far outnumber single men in foreign missionary service. One significant factor that has been changing on the missions scene in very recent years is the increase of non-Western participants, and this includes a large number of highly qualified women.

What has changed the most over the past two centuries has been the acceptance women find as they enter missionary service. Meaningful ministry opportunities for women are more readily available today than they have ever been. The doors have opened wide in virtually every avenue of service, with far fewer obstacles than women faced in prior generations.

But along with the two centuries of progress that women have made in the foreign missionary enterprise, there have been some very grave setbacks. The enthusiasm for missions among women has dramatically declined over the past century. While once women flocked to missionary meetings on the home front and a foreign missionary career was seen as the highest vocation a woman could aspire to, today the perspective has changed. Few young women attend women's missionary society meetings, complaining that they are hum-drum and boring. Yet they themselves offer few ideas for creative alternatives. And plans for a missionary career abroad are too easily set aside for what are believed to be more exiting opportunities women can now enjoy on the home front.

The opportunities abound and the obstacles are few, but unless women recapture the vision that once propelled them into the forefront of missionary service, many of the gains will not be taken advantage of. Helen Barrett Montgomery's challenge decades ago is in many ways more applicable today than it was then: "We have done very little original work. We have made very few demands upon the brains of the women ... and as a result, we have been given over to smallness of vision in our missionary life." Women must go forward in missionary outreach, never forgetting the remarkable heritage that is theirs.

# NOTES

## Introduction

[1] Geoffrey Moorhouse, *The Missionaries* (London: Eyre Methuen, 1973), 175–77.

[2] Ibid., 178.

[3] Patricia R. Hill, *The World Their Household: The American Woman's Foreign Mission Movement and Cultural Transformation, 1870–1920* (Ann Arbor: University of Michigan, 1985), 5–8; R. Pierce Beaver, *American Protestant Women in World Mission: A History of the First Feminist Movement in North America* (Grand Rapids: Eerdmans, 1980), 111.

[4] Helen Barrett Montgomery, *Western Women in Eastern Lands* (New York: Macmillan, 1910), 159.

[5] Donald C. Lord, *Mo Bradley and Thailand* (Grand Rapids: Eerdmans, 1969), 43.

## Part I

[1] Mrs. James F. Holcomb, "Correspondence," *Woman's Work for Woman* 12 (1882):300.

## Chapter 1

[1] Louis Bobe, *Hans Egede: Colonizer and Missionary of Greenland* (Copenhagen: Rosenkilde and Bagger, 1952), 16, 23.

[2] Ibid., 23, 29.

[3] Ibid., 162, 167, 168, 172.

[4] Mary Drewery, *William Carey: A Biography* (Grand Rapids: Zondervan, 1978), 21.

[5] Ibid., 21–24.

[6] Ibid., 32–33.

[7] S. Pearce Carey, *William Carey* (London: Hodder and Stoughton, 1926), 107.

[8] Drewery, *William Carey*, 44–45.

[9] Carey, *William Carey*, 107.

[10] Ibid., 113.

[11] Drewery, *William Carey*, 51–52.

[12] Ibid., 70; Carey, *William Carey*, 145, 162.

[13] Drewery, *William Carey*, 115, 146.

[14] Oliver Ransford, *David Livingstone: The Dark Interior* (New York: St. Martin's, 1978), 38.

[15] Moorhouse, *The Missionaries*, 116.

[16] Edith Deen, *Great Women of the Christian Faith* (New York: Harper & Row, 1959), 192.

[17] Cecil Northcott, *Robert Moffat: Pioneer in Africa, 1817–1870* (London: Lutterworth, 1961), 189.

[18] Ransford, *David Livingstone*, 39.

[19] Northcott, *Robert Moffat*, 189.

[20] Deen, *Great Women*, 193–94.

[21] Ibid., 194.

[22] Moorhouse, *The Missionaries*, 122.

[23] Deen, *Great Women*, 194; Ransford, *David Livingstone*, 118.

[24] Ibid., 196.

[25] Moorhouse, *The Missionaries*, 146.

[26] Ibid., 146–47.

## Chapter 2

[1] Barbara Welter, "She Hath Done What She Could: Protestant Women's Missionary Careers in Nineteenth-Century America," in Janet Wilson James, *Women in American Religion* (Philadelphia: University of Pennsylvania, 1980), 116–17.

[2] Phebe Hanaford, *Daughters of America; or, Women of the Century* (Augusta, Maine: True and Company, 1883), 487–89.

[3] William Dean, *Memoirs of Mrs. Lucy T. Lord of the Chinese Baptist Missions* (Philadelphia: n.p., 1854), 8–11.

[4] Augustus R. Buckland, *Women in the Mission Field: Pioneers and Martyrs* (New York: Thomas Whittaker, 1895), 44–45.

[5] Buckland, *Women in the Mission Field*, 45–50.

[6] Ibid., 25, 28, 32.

[7] Ibid., 36.

[8] Winifred Mathews, *Dauntless Women: Stories of Pioneer Wives* (Freeport, N.Y.: Books for Libraries Press, 1947), 109–13.

[9] Ibid., 118.

[10] Courtney Anderson, *To the Golden Shore: The Life of Adoniram Judson* (Grand Rapids: Zondervan, 1972), 84.

[11] James D. Knowles, *Memoirs of Mrs. Ann H. Judson* (Boston: Lincoln and Edmands, 1829), 58.

[12] Ibid., 111–12.

[13] Ibid., 147.

[14] *American Baptist Magazine*, 4 (January 1823): 19.

[15] Joan Jacobs Brumberg, *Mission For Life: The Story of the Family of Adoniram Judson* (New York: The Free Press, 1980), 87–88.

[16] Ibid., 92.

[17] Donald C. Lord, *Mo Bradley and Thailand* (Grand Rapids: Eerdmans, 1969), 52.

[18] Ruth A. Tucker, *From Jerusalem to Irian Jaya: A Biographical History of Christian Missions* (Grand Rapids: Zondervan, 1983), 128–29.

[19] Knowles, *Memoirs*, 103.

[20] Brumberg, *Mission for Life*, 41.

[21] J. Johnston Walsh, *A Memorial of the Futtehgurh Mission and Her Martyred Missionaries* (Philadelphia: Joseph M. Wilson, 1859), 175, 157, 186.

[22] Ibid., 181.

[23] Ibid., 189–90.

[24] Ibid., 190, 305.

## Chapter 3

[1] E. R. Pitman, *Lady Missionaries in Many Lands* (London: Pickering & Inglis, n.d.), 110.

[2] Winifred Mathews, *Dauntless Women: Stories of Pioneer Wives* (Freeport, N.Y.: Books for Libraries Press, 1947), 114–15.

[3] Edith Deen, *Great Women of the Christian Faith* (New York: Harper & Row, 1959), 187.

[4] J. C. Pollock, *Hudson Taylor and Maria: Pioneers in China* (Grand Rapids: Zondervan, 1962), 79.

[5] Ibid., 82–83.

[6] Ibid., 84–98.

[7] Ibid., 173.

[8] Ibid.

[9] Ibid.

[10] Ibid., 182–83.

[11] Ibid., 202.

[12] Ibid.

[13] Ibid., 204, 206.

[14] Deen, *Great Women*, 193–94.

[15] Ruth A. Tucker, *From Jerusalem to Irian Jaya: A Biographical History of Christian Missions* (Grand Rapids: Zondervan, 1983), 190.

[16] Rosalind Goforth, *Goforth of China* (Grand Rapids: Zondervan, 1937), 156.

[17] Ibid., 156–57.

[18] Ibid., 157.

## Chapter 4

[1] Elisabeth Elliot Leitch, "The Place of Women in World Missions," in *Jesus Christ: Lord of the Universe, Hope of the World*, ed. by David M. Howard (Downers Grove: InterVarsity Press, 1974), 124–25.

[2] Jane Hunter, *The Gospel of Gentility: American Women Missionaries in Turn-of-the-Century China* (New Haven: Yale University Press, 1974), 88.

[3] Nancy F. Cott, *The Bonds of Womanhood: "Woman's Sphere" in New England, 1780–1835* (New Haven: Yale University Press, 1977), 140–41.

[4] Leecy A. Barnett, "Hundreds of Pious Women: Presbyterian Women Missionaries to the American Indians, 1833–1893 " (M.A. Thesis, Trinity Evangelical Divinity School, 1985), 127.

[5] Robert Speer, *Servants of the King* (New York: Interchurch Press, 1909), 144.

[6] Barnett, *Pious Women*, 129.

[7] Mrs. Ethan Curtis, "The Reflex Influence of Missions," *Missionary Review of the World*, 5 (March 1982): 183.

[8] James Thoburn, *Life of Isabella Thoburn* (Cincinnati: Jennings and Pye, 1903); quoted in Barbara Welter, "She Hath Done What She Could: Protestant Women's Missionary Careers in Nineteenth-Century America," in Janet Wilson James, *Women in American Religion* (Philadelphia: University of Pennsylvania, 1980), 120.

[9] Mrs. James F. Holcomb, Correspondence, *Woman's Work for Woman*, 12 (1882): 300; Frederick B. Hoyt, " 'When a Field was Found too Difficult for a Man, a Woman Should be Sent': Adele M. Fielde in Asia, 1865–1890," *The Historian* 44 (May 1982): 317.

[10] Quoted in Leslie A. Flemming, "Women and Witness: American Presbyterian Women Missionaries in North India, 1870–1910" (Paper delivered at Wheaton College, June 17, 1986).

[11] John R. Rice, *Bobbed Hair, Bossy Wives, and Women Preachers* (Murfreesboro, Tenn.: Sword of the Lord, 1941), 64–65.

[12] Pearl S. Buck, *The Exile* (New York: Reynal & Hitchcock, 1936), 283.

[13] Irwin Hyatt, *Our Ordered Lives Confess: Three Nineteenth-Century American Missionaries in East Shantung* (Cambridge, Mass.: Harvard University Press, 1976), 95.

[14] Ibid., 99.

[15] Ibid., 104.

[16] Ibid., 104–105.

[17] Ibid., 106.

[18] Ibid., 115, 117.

[19] Ibid., 113.

[20] Ruth A. Tucker, *From Jerusalem to Irian Jaya: A Biographical History of Christian Missions* (Grand Rapids: Zondervan, 1983), 238.

[21] Catherine Allen, *The New Lottie Moon Story* (Nashville: Broadman, 1980), 288.

[22] Buck, *Exile*, 77–78, 83, 90, 92.

[23] Ibid., 172, 167.

[24] Theodore F. Harris, *Pearl S. Buck: A Biography* (New York: John Day, 1969), 28.

[25] Buck, *Exile*, 129, 188.

[26] Nora Stirling, *Pearl Buck: A Woman in Conflict* (New York: New Century Publishers, 1983), 9, 12.

[27] Buck, *Exile*, 130, 198, 147, 188.

[28] Ibid., 251, 278.

[29] Ibid., 264, 191–92.

[30] Ibid., 280–81.

[31] Ibid., 313–14.

[32] *Missionary Review of the World* 11 (November 1898): 873–74.

[33] Dr. and Mrs. Howard Taylor, *J. Hudson Taylor: God's Man in China* (Chicago: Moody, 1978), 208.

[34] Phyllis Thompson, *Each to Her Own Post* (London: Hodder and Stoughton, 1982), 57–59.

## Chapter 5

[1] Neil Gunson, *Messengers of Grace: Evangelical Missionaries in the South Seas, 1797–1860* (New York: Harper & Row, 1960), 202.

[2] Ibid., 164–65.

[3] Ibid., 154.

[4] Leecy Barnett, "Hundreds of Pious Women: Presbyterian Women Missionaries to the American Indians, 1833–1893" (M.A. Thesis, Trinity Evangelical Divinity School, 1985), 65–66.

[5] Ibid., 67.

[6] Ruth A. Tucker, *From Jerusalem to Irian Jaya: A Biographical History of Christian Missions* (Grand Rapids: Zondervan, 1983), 98.

[7] Ibid., 100.

[8] Opal Sweazea Allen, *Narcissa Whitman: An Historical Biography* (Portland: Binfords & Mort, 1959), 61.

[9] Nard Jones, *The Great Command: The Story of Marcus and Narcissa Whitman and the Oregon Country Pioneers* (Boston: Little, Brown, and Co., 1959), 202, 229.

[10] Clifford M. Drury, ed., *First White Women Over the Rockies: Diaries, Letters, and Biographical Sketches of the Six Women of the Oregon Mission who made the Overland Journey in 1836 and 1938*, Vol. 3 (Glendale: Arthur H. Clark, 1966), 110.

[11] Ibid., 113–14.

[12] Ibid., 114.

[13] Ibid., 115.

[14] Tucker, *From Jerusalem to Irian Jaya*, 101.

[15] J. C. Pollock, *Hudson Taylor and Maria: Pioneers in China* (Grand Rapids: Zondervan, 1976), 147.

[16] Pat Barr, *To China With Love: The Lives and Times of Protestant Missionaries in China, 1860–1900* (Garden City, N.Y.: Doubleday, 1973), 9–10, 29.

[17] Ibid., 30.

[18] Ibid., 30–31.

[19] Ibid., 31.

[20] Pollock, *Hudson Taylor and Maria*, 89.

[21] Ibid., 89–95.

[22] Barr, *To China With Love*, 32.

[23] Phyllis Thompson, *Each To Her Own Post* (London: Hodder and Stoughton, 1982), 53.

[24] Barr, *To China With Love*, 50.

[25] Ibid., 50–51.

[26] Thompson, *Each To Her Own Post*, 58–61.

[27] Irwin T. Hyatt, Jr., *Our Ordered Lives Confess: Three Nineteenth-Century American Missionaries in East Shantung* (Cambridge, Mass.: Harvard University Press, 1976), 6–7.

[28] Ibid., 8.

[29] Ibid., 40.

[30] Ibid., 40–41.

[31] Ibid., 46.

[32] Ibid., 55, 61–62.

[33] Ibid., 235.

## Part II

[1] Leslie A. Flemming, "Women and Witness: American Presbyterian Women Missionaries in North India, 1870–1910," paper delivered at Wheaton College, June 17, 1986, 11–12.

## Chapter 6

[1] Joan Jacobs Brumberg, *Mission for Life* (New York: The Free Press, 1980), 88.

[2] Albert L. Vail, *Mary Webb and the Mother Society* (Philadelphia: American Baptist Publication Society, 1914), ii.

[3] R. Pierce Beaver, *American Protestant Women in World Mission: A History of the First Feminist Movement in North America* (Grand Rapids: Eerdmans, 1980) 13–14.

[4] Ibid., 24.

[5] Vail, *Mary Webb*, 8–9.

[6] Ibid., 28–29.

[7] Inez Haynes Irwin, *Angels and Amazons: A Hundred Years of American Women* (New York: Arno Press, 1974), 52.

[8] Leon McBeth, *Women in Baptist Life* (Nashville: Broadman, 1979), 77.

[9] Ibid., 77–78.

[10] Ibid., 78.

[11] Ibid., 77.

[12] Vail, *Mary Webb*, 65–68, 107.

[13] Mary R. Parkman, *Heroines of Service* (New York: The Century Co., 1917), 15–16.

[14] Ibid., 20–22.

[15] Annie Ryder Gracey, *Eminent Missionary Women* (New York: Eaton & Mains, 1898), 4–5.

[16] Patricia Hill, *The World Their Household: The American Woman's Foreign Mission Movement and Cultural Transformation, 1870–1920* (Ann Arbor: University of Michigan, 1985), 42.

[17] Gracey, *Eminent Missionary Women*, 6, 9.


## Chapter 7

[1] Francis Parkman, *The Jesuits in North America in the Seventeenth Century* (Boston: Little, Brown, and Company, 1868), 278.

[2] Stephen Neill, *A History of Christian Missions* (New York: Penguin, 1964), 423.

[3] Glenn D. Kittler, *The Woman God Loved* (Garden City: Hanover House, 1959), 58.

[4] Henri Daniel-Rops, *The Heroes of God* (New York: Hawthorne Books, 1959), 154–55.

[5] Ibid., 162.

[6] Kittler, *The Woman God Loved*, 148.

[7] Ibid., 176–77, 180.

[8] Daniel-Rops, *The Heroes of God*, 163.

[9] Kittler, *The Woman God Loved*, 214.

[10] Ibid., 225.

[11] Ibid., 225.

[12] Ibid., 226.

[13] Ibid., 227.

[14] Elliott Wright, *Holy Company: Christian Heroes and Heroines* (New York: Macmillan, 1980), 93–94.

[15] Lorry Lutz, *Born to Lose, Bound to Win: The Amazing Journey of Mother Eliza George* (Irvine, Calif.: Harvest House, 1980), 33.

[16] Ibid., 37.

[17] Ibid., 46–47.

[18] Ibid., 54, 56, 61.

[19] Ibid., 71, 77.

[20] Ibid., 75, 118.

[21] Ibid., 122.

[22] Ibid., 137–38.

[23] Ibid., 184.


## Chapter 8

[1] Timothy L. Smith, *Revivalism and Social Reform: American Protestantism on the Eve of the Civil War* (Gloucester, Mass.: Peter Smith, 1976), 169.

[2] Ibid., 170.

[3] Flora Larsson, *My Best Men are Women* (London: Hodder and Stoughton, 1974), 33–35.

[4] Patricia Hill, *The World Their Household: The American Woman's Foreign Mission Movement and Cultural Transformation, 1870–1920* (Ann Arbor: University of Michigan, 1985), 45.

[5] Mary E. A. Chamberlain, *Fifty Years in Foreign Fields: A History of Five Decades of the Woman's Board of Foreign Missions, Reformed Church in America* (New York: Woman's Board of Foreign Missions, Reformed Church in America, 1925), 5–6.

[6] Annie Ryder Gracey, *Eminent Missionary Women* (New York: Eaton & Mains, 1898), 18.

[7] Carma Van Liere, "Sarah Doremus: Reformed Church Saint," *The Church Herald* (October 4, 1985), 17.

[7] Ibid., 17.

[9] Chamberlain, *Fifty Years*, 6.

[10] Louis L. King, "Mother Whittemore's Miracles," *The Alliance Witness* (January 21, 1987), 20.

[11] Ibid., 20.

[12] Phyllis Thompson, *Each To Her Own Post* (London: Hodder and Stoughton, 1982), 78–79.

[13] Ibid., 78.

[14] Charles Edwin Jones, *Perfectionist Persuasion: The Holiness Movement and American Methodism, 1867–1936* (Metuchen N.J.: Scarecrow, 1974), 189–94.

## Chapter 9

[1] Ruth A. Tucker, *From Jerusalem to Irian Jaya: A Biographical History of Christian Missions* (Grand Rapids: Zondervan, 1983), 148, 314, 331.

[2] Opel Sweazea Allen, *Narcissa Whitman: An Historical Biography* (Portland, Ore.: Binfords & Mort, 1959), 47, 54, 84, 131.

[3] Rosemary Cunningham, *Under a Thatched Roof in a Brazilian Jungle* (Grand Rapids: Zondervan, 1955), 11.

[4] Ibid., 11, 92.

[5] Tucker, *From Jerusalem to Irian Jaya*, 159.

[6] Ibid., 161–62.

[7] Miriam Adeney, "Esther Across Cultures: Indigenous Leadership Roles for Women," *Missiology* XV (July 1987): 324.

[8] W. P. Livingstone, *Mary Slessor of Calabar: Pioneer Missionary* (London: Hodder & Stoughton, 1915), 51, 57.

[9] Ibid., 65.

[10] James Buchan, *The Expendable Mary Slessor* (New York: Seabury Press, 1981), 66.

[11] Livingstone, *Mary Slessor*, 114.

[12] Ibid., 135.

[13] Carol Christian and Gladys Plummer, *God and One Red Head: Mary Slessor of Calabar* (Grand Rapids: Zondervan, 1970), 177.

[14] Tucker, *From Jerusalem to Irian Jaya*, 162–63.

[15] Mildred Cable and Francesca French, *Something Happened* (London: Hodder & Stoughton, 1934), 122.

[16] Ibid., 123.

[17] Phyllis Thompson, *Desert Pilgrim* (Lincoln, Neb.: Back to the Bible, 1957), 14.

[18] Ibid., 15.

[19] Ibid., 21–22.

[20] Cable and French, *Something Happened*, 142.

[21] Ibid., 145, 159, 163.

[22] Ibid., 165–66.

[23] Thompson, *Desert Pilgrim*, 70.

[24] Cable and French, *Something Happened*, 226–27.

[25] Ibid., 280.

## Chapter 10

[1] Ruth Hitchcock, *The Good Hand of Our God* (Elgin, Ill.: David C. Cook, 1975), 14–15.

[2] Leecy A. Barnett, "Hundreds of Pious Women: Presbyterian Women Missionaries to the American Indians, 1833–1893" (Trinity Evangelical Divinity School, M.A. Thesis, 1985), 114–15.

[3] Daniel C. Eddy, *Heroines of the Missionary Enterprise* (London: Arthur Hall, Virtue, and Co., n.d.), 240, 124–25.

[4] Ibid., 128.

[5] Ibid., 128, 130, 134.

[6] Ibid., 130, 135, 138.

[7] Ibid., 131, 137.

[8] Ibid., 140.

[9] Barnett, *Hundreds of Pious Women*, 116–17.

[10] Michael C. Coleman, "Christianizing and Americanizing the Nez Perce: Sue L. McBeth and her Attitudes to the Indians," *Journal of Presbyterian History*, Vol. 53 (Winter 1975), 339–40.

[11] Barnett, *Hundreds of Pious Women*, 117.

[12] Coleman, "Christianizing and Americanizing the Nez Perce," 342.

[13] Ibid., 342.

[14] Barnett, *Hundreds of Pious Women*, 118.

[15] Coleman, "Christianizing and Americanizing the Nez Perce," 347.

[16] Ibid., 351.

[17] Maria Nilsen, with Paul H. Sheetz, *Malla Moe* (Chicago: Moody Press, 1956), 26.

[18] Ibid., 27–29.

[19] Alan H. Winquist, "Scandinavian-American Missions in Southern Africa and Zaire," Unpublished paper delivered at the Billy Graham Center, Wheaton, Illinois (June 1986), 14.

[20] Ibid., 15.

[21] Letter from Grace Sanders, February 10, 1940, Moe Collection 280, box 2, folder 5, Archives of the Billy Graham Center, quoted in Winquist, "Scandinavian-American Missions," 14.

[22] Winquist, "Scandinavian-American Missions," 14.

[23] Nilsen, *Malla Moe*, 174–75.

[24] Ibid., 166.

[25] Ibid., 135.

[26] Fredrik Franson, "Prophesying Daughters," Unpublished Paper, Stockholm, Sweden, 1897, 2.

[27] Janette Hassey, *No Time for Silence: Evangelical Women in Public Ministry Around the Turn of the Century* (Grand Rapids: Zondervan, 1986), 145.

## Chapter 11

[1] C. S. Winchell, "Mary Clarke Nind," *Woman's Missionary Friend* 37 (November 1905): 382–83.

2 Patricia Hill, *The World Their Household: The American Woman's Foreign Mission Movement and Cultural Transformation, 1870-1920* (Ann Arbor: University of Michigan, 1985), 87–89.

3 Bobbie Sorrill, *Annie Armstrong: Dreamer in Action* (Nashville: Broadman, 1984), 19, 32, 39, 57, 59, 68, 77, 81.

4 Ibid., 83.

5 Ibid., 267.

6 Ibid., 93–95.

7 Ibid., 165, 168, 171.

8 Ibid., 156, 127–28.

9 Ibid., 204–206.

10 Ibid., 218, 221–26.

11 Ibid., 228–29.

12 Ibid., 230, 233, 235, 251.

13 Ibid., 123, 180, 182.

14 Ibid., 253.

15 R. Pierce Beaver, *American Protestant Women in World Mission: A History of the First Feminist Movement in North America* (Grand Rapids: Eerdmans,

16 Hill, *The World Their Household* 143.

17 Helen Barrett Montgomery, *Helen Barrett Montgomery: From Campus to World Citizenship* (London: Fleming H. Revell, 1940), 22.

18 Ibid., 24.

19 Ibid., 29.

20 Ibid., 31, 34, 37.

21 Ibid., 38, 44.

22 Ibid., 46, 65.

23 Ibid., 72–73, 76.

24 Ibid., 78.

25 Albert Beaven, "Helen of Rochester," in Montgomery, *Helen Barrett Montgomery*, 88, 90, 92.

26 Mrs. Curtis Lee Laws, "Her Baptist World," in Montgomery, *Helen Barrett Montgomery*, 109.

27 Louise A. Cattan, *Lamps are for Lighting: The Story of Helen Barrett Montgomery and Lucy Waterbury Peabody* (Grand Rapids: Eerdmans, 1972), 36–43.

28 Helen Barrett Montgomery, *The King's Highway: A Study of Present Conditions on the Foreign Field* (West Medford, Mass.: The Central Committee on the United Study of Foreign Missions, 1915), 244–48.

29 Helen Barrett Montgomery, *Western Women in Eastern Lands* (New York: Macmillan, 1910), 243–44.

30 Cattan, *Lamps Are for Lighting*, 66–75.

31 Hill, *The World Their Household*, 1985.

32 Cattan, *Lamps Are for Lighting*, 103, 108.

33 Geoffrey Moorhouse, *The Missionaries* (London: Eyre Methuen, 1973), 276.

34 Phyllis Thompson, *Each To Her Own Post* (London: Hodder and Stoughton, 1982), 83–84.

35 Mildred Cable and Francesca French, *A Woman Who Laughed* (Philadelphia: China Inland Mission, 1934), 48.

36 Ibid., 61, 63.

37 Ibid., 50–51, 54.

38 Ibid., 82–85.

39 Ibid., 105–106.

40 Ibid., 121, 135.

41 Ibid., 138–40.

42 Ibid., 143–44.

43 Ibid., 144.

44 Ibid., 146–47.

45 Ibid., 156.

46 Ibid., 154–55.

47 Ibid., 165.

48 Ibid., 191.

49 Ibid., 231.

## Chapter 12

1 Patricia R. Hill, *The World Their Household: The American Woman's Foreign Mission Movement and Cultural Transformation, 1870–1920* (Ann Arbor: University of Michigan, 1985), 49.

2 Ibid., 133.

3 Barbara Welter, "She Hath Done What She Could: Protestant Women's Missionary Careers in Nineteenth-Century America," in Janet Wilson James, ed., *Women in American Religion* (Philadelphia: University of Pennsylvania, 1980), 118.

4 J. Waskom Pickett, *Christian Mass Movements in India* (New York: Abingdon, 1933), 193.

5 Susan R. Janvier, "Inside Zenanas of Allahabad," *Woman's Work for Women*, 8 (August 1898): 216.

6 Shirley S. Garrett, "Images of Chinese Women," in John and Ellen Low Webster, eds., *The Church and Women in the Third World* (Philadelphia: Westminster, 1985), 27.

7 E. R. Pitman, *Lady Missionaries in Many Lands* (London: Pickering & Inglis, n.d.), 149.

8 Eliza Gillett Bridgman, *Daughters of China; or, Sketches of Domestic Life in the Celestial Empire* (New York: Robert Carter & Brothers, 1953), viii.

9 Helen N. Stevens, *Memorial Biography of Adele M. Fielde: Humanitarian* (New York: The Fielde Memorial Committee, 1918), 80.

10 Ibid., 86.

[11] Frederick B. Hoyt, "'When a Field was Found too Difficult for a Man, A Woman should be Sent': Adele M. Fielde in Asia, 1865–1890," *The Historian*, 44 (May 1982): 318–22.

[12] Stevens, *Memorial Biography*, 111.

[13] Ibid., 115.

[14] Ibid., 119.

[15] Ibid., 125.

[16] Hoyt, "When a Field Was Found Too Difficult," 334.

[17] Beaver, *American Protestant Women*, 119.

[18] Winburn T. Thomas, *Protestant Beginnings in Japan: The First Three Decades, 1859-1889* (Rutland, Vt.: Charles E. Tuttle, 1959), 108.

[19] Margaret E. Burton, *Women Workers of the Orient* (West Bedford, Ma.: Central Committee on the United Study of Foreign Missions, 1918), 223–24.

[20] Arthur T. Pierson, *The New Acts of the Apostles* (New York: Baker & Taylor, l894), 342.

[21] Augustus R. Buckland, *Women in the Mission Field* (New York: Thomas Whittaker, 1895), 86, 90.

[22] Ibid., 88.

[23] Ibid., 89.

[24] M. Geraldine Taylor, *Margaret King's Vision* (Philadelphia: China Inland Mission, 1934), ix.

[25] Ibid., ix.

[26] Ibid., 27.

[27] Ibid., 38.

[28] Phyllis Thompson, *Each To Her Own Post* (London: Hodder and Stoughton, 1982), 73–74.

[29] Ibid., 74.

[30] Taylor, *Margaret King's Vision*, 114.

[31] Ibid., 131.

[32] Thompson, *Each To Her Own Post*, 75.

[33] Taylor, *Margaret King's Vision*, 112, 121.

[34] Thompson, *Each To Her Own Post*, 87.

[35] Ibid., 89, 92–93.

[36] Ibid., 93–94.

[37] Ibid., 95–96.

[38] Ibid., 82, 98.

## Chapter 13

[1] Phyllis Thompson, *Desert Pilgrim* (Lincoln, Neb.: Back to the Bible, 1957), 11, 33.

[2] Ibid., 34–35.

[3] Elisabeth Elliot, *A Chance To Die: The Life and Legacy of Amy Carmichael* (Old Tappan, N.J.: Revell, 1987), 37–38.

[4] Frank Houghton, *Amy Carmichael of Dohnavur* (London: Society for the Propagation of Christian Knowledge, 1954), 78.

[5] Ibid., 73.

[6] Ibid., 88–89.

[7] Ibid., 105.

[8] Sherwood Eddy, *Pathfinders of the World Missionary Crusade* (Nashville: Abingdon, 1945), 126.

[9] Houghton, *Amy Carmichael*, 117–18.

[10] Ibid., 121–22.

[11] Ibid., 135–36.

[12] Ibid., 62.

[13] Ibid., 247.

[14] Eddy, *Pathfinders*, 126–27.

[15] Houghton, *Amy Carmichael*, 213.

[16] Eddy, *Pathfinders*, 127.

[17] Tucker, *From Jerusalem to Irian Jaya: A Biographical History of Christian Missions* (Grand Rapids: Zondervan, 1983), 242.

[18] Louise Walker, "Lillian Trasher: Mother to Thousands in Egypt," Unpublished manuscript (Springfield, Mo., 1986), 1, taken from Adele Dalton, *Letters From Lillian* (Springfield, Mo.: Assemblies of God Division of Foreign Missions, n.d.)

[19] Lester F. Sumrall, *Lillian Trasher: The Nile Mother* (Springfield, Mo.: Gospel Publishing House, 1951), 12–13.

[20] Walker, "Lillian Trasher," 1–2.

[21] Sumrall, *Lillian Trasher*, 113–29.

[22] Walker, "Lillian Trasher," 3.

[23] Ibid., 4.

[24] Ibid., 5.

## Chapter 14

[1] Shirley S. Garrett, "Sisters All: Feminism and the American Women's Missionary Movement," in Torben Christensen and William R. Hutchinson, eds., *Missionary Ideologies in the Imperialist Era: 1880–1920* (Denmark: Aros, 1982), 225.

[2] Ibid., 226.

[3] R. Pierce Beaver, *American Protestant Women in World Mission: A History of the First Feminist Movement in North America* (Grand Rapids: Eerdmans, 1980), 79.

[4] Ibid., 81.

[5] Christiana Tsai, *Queen of the Dark Chamber* (Chicago: Moody, 1953), 67–68.

[6] Ibid., 68, 71–72.

[7] Ibid., 83–88.

[8] Ibid., 184.

[9] Sherwood Eddy, *Pathfinders of the World Missionary Crusade* (Nashville: Abingdon, 1945), 93.

[10] Beaver, *American Protestant Women*, 123.

[11] James. M. Thoburn, *Life of Isabella Thoburn* (New York: Eaton and Mains, 1903), 148–49.

[12] Ibid., 192.

[13] Eddy, *Pathfinders*, 94.

[14] Ibid., 94.

[15] Thoburn, *Isabella Thoburn*, 360–62.

[16] Pandita Ramabai, *The High-Caste Hindu Woman* (London: George Bell and Sons, 1888), xxi.

[17] Helen S. Dyer, *Pandita Ramabai: Her Vision, Her Mission and Her Triumph of Faith* (London: Pickering & Inglis, n.d.), 24.

[18] Shamsundar Manohar Adhav, *Pandita Ramabai* (Madras: The Christian Literature Society, 1979), 6–8, 131.

[19] Ibid., 131.

[20] Ibid., 141–42.

[21] Ibid., 42.

[22] Nancy Hardesty, *Great Women of the Faith* (Grand Rapids: Baker, 1980), 128.

[23] Dyer, *Pandita Ramabai*, 71.

[24] Ibid., 86, 113–14.

[25] Ibid., 115–16.

[26] Adhav, *Pandita Ramabai*, 19.

[27] Elliott Wright, *Holy Company: Christian Heroes and Heroines* (New York: Macmillan, 1980), 44.

[28] Dyer, *Pandita Ramabai*, 136.

[29] Wright, *Holy Company*, 45.

## Chapter 15

[1] Dorothy Clarke Wilson, *Palace of Healing: The Story of Dr. Clara Swain, First Woman Missionary Doctor and the Hospital She Founded* (New York: McGraw-Hill, 1968), passim.

[2] Annie Ryder Gracey, *Eminent Missionary Women* (New York: Eaton & Mains, 1898), 214–15.

[3] Winifred Mathews, *Dauntless Women: Stories of Pioneer Wives* (Freeport, N.Y.: Books for Libraries Press, 1947), 148.

[4] Ibid., 149.

[5] Ibid., 158.

[6] Ibid., 159–60.

[7] Leecy Barnett, *Hundreds of Pious Women: Presbyterian Women Missionaries to the American Indians, 1833–1893* (Trinity Evangelical Divinity School, M.A. Thesis, 1985), 61.

[8] Nancy Boyd, *Emissaries: The Overseas work of the American YWCA, 1895–1970* (New York: The Woman's Press, 1986), 3–5.

[9] Ibid.

[10] Robert E. Speer, *Servants of the King* (New York: Interchurch Press, 1909), 94.

[11] Ibid., 95.

[12] Ibid., 96.

[13] Ibid., 98–99.

[14] James and Marti Hefley, *By Their Blood: Christian Martyrs of the 20th Century* (Milford, Mich.: Mott Media, 1979), 46.

[15] Speer, *Servants of the King*, 100.

[16] Ibid., 103.

[17] Hefleys, *By Their Blood*, 46.

[18] Speer, *Servants of the King*, 107.

[19] Ibid., 108–109.

[20] Dorothy Clarke Wilson, "The Legacy of Ida S. Scudder," *International Bulletin of Missionary Research*, 1 (January 1985): 26.

[21] Dorothy Clarke Wilson, *Dr. Ida: The Story of Dr. Ida Scudder of Vellore* (New York: McGraw-Hill, 1959), 22.

[22] Mary Pauline Jeffrey, *Dr. Ida: India* (New York: Fleming H. Revell, 1938), 49–51.

[23] Ruth A. Tucker, *From Jerusalem to Irian Jaya: A Biographical History of Christian Missions* (Grand Rapids: Zondervan, 1983), 334.

[24] Wilson, *Dr. Ida*, 286.

[25] Tucker, *From Jerusalem to Irian Jaya*, 337.

[26] Phyllis Thompson, *Each to Her Own Post* (London: Hodder and Stoughton, 1982), 133–35.

[27] Ibid., 136–37.

[28] Ibid., 140–41.

[29] Ibid., 143–44.

[30] Isobel Kuhn, *Assent to the Tribes* (Chicago: Moody, 1956), 198.

[31] Thompson, *Each to Her Own Post*, 144–45.

[32] Ibid., 148, 152–53.

[33] Ibid., 150.

[34] Ibid., 154–55.

[35] Ibid., 156–57.

## Chapter 16

[1] Clarence W. Hall, *Adventurers for God* (New York: Harper & Row, 1959), 119.

[2] Ethel Wallis and Mary Bennett, *Two Thousand Tongues to Go* (New York: Harper & Row, 1959), 98.

[3] Eunice V. Pike, *Not Alone* (Chicago: Moody Press, 1964), 10.

4 Eunice V. Pike, *Words Wanted* (Huntington Beach, Ca.: Wycliffe Bible Translators, 1958), 8–9.

5 Pike, *Not Alone*, 78.

6 Pike, *Words Wanted*, 50–52.

7 Ibid., 55, 148, 185.

8 Helen W. Kooiman, *Cameos: Women Fashioned by God* (Wheaton: Tyndale, 1971), 68–69.

9 Ibid., 70–71.

10 Ibid., 71–72.

11 Ibid., 73–74.

12 Ruth A. Tucker, *From Jerusalem to Irian Jaya: A Biographical History of Christian Missions* (Grand Rapids: Zondervan, 1983), 363.

13 Clarence W. Hall, *Miracle on the Sepik* (Costa Mesa, Calif.: Gift Publications, 1980), 5.

14 Ibid., 3, 8.

15 Ibid., 8–9.

16 Ibid., 14.

17 Ibid., 18.

18 Ibid., 18–19.

19 Ibid., 20.

20 Ibid., 21.

21 Ibid., 24.

22 Ibid., 28.

23 Ibid., 33–34.

24 Ibid., 40, 53–54.

## Chapter 17

1 Mabel Francis with Gerald B. Smith, *One Shall Chase a Thousand* (Harrisburg: Christian Publications, 1968), 32–33.

2 Ibid., 33–34.

3 Ibid., 34–38.

4 Ibid., 22–23.

5 Ibid., 44, 48.

6 Robert L. Niklaus, John S. Sawin, and Samuel J. Stoesz, *All For Jesus: God at Work in the Christian and Missionary Alliance Over One Hundred Years* (Camp Hill, PA: Christian Publications, 1986), 195.

7 Francis, *One Shall Chase*, 56–60.

8 Ibid., 63, 67, 75–79.

9 Ibid., 89.

10 Niklaus et al, *All For Jesus*, 201.

11 Leslie Andrews, "Restricted Freedom: A. B. Simpson's View of Women in Ministry," in David F. Hartzfeld and Charles Nienkirchen, eds., *The Birth of a Vision* (Beaverlodge, Alberta: Buena Book Services, 1986), 219.

12 Andrews, "Restricted Freedom," 220.

13 A. B. Simpson, *When the Comforter Came* (New York: Christian Publications, 1911), 11.

14 Ibid., 11.

15 Ruth A. Tucker, *From Jerusalem to Irian Jaya: A Biographical History of Christian Missions* (Grand Rapids: Zondervan, 1983), 249–50.

16 Phyllis Thompson, *A Transparent Woman: The Compelling Story of Gladys Aylward* (Grand Rapids: Zondervan, 1971), 20.

17 Tucker, *From Jerusalem to Irian Jaya*, 251.

18 Alan Burgess, *The Small Woman* (New York: Dutton, 1957), 29.

19 Tucker, *From Jerusalem to Irian Jaya*, 251.

20 Burgess, *The Small Woman*, 110.

21 Tucker, *From Jerusalem to Irian Jaya*, 252–253.

22 Burgess, *The Small Woman*, 123–28.

23 Ibid., 162.

24 Ibid., 166.

25 Tucker, *From Jerusalem to Irian Jaya*, 253.

26 Burgess, *The Small Woman*, 197.

27 Thompson, *A Transparent Woman*, 73–74.

28 Burgess, *The Small Woman*, 214, 217; Thompson, *The Transparent Woman*, 83.

29 Tucker, *From Jerusalem to Irian Jaya*, 254.

30 Ibid., 431.

31 Ibid., 430.

32 James and Marti Hefley, *No Time for Tombstones: Life and Death in the Vietnamese Jungle* (Wheaton: Tyndale, 1976), 87, 91.

33 James and Marti Hefley, *By Their Blood: Christian Martyrs of the 20th Century* (Milford, MI: Mott, 1979), 131.

## Chapter 18

1 J. Herbert Kane, *Life and Work on the Mission Field* (Grand Rapids: Baker, 1980), 143.

2 Louise A. Cattan, *Lamps are for Lighting: The Story of Helen Barrett Montgomery and Lucy Waterbury Peabody* (Grand Rapids: Eerdmans, 1972), 38.

3 Ruth A. Tucker, "Female Mission Strategists: A Historical and Contemporary Perspective," *Missiology*, 15 (January 1987): 86–87.

4 Tucker, *From Jerusalem to Irian Jaya*, 397.

5 Thomas E. and Elizabeth S. Brewster, "Bonding and the Missionary Task" in Ralph Winter and Steven Hawthorne, eds., *Perspectives on the World Christian Movement* (Pasadena: William Carey Library, 1981), 452.

6 Kenneth Cragg, "Constance E. Padwick, 1886–1968," *The Muslim World*, 59 (January 1969): 29–30.

7 Ibid., 30.

[8] William Richey Hogg, *Ecumenical Foundations: A History of The International Missionary Council and its Nineteenth Century Background* (New York: Harper, 1952), 325.

[9] Gordon Hewitt, *The Problems of Success: A History of the Church Missionary Society, 1910–1942*, Vol. 1 (London: SCM Press, 1971), 314–16.

[10] Carl F. Hallencreutz, *Kraemer Towards Tambaram: A Study in Hendrik Kraemer's Missionary Approach* (Uppsala: Almquist and Wiksells, 1966), 273.

[11] Constance Padwick, "North African Reverie," *International Review of Missions*, 17 (1938): 351.

[12] Ibid., 251.

[13] Agnes De Selincourt, "Signs of Progress in India" in Annie Van Sommer and Samuel Zwemer, *Daylight in the Harem: A New Era for Moslem Women* (New York: Fleming H. Revell, 1911), 57–58.

[14] Constance E. Padwick, *Henry Martyn: Confessor of the Faith* (London, 1922), 108, 149, 151.

[15] Padwick, *Call to Istanbul* (London: Longmans, Green and Co., 1958), ix.

[16] B. V. Subbamma, *New Patterns for Discipling Hindus* (Pasadena: William Carey Library, 1970), 30.

[17] Donald McGavran, "Forward," in *New Patterns for Discipling Hindus*, xiii.

[18] Subbamma, *New Patterns*, 46–47.

[19] Phyllis Thompson, *Capturing Voices: The Story of Joy Ridderhof* (London: Hodder and Stoughton, 1978), 52.

[20] Ibid., 52.

[21] Ibid., 53, 59, 62.

[22] Ibid., 77–78.

[23] Phyllis Thompson, *Faith By Hearing: The Story of Gospel Recordings* (Hongkong: The Alliance Press, 1960), 41.

## Chapter 19

[1] Elisabeth Elliot, *These Strange Ashes* (San Francisco: Harper & Row, 1979), 72–73.

[2] Ibid., 73.

[3] Ibid., 75.

[4] Ibid., 44–45.

[5] Ibid., 85.

[6] Ibid., 82–83.

[7] Ibid., 108–109.

[8] Ibid., 127.

[9] Elisabeth Elliot, *No Graven Image* (New York: Harper & Row, 1966), 84.

[10] Ibid., 87.

[11] Ibid., 106.

[12] Ibid., 237.

[13] Ruth A. Tucker, *From Jerusalem to Irian Jaya: A Biographical History of Christian Missions* (Grand Rapids: Zondervan, 1983), 318.

[14] Elisabeth Elliot, "Thirty Years Later: The Auca Massacre," *Christian Life* (April 1986): 28.

[15] Carolyn L. Canfield, *One Vision Only* (Chicago: Moody, 1959), 10, 177, 186.

[16] Isobel Kuhn, *By Searching* (Chicago: Moody, 1959), 8.

[17] Ibid., 15.

[18] Ibid., 119.

[19] Ibid., 119–122.

[20] Ibid., 152.

[21] Canfield, *One Vision Only*, 51–131 (*Vistas* is Part II of *One Vision Only*).

[22] Ibid., 51.

[23] Ibid., 69.

[24] Ibid., 72–74.

[25] Ibid., 138–39.

[26] Ibid., 138.

[27] Ibid., 139–40.

[28] Ibid., 149.

[29] Isobel Kuhn, *Assent to the Tribes* (Chicago: Moody, 1956), 17.

[30] Canfield, *One Vision Only*, 165.

[31] Ibid., 165.

[32] Kuhn, *Assent to the Tribes*, 174.

[33] Ibid., 255–56.

[34] Ibid., 131.

[35] Canfield, *One Vision Only*, 179–80.

[36] Ibid., 182–83.

[37] Ibid., 184.

## Chapter 20

[1] Leecy Barnett, *Hundreds of Pious Women: Presbyterian Women Missionaries to the American Indians, 1833–1893* (Trinity Evangelical Divinity School, M.A. Thesis, 1985), 39.

[2] Ruth T. Shaffer, *Road to Kilimanjaro: An American Family in Maasailand* (Grand Rapids: Four Corners Press, 1985), 27, 30, 41.

[3] Ibid., 46–47.

[4] Ibid., 49–50.

[5] Ibid., 97, 79.

[6] Ibid., 79.

[7] Ibid., 101–102.

[8] Ibid., 102.

[9] Ibid., 112–13.

[10] Ibid., 228–29.

[11] Lillian Dickson, *These My People* (Grand Rapids: Zondervan, 1958), 7–8.

[12] Ibid., 20–21.

[13] Ibid., 31, 32.

[14] Ibid., 65, 93, 96.

[15] Ibid., 4, 112–13.

[16] Ibid., 113.

[17] Ibid., 88–89.

[18] Ibid., 119.

[19] Ibid., 119–120.

[20] Don Richardson, *Lords of the Earth* (Glendale, Calif.: Regal, 1977), 118–122.

[21] Ibid., 125–30.

[22] Ibid., 206, 214–15.

[23] Ibid., 221.

[24] Ibid., 228–29, 238.

[25] Ibid., 239–40.

[26] Ibid., 220, 241, 246, 256.

[27] Ibid., 257–58.

[28] Ibid., 259–60, 289–306.

## Chapter 21

[1] Carolyn L. Canfield, *One Vision Only* (Chicago: Moody, 1959), 127.

[2] Ibid., 130.

[3] Ibid., 130.

[4] William Paton, *Alexander Duff: Pioneer of Missionary Education* (New York: Doran, 1922), 220.

[5] Jane Hunter, *The Gospel of Gentility: American Women Missionaries in Turn-of-the-Century China* (New Haven: Yale University, 1984), 119.

[6] Dorothy Clarke Wilson, *Climb Every Mountain: The Story of Granny Brand* (London: Hodder and Stoughton, 1976), 32–33, 42.

[7] Ibid., 51, 55.

[8] Ibid., 69.

[9] Ibid., 73, 77.

[10] Ibid., 77.

[11] Ibid., 92–95, 101.

[12] Ibid., 106, 110.

[13] Ibid., 131, 138, 148, 153, 170, 211.

[14] Doris Van Stone with Erwin W. Lutzer, *Dorie: The Girl Nobody Loved* (Chicago: Moody, 1979), 100–101.

[15] Ibid., 115–17, 122.

[16] Ibid., 132.

[17] Ibid., 132–33.

[18] Ibid., 131–33.

[19] Ibid., 134–35.

[20] Ibid., 136–37, 140.

## Chapter 22

[1] Jane Hunter, *The Gospel of Gentility: American Women Missionaries in Turn-of-the-Century China* (New Haven: Yale University, 1984), 66–68, 80.

[2] Daniel C. Eddy, *Heroines of the Missionary Enterprise* (London: Arthur Hall, Virtue, and Co., n.d.), 124.

[3] Lillian Dickson, *These My People* (Grand Rapids: Zondervan, 1958), 76.

[4] Jeannie Lockerbie, *By Ones and By Twos: Single and Double Missionaries* (Pasadena: William Carey Library, 1983), 29, 1, 5.

[5] Evelyn Stenbock, *"Miss Terri": The Story of Maude Cary, Pioneer GMU Missionary in Morocco* (Lincoln, Neb.: Good News Broadcasting, 1970), 30.

[6] Ibid., 46.

[7] Ibid., 48.

[8] Ibid., 53.

[9] Ibid., 58.

[10] Ibid., 52.

[11] Ibid., 59.

[12] Ibid., 60.

[13] Ibid., 71.

[14] Ruth A. Tucker, *From Jerusalem to Irian Jaya: A Biographical History of Christian Missions* (Grand Rapids: Zondervan, 1983), 245.

[15] Ibid., 245.

[16] Stenbock, *"Miss Terri"*, 103.

[17] Ibid., 113–14.

[18] Ibid., 139.

[19] Alan Burgess, *Daylight Must Come: The Story of a Courageous Woman Doctor in the Congo* (New York: Dell, 1975), 135.

[20] Tucker, *From Jerusalem to Irian Jaya*, 257.

[21] Helen Roseveare, "A HIS Interview with Helen Roseveare," *HIS* (January 1977), 18.

[22] Tucker, *From Jerusalem to Irian Jaya*, 258.

[23] Burgess, *Daylight Must Come*, 45.

[24] Ibid., 33.

[25] Roseveare, "A HIS Interview," 19.

[26] Tucker, *From Jerusalem to Irian Jaya*, 259.

[27] Helen Roseveare, "I'm Single," *Moody Monthly* (December 1976), 54.

[28] Roseveare, "A HIS Interview," 19.

[29] Ibid., 19.

## Chapter 23

[1] Vinson Synan, *The Holiness-Pentecostal Movement in the United States* (Grand Rapids: Eerdmans, 1971), 101–103.

[2] Jim Montgomery, *New Testament Fire in the Philippines* (Manila: Church Growth Research in the Philippines, 1972), 10.

[3] Ibid., 73.

[4] Ibid., 75–79.

[5] Ibid., 80–83.

[6] Mildred Larson and Lois Dodds, *Treasure in Clay Pots: An Amazon People on the Wheel of Change* (Dallas: Person to Person Books, 1985), 14.

[7] Ibid., 14.

[8] Ibid., 36.

[9] Ibid., 53.

[10] Ibid., 203.

[11] Ibid., 204.

[12] Ibid., 205.

[13] Ibid., 222.

[14] Ibid., 226.

[15] Ibid.

## Chapter 24

[1] Helen Barrett Montgomery, *Western Women in Eastern Lands* (New York: Macmillan, 1910), 114.

[2] Ruth A. Tucker, "The Role of Bible Women in World Evangelism," *Missiology*, 13 (April 1985): 143.

[3] Alice Chai, "Korean Women in Hawaii, 1903–1945," in Hilah Thomas and Rosemary Keller, eds., *Women in New Worlds: Historical Perspectives on Wesleyan Tradition* (Nashville: Abingdon, 1981), 330.

[4] Charles W. Forman, "Sing to the Lord a New Song': Women in the Churches of Oceania," in Denise O'Brien and Sharon W. Tiffany, eds., *Rethinking Women's Roles: Perspectives From the Pacific* (Los Angeles: University of California, 1984), 160–61.

[5] Kathleen Bliss, *The Service and Status of Women in the Churches* (London: SCM, 1952), 64.

[6] Ruth A. Tucker, "African Women's Movement Finds Massive Response," *Evangelical Missions Quarterly*, 22 (July 1986): 284–87.

[7] Juliet Thomas, "What Is the Church Doing to Elevate the Status of Women in India?," *Christianity Today* (October 17, 1986): 47.

[8] W. Harold Fuller, " 'Wonder Woman' Patricia Kim," *SIM Now* (May/June 1986): 4–5.

[9] John Maust, "Rosario Rivera: Reaching Lima's Children," *Missiology*, 15 (July 1987): 340–41.

[10] Ibid., 341–42.

[11] Ibid., 342.

[12] Ibid., 343.

[13] Ibid., 343–44.

[14] Ibid., 344–45.

[15] Ibid., 346.

[16] Young Sawa Kim, "My Journey in Mission: A Korean-Japanese Woman Pastor's Story," *Missiology*, 15 (July 1987): 347.

[17] Ibid., 348–49.

[18] Ibid., 349–50.

[19] Ibid., 350–51.

[20] Ibid., 351.

[21] Ibid., 352–53.

[22] Ibid., 355.

[23] Courtney Tower, "Mother Teresa's Work of Grace," *Reader's Digest* (December 1987), 167–75.

[24] Edward Le Joly, S. J., *Mother Teresa of Calcutta: A Biography* (San Francisco: Harper & Row, 1983), 8.

[25] Ibid., 13.

[26] Eileen Egan, *Such a Vision of the Street: Mother Teresa—The Spirit and the Work* (Garden City, N.Y.: Doubleday, 1985): 25.

[27] Tower, "Mother Teresa's Work," 168–75.

[28] Egan, *Such A Vision*, 90–91, 155, 243.

[29] Ibid., 365–66, 192.

[30] Tower, "Mother Teresa's Work," 243.

[31] Ibid., 228.

[32] Ibid., 175.

[33] Malcolm Muggeridge, *Something Beautiful for God* (Garden City, N.Y.: Image Books, 1971), 37.

[34] Egan, *Such A Vision*, 357.

[35] Dee Jepson, *Women Beyond Equal Rights* (Waco: Word Books, 1984), 52.

[36] Ibid., 53.

# BIBLIOGRAPHY

Adeney, Miriam. "Esther Across Cultures: Indigenous Leadership Roles for Women." *Missiology*. 15 (July 1987): 323–37.

Adhav, Shamsundar Manohar. *Pandita Ramabai*. Madras: The Christian Literature Society, 1979.

Allen, Catherine. *The New Lottie Moon Story*. Nashville: Broadman, 1980.

Allen, Opal Sweazea. *Narcissa Whitman: An Historical Biography*. Portland, Ore.: Binfords & Mort, 1959.

Anderson, Courtney. *To the Golden Shore: The Life of Adoniram Judson*. Grand Rapids: Zondervan, 1972.

Andrews, Leslie. "Restricted Freedom: A. B. Simpson's View of Women in Ministry." In David F. Hartzfeld and Charles Nienkirchen, eds., *The Birth of a Vision*. Beaverlodge, Alberta: Buena Book Services, 1986.

Barnett, Leecy A. *Hundreds of Pious Women: Presbyterian Women Missionaries to the American Indians, 1833–1893*. Trinity Evangelical Divinity School: M. A. Thesis, 1985.

Barr, Pat. *To China With Love: The Lives and Times of Protestant Missionaries in China, 1860–1900*. Garden City, N.Y.: Doubleday, 1973.

Beaver, R. Pierce. *American Protestant Women in World Mission: A History of the First Feminist Movement in North America*. Grand Rapids: Eerdmans, 1980.

Bliss, Kathleen. *The Service and Status of Women in the Churches*. London: SCM, 1952.

Bobe, Louis. *Hans Egede: Colonizer and Missionary of Greenland*. Copenhagen: Rosenkilde and Bagger, 1952.

Boyd, Nancy. *Emissaries: The Overseas Work of the American YWCA, 1895–1970*. New York: The Woman's Press, 1986.

Brewster, Thomas E. and Elizabeth S. "Bonding and the Missionary Task." In Ralph Winter and Steven Hawthorne, eds., *Perspectives on the World Christian Movement*. Pasadena: William Carey Library, 1981. Pages 452-464.

Bridgman, Eliza Gilett. *Daughters of China; or, Sketches of Domestic Life in the Celestial Empire*. New York: Robert Carter & Brothers, 1953.

Brumberg, Joan Jacobs. *Mission For Life: The Story of the Family of Adoniram Judson*. New York: The Free Press, 1980.

Buchan, James. *The Expendable Mary Slessor*. New York: Seabury Press, 1981.

Buck, Pearl S. *The Exile*. New York: Reynal & Hitchcock, 1936.

Buckland, Augustus R. *Women in the Mission Field: Pioneers and Martyrs*. New York: Thomas Whittaker, 1895.

Bueltmann, A. J. *White Queen of the Cannibals: The Story of Mary Slessor*. Chicago: Moody, n.d.

Bulifant, Josephine. *Forty Years in the African Bush*. Grand Rapids: Zondervan, 1950.

Burgess, Alan. *Daylight Must Come: The Story of a Courageous Woman Doctor in the Congo.* New York: Dell, 1975.

Burgess, Alan. *The Small Woman.* New York: Dutton, 1957.

Burton, Margaret E. *Women Workers of the Orient.* West Bedford, Ma.: Central Committee on the United Study of Foreign Missions, 1918.

Cable, Mildred and French, Francesca. *A Woman Who Laughed.* Philadelphia: China Inland Mission, 1934.

Cable, Mildred and French, Francesca. *Ambassadors for Christ.* Chicago: Moody, n.d.

Cable, Mildred and French, Francesca. *Something Happened.* London: Hodder & Stoughton, 1934.

Canfield, Carolyn L. *One Vision Only.* Chicago: Moody, 1959.

Carey, S. Pearce. *William Carey.* London: Hodder and Stoughton, 1926.

Cattan, Louise A. *Lamps are for Lighting: The Story of Helen Barrett Montgomery and Lucy Waterbury Peabody.* Grand Rapids: Eerdmans, 1972.

Chai, Alice. "Korean Women in Hawaii, 1903–1945." In Hilah Thomas and Rosemary Keller, eds., *Women in New Worlds: Historical Perspectives on Wesleyan Tradition.* Nashville: Abingdon, 1981. Pages 328–344.

Chamberlain, Mary E. A. *Fifty Years in Foreign Fields: A History of Five Decades of the Woman's Board of Foreign Missions, Reformed Church in America.* New York: Woman's Board of Foreign Missions, Reformed Church in America, 1925.

Christian, Carol and Plummer, Gladys. *God and One Red Head: Mary Slessor of Calabar.* Grand Rapids: Zondervan, 1970.

Coleman, Michael C. "Christianizing and Americanizing the Nez Perce: Sue L. McBeth and her Attitudes to the Indians." *Journal of Presbyterian History.* 53 (Winter 1975): 339–361.

Cott, Nancy F. *The Bonds of Womanhood: "Woman's Sphere" in New England, 1780–1835.* New Haven: Yale University Press, 1977.

Cragg, Kenneth. "Constance E. Padwick, 1886–1968." *The Muslim World.* 59 (January 1969) 29–39.

Cunningham, Rosemary. *Under a Thatched Roof in a Brazilian Jungle.* Grand Rapids: Zondervan, 1955.

Daniel-Rops, Henri. *The Heroes of God.* New York: Hawthorne Books, 1959.

De Selincourt, Agnes. "Signs of Progress in India." In Annie Van Sommer and Samuel Zwemer, *Daylight in the Harem: A New Era for Moslem Women.* New York: Fleming H. Revell, 1911.

Dean, William. *Memoirs of Mrs. Lucy T. Lord of the Chinese Baptist Missions.* Philadelphia: n.p., 1854.

Deen, Edith. *Great Women of the Christian Faith.* New York: Harper & Row, 1959.

Dickson, Lillian. *These My People.* Grand Rapids: Zondervan, 1958.

Drewery, Mary. *William Carey: A Biography.* Grand Rapids: Zondervan, 1978.

Drury, Clifford M., ed. *First White Women Over the Rockies: Diaries, Letters, and Biographical Sketches of the Six Women of the Oregon Mission Who Made the Overland Journey in 1836 and 1938.* 3 vols. Glendale, Calif.: Arthur H. Clark, 1966.

Dyer, Helen S. *Pandita Ramabai: Her Vision, Her Mission and Her Triumph of Faith.* London: Pickering & Inglis, n.d.

Eddy, Daniel C. *Heroines of the Missionary Enterprise.* London: Arthur Hall, Virtue, and Co., n.d.

Eddy, Sherwood. *Pathfinders of the World Missionary Crusade.* Nashville: Abingdon, 1945.

Egan, Eileen. *Such a Vision of the Street: Mother Teresa—The Spirit and the Work.* Garden City, N.Y.: Doubleday, 1985.

Elliot, Elisabeth. *A Chance to Die: The Life and Legacy of Amy Carmichael.* Old Tappan, N.J.: Revell, 1987.

Elliot, Elisabeth. *No Graven Image.* New York: Harper & Row, 1966.

Elliot, Elisabeth. *These Strange Ashes.* San Francisco: Harper & Row, 1979.

Elliot Leitch, Elisabeth. "The Place of Women in World Missions." In David M. Howard, ed. *Jesus Christ: Lord of the Universe, Hope of the World.* Downers Grove: InterVarsity Press, 1974.

Elliot, Elisabeth. "Thirty Years Later: The Auca Massacre," *Christian Life.* (April 1986): 26–29.

Elliot, Elisabeth. *Through Gates of Splendor.* New York: Harper & Row, 1958

Flemming, Leslie A. "Women and Witness: American Presbyterian Women Missionaries in North India, 1870–1910." Paper delivered at Wheaton College, June 17, 1986.

Forman, Charles W. " 'Sing to the Lord a New Song': Women in the Churches of Oceania." In Denise O'Brien and Sharon W. Tiffany, eds., *Rethinking Women's Roles: Perspectives From the Pacific.* Los Angeles: University of California, 1984.

Francis, Mabel with Smith, Gerald B. *One Shall Chase ?? a Thousand.* Harrisburg: Christian Publications, 1968.

Franson, Fredrik. "Prophesying Daughters," Unpublished Paper, Stockholm, Sweden, 1897.

Fuller, W Harold. " 'Wonder Woman' Patricia Kim." *SIM Now.* (May/June 1986): 4–6.

Garrett, Shirley S. "Images of Chinese Women." In John and Ellen Low Webster, eds., *The Church and Women in the Third World.* Philadelphia: Westminster, 1985. Pages 21–34.

Garrett, Shirley S. "Sisters All: Feminism and the American Women's Missionary Movement." In Torben Christensen and William R. Hutchinson, eds., *Missionary Ideologies in the Imperialist Era: 1880–1920.* Denmark: Aros, 1982.

Goforth, Rosalind. *Climbing: Memories of a Missionary's Wife.* Chicago: Moody, n.d.

Goforth, Rosalind. *Goforth of China.* Grand Rapids: Zondervan, 1937.

Gracey, Annie Ryder. *Eminent Missionary Women.* New York: Eaton & Mains, 1898.

Gunson, Neil. *Messengers of Grace: Evangelical Missionaries in the South Seas, 1797–1860.* New York: Harper & Row, 1960.

Hall, Clarence W. *Adventurers for God.* New York: Harper & Row, 1959.

Hanaford, Phebe. *Daughters of America; or, Women of the Century.* Augusta, Maine: True and Company, 1883.

Hardesty, Nancy. *Great Women of the Faith.* Grand Rapids: Baker, 1980.

Harris, Theodore F. *Pearl S. Buck: A Biography.* New York: John Day, 1969.

Hassey, Janette. *No Time for Silence: Evangelical Women in Public Ministry Around the Turn of the Century.* Grand Rapids: Zondervan, 1986.

Hefley, James and Marti. *By Their Blood: Christian Martyrs of the 20th Century.* Milford, Mich.: Mott Media, 1979.

Hefley, James and Marti. *No Time for Tombstones: Life and Death in the Vietnamese Jungle.* Wheaton: Tyndale, 1976.

Hill, Patricia R. *The World Their Household: The American Woman's Foreign Mission Movement and Cultural Transformation, 1870–1920.* Ann Arbor: University of Michigan, 1985.

Hitchcock, Ruth. *The Good Hand of Our God.* Elgin, Ill.: David C. Cook, 1975.

Hitt, Russell T. *Sensei: The Life Story of Irene Webster-Smith.* New York: Harper & Row, 1965.

Houghton, Frank. *Amy Carmichael of Dohnavur.* London: Society for the Propagation of Christian Knowledge, 1954.

Hoyt, Frederick B. " 'When a Field was Found too Difficult for a Man, a Woman Should be Sent': Adele M. Fielde in Asia, 1865–1890." *The Historian* 44 (May 1982): 314–334.

Hull, Eleanor. *Women Who Carried the Good News: The History of the Woman's American Baptist Home Mission Society.* Valley Forge, Pa.: Judson Press, 1975.

Hunter, Jane. *The Gospel of Gentility: American Women Missionaries in Turn-of-the-Century China.* New Haven: Yale University, 1984.

Hyatt, Irwin. *Our Ordered Lives Confess: Three Nineteenth-Century American Missionaries in East Shantung.* Cambridge, Mass.: Harvard University, 1976.

Irwin, Inez Haynes. *Angels and Amazons: A Hundred Years of American Women.* New York: Arno Press, 1974.

Janvier, Susan R. "Inside Zenanas of Allahabad." *Woman's Work for Women.* 8 (August 1898).

Jeffrey, Mary Pauline. *Dr. Ida: India.* New York: Fleming H. Revell, 1938.

Jepson, Dee. *Women Beyond Equal Rights.* Waco: Word Books, 1984.

Jones, Charles Edwin. *Perfectionist Persuasion: The Holiness Movement and American Methodism, 1867–1936.* Metuchen N.J.: Scarecrow, 1974.

Jones, Nard. *The Great Command: The Story of Marcus and Narcissa Whitman and the Oregon Country Pioneers.* Boston: Little, Brown, and Co., 1959.

Kane, J. Herbert. *Life and Work on the Mission Field.* Grand Rapids: Baker, 1980.

Kim, Young Sawa. "My Journey in Mission: A Korean-Japanese Woman Pastor's Story." *Missiology.* 15 (July 1987): 347–56.

King, Louis L. "Mother Whittemore's Miracles," *The Alliance Witness* (January 21, 1987): 20–22.

Kittler, Glenn D. *The Woman God Loved.* Garden City: Hanover House, 1959.

Knowles, James D. *Memoirs of Mrs. Ann H. Judson.* Boston: Lincoln and Edmands, 1829.

Kooiman, Helen W. *Cameos: Women Fashioned by God.* Wheaton: Tyndale, 1971.

Kuhn, Isobel. *Ascent to the Tribes.* Chicago: Moody, 1956.

Kuhn, Isobel. *By Searching.* Chicago: Moody, 1959.

Larson, Mildred and Dodds, Lois. *Treasure in Clay Pots: An Amazon People on the Wheel of Change.* Dallas: Person to Person Books, 1985.

Larsson, Flora. *My Best Men are Women.* London: Hodder and Stoughton, 1974.

Le Joly, Edward, S. J. *Mother Teresa of Calcutta: A Biography.* San Francisco: Harper & Row, 1983.

Livingstone, W. P. *Mary Slessor of Calabar: Pioneer Missionary.* London: Hodder & Stoughton, 1915.

Lockerbie, Jeannie. *By Ones and By Twos: Single and Double Missionaries.* Pasadena: William Carey Library, 1983.

Lord, Donald C. *Mo Bradley and Thailand.* Grand Rapids: Eerdmans, 1969.

Lutz, Lorry. *Born to Lose, Bound to Win: The Amazing Journey of Mother Eliza George.* Irvine, Calif.: Harvest House, 1980.

Mathews, Winifred. *Dauntless Women: Stories of Pioneer Wives.* Freeport, N.Y.: Books for Libraries Press, 1947.

Maust, John. "Rosario Rivera: Reaching Lima's Children." *Missiology.* 15 (July 1987): 339–46.

McBeth, Leon. *Women in Baptist Life.* Nashville: Broadman, 1979.

Montgomery, Helen Barrett. *Helen Barrett Montgomery: From Campus to World Citizenship.* London: Fleming H. Revell, 1940.

Montgomery, Jim. *New Testament Fire in the Philippines.* Manila: Church Growth Research in the Philippines, 1972.

Moorhouse, Geoffrey. *The Missionaries.* London: Eyre Methuen, 1973.

Muggeridge, Malcolm. *Something Beautiful for God.* Garden City, N.Y.: Image Books, 1971.

Neill, Stephen. *A History of Christian Missions.* New York: Penguin, 1964.

Niklaus, Robert L., Sawin, John S. and Stoesz, Samuel J. *All For Jesus: God at Work in the Christian and Missionary Alliance Over One Hundred Years.* Camp Hill, Pa.: Christian Publications, 1986.

Nilsen, Maria with Paul H. Sheetz, *Malla Moe.* Chicago: Moody Press, 1956.

Northcott, Cecil. *Robert Moffat: Pioneer in Africa, 1817–1870.* London: Lutterworth, 1961.

Padwick, Constance. "North African Reverie." *International Review of Missions.* 17 (1938): 341–54.

Parkman, Francis. *The Jesuits in North America in the Seventeenth Century.* Boston: Little, Brown, and Company, 1868.

Parkman, Mary R. *Heroines of Service.* New York: The Century Co., 1917.

Paton, William. *Alexander Duff: Pioneer of Missionary Education.* New York: Doran, 1922.

Pickett, J. Waskom. *Christian Mass Movements in India.* New York: Abingdon, 1933.

Pierson, Arthur T. *The New Acts of the Apostles.* New York: Baker & Taylor, 1894.

Pike, Eunice V. *Not Alone.* Chicago: Moody Press, 1964.

Pike, Eunice V. *Words Wanted.* Huntington Beach, Ca.: Wycliffe Bible Translators, 1958.

Pitman, E. R. *Lady Missionaries in Many Lands.* London: Pickering & Inglis, n.d.

Pollock, J. C. *Hudson Taylor and Maria: Pioneers in China.* Grand Rapids: Zondervan, 1962.

Ramabai, Pandita. *The High-Caste Hindu Woman.* London: George Bell and Sons, 1888.

Ransford, Oliver. *David Livingstone: The Dark Interior.* New York: St. Martin's, 1978.

Rice, John R. *Bobbed Hair, Bossy Wives, and Women Preachers.* Murfreesboro, Tenn.: Sword of the Lord, 1941.

Richardson, Don. *Lords of the Earth.* Glendale, Calif.: Regal, 1977.

Roseveare, Helen. "A HIS Interview with Helen Roseveare." *HIS.* (January 1977): 16–19.

Roseveare, Helen. *Give Me This Mountain.* London: Inter-Varsity Fellowship, 1966.

Roseveare, Helen. *He Gave Us a Valley.* Downers Grove: InterVarsity, 1976.

Roseveare, Helen. "I'm Single." *Moody Monthly.* (December 1976): 53–54.

Roseveare, Helen. *Living Sacrifice.* Chicago: Moody, 1979.

Sands, Audrey Lee. *Single and Satisfied.* Wheaton: Tyndale, 1971.

Shaffer, Ruth T. *Road to Kilimanjaro: An American Family in Maasailand.* Grand Rapids: Four Corners Press, 1985.

Simpson, A. B. *When the Comforter Came.* New York: Christian Publications, 1911.

Smith, Timothy L. *Revivalism and Social Reform: American Protestantism on the Eve of the Civil War.* Gloucester, Mass.: Peter Smith, 1976.

Sorrill, Bobbie. *Annie Armstrong: Dreamer in Action.* Nashville: Broadman, 1984.

Speer, Robert. *Servants of the King.* New York: Interchurch Press, 1909.

Stenbock, Evelyn. *"Miss Terri": The Story of Maude Cary, Pioneer GMU Missionary in Morocco.* Lincoln, Neb.: Good News Broadcasting, 1970.

Stevens, Helen N. *Memorial Biography of Adele M. Fielde: Humanitarian.* New York: The Fielde Memorial Committee, 1918.

Stirling, Nora. *Pearl Buck: A Woman in Conflict*. New York: New Century Publishers, 1983.

Subbamma, B. V. *New Patterns for Discipling Hindus*. Pasadena: William Carey Library, 1970.

Sumrall, Lester F. *Lillian Trasher: The Nile Mother*. Springfield, Mo.: Gospel Publishing House, 1951.

Synan, Vinson. *The Holiness-Pentecostal Movement in the United States*. Grand Rapids: Eerdmans, 1971.

Taylor, Geraldine M. *Margaret King's Vision*. Philadelphia: China Inland Mission, 1934.

Taylor, Dr. and Mrs. Howard. *J. Hudson Taylor: God's Man in China*. Chicago: Moody, 1978.

Thoburn, James. *Life of Isabella Thoburn*. Cincinnati: Jennings and Pye, 1903.

Thomas, Juliet. "What Is the Church Doing to Elevate the Status of Women in India?" *Christianity Today*. (October 17, 1986): 47.

Thomas, Winburn T. *Protestant Beginnings in Japan: The First Three Decades, 1859–1889*. Rutland, Vt.: Charles E. Tuttle, 1959.

Thompson, Phyllis. *Capturing Voices: The Story of Joy Ridderhof*. London: Hodder and Stoughton, 1978.

Thompson, Phyllis. *A Transparent Woman: The Compelling Story of Gladys Aylward*. Grand Rapids: Zondervan, 1971.

Thompson, Phyllis. *Desert Pilgrim*. Lincoln, Neb.: Back to the Bible, 1957.

Thompson, Phyllis. *Each to Her Own Post*. London: Hodder and Stoughton, 1982.

Thompson, Phyllis. *Faith By Hearing: The Story of Gospel Recordings*. Hongkong: The Alliance Press, 1960.

Tower, Courtney. "Mother Teresa's Work of Grace." *Reader's Digest*. (December 1987): 164–248.

Tsai, Christiana. *Queen of the Dark Chamber*. Chicago: Moody, 1953.

Tucker, Ruth A. "African Women's Movement Finds Massive Response." *Evangelical Missions Quarterly*. 22 (July 1986): 282–90.

Tucker, Ruth A. and Liefeld, Walter L. *Daughters of the Church: Women and Ministry From New Testament Times to the Present*. Grand Rapids: Zondervan, 1987.

Tucker, Ruth A. "Female Mission Strategists: A Historical and Contemporary Perspective." *Missiology*. 15 (January 1987): 73–89.

Tucker, Ruth A. *From Jerusalem to Irian Jaya: A Biographical History of Christian Missions*. Grand Rapids: Zondervan, 1983.

Tucker, Ruth A. "The Role of Bible Women in World Evangelism." *Missiology*. 13 (April 1985): 133–46.

Vail, Albert L. *Mary Webb and the Mother Society*. Philadelphia: American Baptist Publication Society, 1914.

Van Liere, Carma. "Sarah Doremus: Reformed Church Saint," *The Church Herald*. (October 4, 1985): 16–17.

Van Stone, Doris with Lutzer, Erwin W. *Dorie: The Girl Nobody Loved*. Chicago: Moody, 1979.

Walker, Louise. "Lillian Trasher: Mother to Thousands in Egypt." Unpublished manuscript. Springfield, Mo., 1986.

Wallis, Ethel and Bennett, Mary. *Two Thousand Tongues to Go*. New York: Harper & Row, 1959.

Walsh, J. Johnston. *A Memorial of the Futtehgurh Mission and Her Martyred Missionaries*. Philadelphia: Joseph M. Wilson, 1859.

Welter, Barbara. "She Hath Done What She Could: Protestant Women's Missionary Careers in Nineteenth-Century America." In Janet Wilson James, *Women in American Religion*. Philadelphia: University of Pennsylvania, 1980. Pages 111–125.

Wilson, Dorothy Clarke. *Climb Every Mountain: The Story of Granny Brand*. London: Hodder and Stoughton, 1976.

Wilson, Dorothy Clarke. *Palace of Healing: The Story of Dr. Clara Swain, First Woman Missionary Doctor and the Hospital She Founded*. New York: McGraw-Hill, 1968.

Wilson, Dorothy Clarke. "The Legacy of Ida S. Scudder." *International Bulletin of Missionary Research*. 1 (January 1985): 26–30.

Winchell, C. S. "Mary Clarke Nind." *Woman's Missionary Friend*. 37 (November 1905).

Winquist, Alan H. "Scandinavian-American Missions in Southern Africa and Zaire." Unpublished paper delivered at Wheaton College, Wheaton, Illinois, June 1986.

Wright, Elliott. *Holy Company: Christian Heroes and Heroines*. New York: Macmillan, 1980.

# SUBJECT INDEX